"Reitz presents Marcuse anew as a social justice educator. The volume raises the profile of critical political economy and critical pedagogy in Marcuse studies. It explicates the theoretical foundations of Marcuse's radical socialist humanism. Critical pedagogy now benefits from a re-evaluation of Marcuse's works, especially what I call 'revolutionary critical pedagogy.'"

Peter McLaren, *Professor Emeritus at the School of Education and Information Studies, University of California, Los Angeles*

"There are no other books that do with Marcuse what this book does in a comprehensive way, providing a coherent presentation of the work of Marcuse and its wide relevance to a number of topics. The social conditions of our times politically, economically, and culturally warrant the rediscovery of Marcuse's work and most especially, its ongoing implications for the conditions of our time—and Charles Reitz is absolutely the right scholar to lead the way."

Lauren Langman, *Professor of Sociology, Loyola University, Chicago*

"*Herbert Marcuse as Social Justice Educator* addresses some of the key issues of our time by presenting the importance of Herbert Marcuse's ideas for social justice education. Charles Reitz has long been one of the major scholars on the work and influence of Marcuse in the field of education, ecology, social critique, and progressive politics and this book will be his most important work—his crowning achievement in writing many books on Marcuse, education, social justice, and liberation."

Douglas Kellner, *George Kneller Chair, University of California, Los Angeles and author of* Media Culture: Cultural Studies, Identity, and Politics in the Contemporary Moment *(2nd ed., Routledge, 2020)*

Herbert Marcuse as Social Justice Educator

Demonstrating the continued relevance of Marcuse's work, *Herbert Marcuse as Social Justice Educator* details how his teachings remain a countervailing force to the conventional wisdom in intellectual and political matters today.

By drawing on Marcuse's critical analysis of the political economy, a profound concern for environmental issues, and an explicit critique of educational philosophy, this book illuminates not only the content and contours of Marcuse's work but its importance for developing critical social scientific thinking and theoretical insight into contemporary issues such as genocide and ecocide, fascism and democratic crises, political economy and social inequality, and the role of culture and media in forming compliant consumer-citizens.

From Charles Reitz, a prominent leader in Marcuse studies, this book will be an essential guide for instructors, students, and learners in sociology, social theory, political science, and environmental studies.

Charles Reitz is the author of *The Revolutionary Ecological Legacy of Herbert Marcuse* (2023), *Ecology and Revolution: Herbert Marcuse and the Challenge of a New World System Today* (2019) and *Philosophy & Critical Pedagogy: Insurrection & Commonwealth* (2016); editor of *Crisis and Commonwealth: Marcuse, Marx, McLaren* (2015); and author of *Art, Alienation and the Humanities: A Critical Engagement with Herbert Marcuse* (2000). He served for several years on the Board of Directors of the International Herbert Marcuse Society.

Critical Interventions

The Public in Peril: Trump and the Menace of American Authoritarianism
Henry A. Giroux

Learning to Save the Future: Education After Economism and Digital Determinism
Alexander J. Means

Ecology and Revolution: Herbert Marcuse and the Challenge of a New World System Today
Charles Reitz

Anxious Creativity: When Imagination Fails
David Trend

Rising Fascism in America: It Can Happen Here
Anthony R. DiMaggio

Rethinking Higher Education and the Crisis of Legitimation in Europe
Ourania Filippakou

Horizons of the Future: Science Fiction, Utopian Imagination, and the Politics of Education
Graham B. Slater

Surveillance Education: Navigating the Conspicuous Absence of Privacy in Schools
Nolan Higdon and Allison Butler

Culture, Power and Education: Representation, Interpretation, Contestation
Peter Mayo

Herbert Marcuse as Social Justice Educator: A Critical Introduction
Charles Reitz

Herbert Marcuse as Social Justice Educator
A Critical Introduction

Charles Reitz

NEW YORK AND LONDON

Designed cover image: Shutterstock #2457060817, Phil Pasquini

First published 2025
by Routledge
605 Third Avenue, New York, NY 10158

and by Routledge
4 Park Square, Milton Park, Abingdon, Oxon OX14 4RN

Routledge is an imprint of the Taylor & Francis Group, an informa business

© 2025 Charles Reitz

The right of Charles Reitz to be identified as author of this work has been asserted in accordance with sections 77 and 78 of the Copyright, Designs and Patents Act 1988.

All rights reserved. No part of this book may be reprinted or reproduced or utilized in any form or by any electronic, mechanical, or other means, now known or hereafter invented, including photocopying and recording, or in any information storage or retrieval system, without permission in writing from the publishers.

Trademark notice: Product or corporate names may be trademarks or registered trademarks, and are used only for identification and explanation without intent to infringe.

ISBN: 978-1-032-94594-1 (hbk)
ISBN: 978-1-032-94593-4 (pbk)
ISBN: 978-1-003-57158-2 (ebk)

DOI: 10.4324/9781003571582

Typeset in Sabon
by Taylor & Francis Books

Jerome Heckmann, in memoriam

Contents

	Acknowledgments	x
1	Campus Opposition to Genocide and Ecocide in Gaza Today: Marcuse on Israel's Historical Injustice in Palestine	1
2	Herbert Marcuse as Social Justice Educator: The Liberal Arts and Sciences, Critical Political Economy, Ecopedagogy	24
3	Marcuse as Antifascist Social Critic	57
4	The Activist Legacy of *One-Dimensional Man*	73
5	What Makes Higher Education *Higher*?: The Philosophical Foundations for Critical Social Research	86
6	Critical Teaching and Learning: On the *Origins* of Social Inequality	108
7	Ecosocialism and the Revolutionary Goals of Reason	120
8	Educating the Educator	141
9	Marcuse's Critical Pedagogy as Social Justice Education	151
	Index	164

Acknowledgments

I am much obliged to peer reviewers at Routledge for valuable guidance and encouragement and to Henry A. Giroux for including it in his Critical Interventions series. For superb editorial consideration and courtesy at Routledge, I thank Michael Gibson, Lewis Hodder, Alex Landucci, and Sarah Sibley. Peter McLaren, Lauren Langman, and Douglas Kellner have long shared my enthusiasm for Marcuse, critical pedagogy, and this project on social justice education. They have my immense gratitude for their continuing support. Likewise, I have enjoyed and benefitted from congenial and critical engagement with noted Marcuse scholars Arnold Farr, Andrew Lamas, Imaculada Kangussu, Terry Maley, Sarah Surak, Silvio Carneiro, Savita Singh, Sergio Bedoya Cortés, Rainer Winter, Andrew Feenberg, Javier Sethness Castro, and Peter-Erwin Jansen. Roena Haynie, retired professor of social work education and former Chair of Social Sciences at Avila University, and my spouse of 46 years, supplied knowledgeable criticisms and enhancements to the text. My former social science teaching colleague Stephen Spartan furnished key insights incorporated into Chapter 6. I alone am responsible for shortcomings that remain in this manuscript. Original material in this book is combined with excerpts drawn from writings I have published over the last decade. These are presented in a fully revised and synoptic manner. I wish to acknowledge publishers who generously granted permission to reemploy short passages and to thank also those whose formal permission was not necessary when representing my own work in an extensively revised context: SUNY Press, Peter Lang Publishing, Lexington Books, Springer Nature, Routledge, and Daraja Press. Special thanks to the *Radical Philosophy Review, Fast Capitalism*, the *Review of Radical Political Economics, CounterPunch*, the Brazilian journal of aesthetics and politics, *Das Questões*, the UK's *Theory, Culture & Society*, and Australia's *Sophia*.

Acknowledgments xi

Photo credit: Courtesy of the Frankfurt University Library special collection on Herbert Marcuse. Special thanks to Peter-Erwin Jansen and Harold Marcuse.

Photo commentary: "With Marcuse *to the Left*—or police power *to the Right*"— Imaculada Kangussu, Brazilian Marcuse scholar and philosophy Professor.

1 Campus Opposition to Genocide and Ecocide in Gaza Today

Marcuse on Israel's Historical Injustice in Palestine

This is a book about social justice and education in connection with the central issues of our times, featuring the radical philosophy of Herbert Marcuse. It hopes to do more than bring a discussion of Marcuse up to date; it seeks to explore also the historical context of Marcuse's Marxism and humanism as well as his critical pedagogy in connection with ontological and epistemological issues fundamental to educational philosophy. Herbert Marcuse is the single most important philosopher of our time who embraced, inspired, and participated in the radical movements of his day. He was a transdisciplinary thinker embracing the humanities and social sciences, and this book will follow and renew Marcuse's transdisciplinary project. It must open with the most compelling and disturbing issue concerning contemporary society and history today, the genocide and ecocide in Gaza.

Students across the U.S.A. in 2024 have risen in protest against the genocide and ecocide accompanying the Israel-Gaza war.[1] Given the panic[2] in the corporate mass media and among right-wing Republicans and mainstream Democrats today against the pro-Palestinian campus encampments and occupations, Herbert Marcuse's profoundly radical analysis of a comparable constellation of forces and events renouncing genocide/ecocide in Vietnam must be revisited. Marcuse understood the observable fact of these massive protest movements more fundamentally and philosophically—as expressions of humanity's *political Eros* (Marcuse 2019, 3–4, 16; [1967] 2017, 23).[3]

Erotic energy, Marcuse explained, accounts in no small measure for the radical politicization of individuals within movements for emancipatory social change presenting also new goals, new behavior, a new "language." As *political*, Marcuse understood this Eros in a libidinal yet Platonic way. In sharp contrast to mainstream society's sexual hierarchies, toxic masculinity, and the aggressive sexualization of its commodity culture, the political Eros is neither genital nor gender-binary; it is a generalized sense of energy and exuberance "signifying the affirmation of life … the logos of life" (Feenberg 2018, 272; 2023, 94). The political Eros appears as a resolute and joyous passion for collective liberation, in the manner of Schiller's *Alle Menschen werden Brüder*! i.e. the "Ode to Joy."

The Marcusean perspective in which the political Eros seeks protective care for living things has been most notably elaborated by George Katsiaficas (2024;

DOI: 10.4324/9781003571582-1

2   Herbert Marcuse as Social Justice Educator

2013; 1989). Katsiaficas speaks of "the Eros Effect"—an intuitive revulsion against the brutal destruction of nature or human beings. He sees this as a collective phenomenon, in which thousands of people identify with each other, even across national and ethnic dividing lines, publicly demonstrating in determined yet joyous rebellion for a completely different political reality. People intuitively believe they can "change the direction of the world from war to peace, from racism to solidarity, from external domination to self-determination, from patriotism to humanism" (Katsiaficas 2013, 492). Javier Sethness Castro has recently written a monograph on Marcuse titled, *Eros and Revolution* (2018). He similarly emphasizes that "Eros becomes [Marcuse's] archetypal instinctual and even political alternative to the hegemonic Thanatos as capital, State, and domination" (2018, 99). This characterizes what he calls Marcuse's "Orphic Marxism," the ancient mythological Greek musician Orpheus being the emblem of peace and love.

"The student movement is a vital social and political force" (Marcuse [1971] 2012, 190). From his point of view, campus protests today are but the latest in a series of waves of youthful enthusiasm advocating social justice in terms of the preservation of life and peace around the world—for example, in the erstwhile international demonstrations against the then-impending U.S. war against Iraq (2003); in the Arab Spring (2010); in the international Occupy movement (2011). So too, in to the monumental Black Lives Matter movement (2014); the Women's March after the 2016 election (the largest single-day action in U.S. history—Volpe 2022); the militant opposition to the Dakota Access Pipeline at Standing Rock (2016); the gun safety demonstrations by high school students following the Parkland shootings (2018); the current climate activism of Greta Thunberg, Fridays for Future, and Extinction Rebellion; the French *Mouvement des gilets jaunes*; and the U.S. "strike culture" of actors, writers, and autoworkers in 2023; as well as in the Stop Cop City campaign (2023).

Marcuse understood the social justice movements of our age *as being its civilizing forces*. The organized struggles against racism, sexism, poverty, war, and imperialism were doing their part to educate wide swaths of this country's population outside traditional classrooms about the pernicious forms of alienation and oppression and also about the power of students' deep feelings regarding right and duty. At the University of California San Diego (UCSD) during the late 1960s, Marcuse stood in solidarity with student anti-war protesters and walked among the students and the police officers, who made their presence known. On another occasion, he helped Angela Davis lead the occupation of an administration building—"Eventually we decided to occupy the registrar's office, and Herbert Marcuse was the first person to walk through the door" (Davis 1989).[4]

As Marcuse argued in '60s and early '70s, the world needed to oppose "war crimes being committed against the Vietnamese people" (2019, 1), as well as to combat the resurgent racism, bigoted nationalism, and warlike patriotism (that continue in newer forms today) in the U.S.A.

Today one might say with Marcuse's most famous student, Angela Davis, that this political Eros is expressing itself in the upsurge of social activism—*from*

Ferguson to Palestine. "When we see police repressing protests in Ferguson we have to think about the Israeli police and the Israeli army repressing protests in occupied Palestine" (Davis 2016, 45). Marcuse saw a new militant energy emerge among student activists

> in the early '60s when many of these kids went down to the South and saw, for the first time, how American democracy and equality were really functioning. It was a traumatic shock to them. Then came the war in Southeast Asia as the second traumatic shock.
>
> ([1971] 2012, 195)

Marcuse emphasizes there was really no mysterious explanation for this new militancy: their passion for social justice was an expression of their rejection of the traditional operational values of American society, an expression of a "new sensibility" for radical change.

Marcuse was an émigré to the U.S.A., fleeing the Nazi Third Reich. In 1934 he was the first member of the staff of the Frankfurt Institute for Social Research to arrive in New York City and represent it in exile at Columbia University. In a major departure from what would become the much more cautious politics of the Horkheimer inner circle of the Institute, as well as from the conventional wisdom in U.S. academic circles, Marcuse developed an incisive critique of the culture of commercialism and consumerism in the U.S.A. and also became a supporter of an activist politics against U.S. war-making and U.S.-led globalization.

On Israeli/Palestinian relations Marcuse remarked in 1972—

> The national aspirations of the Palestinian people could be met by the establishment of a national Palestinian state alongside Israel. [This] would be left to the self-determination of the Palestinian people in a referendum under supervision by the United Nations. The optimal solution would be the coexistence of Israelis and Palestinians, Jews and Arabs as equal members of a socialist federation of Middle Eastern states. This is still a utopian prospect.
>
> (Marcuse 2005a, 182)

Of course, "prerequisite to anything must be the idea of the continuation of an Israeli state" (2005a, 181) able to defend itself and "capable of preventing the repetition of the holocaust" (2005a, 180). To be serious as social critics, Marcuse admonishes us, we must understand clearly that we live in a world where another "Auschwitz is still possible" (2019, 49). He never knew how darkly ironic that realization would become.

Going deeply into the complicity of the U.S.A. on issues of genocide and ecocide in North Vietnam, Marcuse's essays "Ecology and Revolution" (1972) and "Ecology and the Critique of Modern Society" (1979) have renewed currency. They were republished in 2019 by the International Herbert Marcuse Society (Marcuse 2019).

4 *Herbert Marcuse as Social Justice Educator*

The genocidal war against people is also "ecocide" insofar as it attacks the sources and resources of life itself. It is no longer enough to do away with people living now; life must also be denied to those who aren't even born yet by burning and poisoning the earth, defoliating the forests, blowing up the dikes. This bloody insanity will not alter the ultimate course of the war, but it is a very clear expression of where contemporary capitalism is at: the cruel waste of productive resources in the imperialist homeland goes hand in hand with the cruel waste of destructive forces and consumption of commodities of death manufactured by the war industry.

(2019, 1–2)

In a very specific sense, the genocide and ecocide in Indochina are the capitalist response to the attempt at revolutionary ecological liberation: the bombs are meant to prevent the people of North Vietnam from undertaking the economic and social rehabilitation of the land. But in a broader sense, monopoly capitalism is waging a war against nature—human nature as well as external nature. For the demands of ever more intense exploitation come into conflict with nature itself, since nature is the source and locus of the life-instincts which struggle against the instincts of aggression and destruction. And the demands of exploitation progressively reduce and exhaust resources: the more capitalist productivity increases, the more destructive it becomes. This is one sign of the internal contradictions of capitalism.

(2019, 2)

The genocidal and ecocidal politics of Lyndon B. Johnson and Benjamin Netanyahu are expressions of a political economic system; so too the complicity of the U.S.A. today. "Genocide, war crimes, crimes against humanity, are not effective arguments against a government which defends property, trade, and commerce at home while it perpetuates its destructive policy abroad" (1969, 67).

Israeli/Palestinian Conflicts of the '60s and '70s

Marcuse addressed the Israeli/Palestinian conflicts of the '60s and '70s in four disparate yet direct statements—"Thoughts on Judaism, Israel, etc." ([1977] 2005a); "Israel is Strong Enough to Concede" ([1972] 2005a); his conversation with Israeli Defense Minister Mosha Dayan ([1971] 2012); and in the "Interview with *Street Journal*" ([1970] 2014).

We owe it to Israeli scholar Zvi Tauber (2013; 2012), who has studied these and other Marcuse materials closely, such that we have a conclusive account of Marcuse's critique of Israeli policies vis à vis Palestine *well prior* to the Israel-Gaza War of 2023–2024:

Marcuse's view regarding the State of Israel stands in contrast to the prevalent Zionist ideology on a crucial matter: he does not recognize the historical-mythical rights of the Jewish people to the Land of Israel, rights ostensibly originating in the Bible or in some belief in the Land's primordial belonging to this people, ostensibly valid throughout history to this day … [T]he very establishment of the State of Israel in 1948 and its conquests in the Six-Day War were for Marcuse also unjust to the Palestinians …

(Tauber 2013, 129)

Marcuse was surprised to hear an explicit admission from then Minister of Defense Moshe Dayan … that the State of Israel was in fact established on Palestinian land.

(Tauber 2013, 129–130)

Tauber makes it clear that Dayan was not apologizing for this fact. Marcuse was struck nonetheless by how this admission undergirded the case one could make that Israel's history is *in fact* that of a colonial settler state. After having been a defender of Israel's policies earlier in his life, by 1970 Marcuse had had a radical change of heart after an Amnesty International report of the Israeli torture of Arab prisoners and learning that 32 children had been killed in a bombing near Cairo (Marcuse [1970] 2014).

Now if these reports are correct, it seems to me that precisely as a Jew and as a member of the New Left, I can no longer defend Israeli policies, and that I have to agree with those who are radically critical of Israel.

(Marcuse [1970] 2014, 354)

Shortly after his death, Marcuse's son Peter and his wife Erica Sherover addressed Herbert's overall relationship to Judaism as follows:

[the] aspect of the Jewish tradition with which Herbert most strongly identified was the importance it places on the struggle for justice in this life, in this world; its insistence on the ongoing effort to "use life to help bring about a better life."

(Peter Marcuse and Erica Sherover, as noted in Sethness Castro 2018, 13)

Coming back to the present, we see that since October 7, 2024, new battles in Washington, D.C. have re-ignited the right-wing culture wars that have been roiling college campuses over the last two decades, now with charges of anti-semitism on campus.[5]

Campus Culture Wars Flare in 2024

Up to now this right-wing culture war has focused on repealing liberal policies in U.S. higher education, targeting affirmative action, equity, diversity and inclusion, and much more, i.e. removing ostensibly woke tenured radicals on the faculty who supposedly enforce political correctness. This latest attempt to curb liberals and the Left features MAGA Republicans like New York

6 Herbert Marcuse as Social Justice Educator

Congresswoman Elise Stefanik offering implicit support to right-wing Israeli politicians today through highly publicized hearings in Washington, D.C. She used her inquisitor's position to evade legitimate criticism of Israeli war crimes and genocide in Gaza.

The right wing's accusations twist the motivation for the recent student protests through a loaded distortion amounting to slander: the students in their account are advocating "genocidal antisemitism," while in their own account the students who were punished at Columbia, the progressive anti-Zionist group Jewish Voice for Peace and Students for Justice in Palestine, aver they were opposing the Israeli occupation of Palestine and advocating ceasefire. "There can be no critique" says Judith Butler …

> … when even calls for ceasefire are considered antisemitic—only those who support Israel's annihilationist war against the Palestinian people in Gaza are exonerated of the charge. The conflation of antisemitism with anti-Zionism can only serve the purposes of extreme censorship, for it constrains those who oppose ongoing Israeli violence, the killing of nearly 18,000 Gazans to date, from expressing moral and political outrage and defending fundamental principles of free expression and political justice.[6]

The UN General Assembly likewise has called for a ceasefire. Regrettably, experts contend that both Israel and Hamas have committed war crimes in the past and are continuing to do so.[7] The student protesters in question were protesting what they contend is a genocide being perpetrated by the Israeli government and its war machine in Gaza; just the opposite of what Congresswoman Stefanik insisted. The investigations by the International Criminal Court (ICC) into war crimes by Israel and Hamas are ongoing and much needed. Israel does not recognize the ICC, but it has agreed to the genocide convention of the United Nations, and the International Court of Justice (ICJ) began to hear the charges of Israeli genocide in Gaza on January 12, 2024, which were brought to the ICJ by South Africa.[8]

Representative Stefanik and others made a grand show of warping the discourse and changing the subject of this protest while at the same time bringing the presidents of prestigious universities to heel in Congress for allegedly acquiescing to campus speakers advocating extreme forms of hate. Like the McCarthy hearings of yore, the interrogation was a public messaging campaign and little other than an explicit intimidation of Left protest. The liberal academics equivocated because the so-called principles of free speech could not allow their universities to sanction the hypothetical mere advocacy of genocidal antisemitism unless such hate speech was simultaneously accompanied by hate crime. Yet Columbia University wasted little time in banning the groups mentioned above. Power has its own language and prerogatives. A billionaire hedge-fund manager, Bill Ackman, undertook an unrelenting pressure campaign to oust the president of Harvard over this issue. He is a wealthy white donor and a member of the 1%.[9] Harvard's board initially declined to fire Claudine Gay, its first black president; but she ultimately stepped away on

Campus Opposition to Genocide and Ecocide in Gaza Today 7

her own. The resignation of the president of the University of Pennsylvania, Elizabeth Magill, was accepted after her appearance before Stefanik.

> After her testimony, Magill faced particular pressure due to the threatened loss of a $100m grant from billionaire Ross Stevens, a UPenn alum. Stevens denounced the university's 'permissive approach' to discrimination against Jews and said he would be nixing the donation as he saw the college's behavior being in breach of its terms.[10]

During the campus struggles of the 1960s, radicals like Herbert Marcuse developed a critique of the free speech fundamentalism of most university administrations. Marcuse advocated the revocation of speech rights to fascists, racists, and any other oppressor of minoritized populations. Marcuse's little-known work "Repressive Tolerance" (1965) reminds us of the truth about freedom of speech in the United States: in theory a right of everyone; in practice, those on the Left have not historically been afforded it. What the culture *does* have is a contest of ideas and a contest for control within our public political sphere and higher education especially. Supporting Marcuse's view is Christopher M. Finan's (2007) comprehensive study *From the Palmer Raids to the Patriot Act: A History of the Fight for Free Speech in America*. This emphasizes that right-wing censorship is a common feature of American politics. He discusses the destruction of the abolitionist presses during the pre-Civil War period of Bleeding Kansas, the suppression of socialists during World War I, to the Palmer Raids, to the Cold War, and the USA Patriot Act, and National Security letters to silence antiwar dissent. There was also the McCarthy era of the 1950s and Governor Ronald Reagan's attacks on Herbert Marcuse during the 1960s. Finan's historical research aids in a critical understanding of political discourse patterns and reinforces Marcuse's critical analysis of the discourse of the time: political activists, radicals, artists, librarians, lawyers, teachers, and students, who have criticized the regnant political orthodoxy, have had to fight for their rights to be heard in the mainstream political arena. Today, there is a rising tide of belligerence expressed by dominant political voices, especially those of the far right, a form of practice with negative impacts on the political culture and higher education today.

The current right-wing culture war reproduces power abuse and domination, and the flare-up is blatantly duplicitous and manipulative. In the recent past, the right wing itself has notoriously attacked campus speech codes that have attempted to restrict hate speech. The New Right or Alt-Right has vigorously asserted a putative political need for an ostensibly democratic society to maintain an absolute tolerance of abusive and even assaultive speech—as protected forms of dissent. These are the free speech fundamentalists or hardliners within both conservative and liberal camps for whom any regulation, even of assaultive speech, is too much. Liberals have met the conservatives more than halfway in this regard, agreeing that hate speech *is* to be tolerated as long as it remains words and *not* hateful or violent deeds.

8   *Herbert Marcuse as Social Justice Educator*

Following the upsurge in conservative racist leadership nationwide under Reagan, Alan Charles Kors and Harvey Silverglate (1998) came to argue many of the major higher education agenda items for the New Right. They explicitly attacked Marcuse with regard to university policies in the U.S.A. David Horowitz (2000; 2006) did likewise a few years later. Central to their arguments was the claim that an ostensible reverse racism *against whites* on the part of a so-called academic Left had betrayed the principle of freedom of speech in the American university in so far as campus codes attempted to regulate speech that was bigoted against ethnic minority groups in our society. Kors and Silverglate organized the Foundation for Individual Rights in Education, or FIRE, to help what they saw as a significant number of right-wing "victims of illiberal policies" subjected to violations of their free speech rights to engage in racist speech on college campuses. David Horowitz formulated an "Academic Bill of Rights" that stressed institutional and professional neutrality with regard to controversial issues, thus permitting no sanctions for even fascist or racist speech. Persons familiar with campus controversies over the last few years know of the cases of Charles Murray at Middlebury College and Milo Yiannopoulos at Berkeley. Students on both campuses demanded "No Free Speech for Racists" and vigorously attempted to interrupt the events. Right-wingers and liberals alike promoted and defended a free speech fundamentalism protecting the academic racism of Murray and the notorious and noxious speech of Yiannopoulos despite the massive antiracist student and faculty protests. Nonetheless, a resurgence of reactionary rhetoric and racist tendencies on the right is intensifying today.

Neoliberal/neoconservative priorities over the last several years have closed many of the academic departments where critical social theorizing previously found a home. Indeed, today, the reigning political circle around Florida's governor Ron DeSantis is making its cultural counterrevolution explicit. Christopher F. Rufo, who orchestrated the right's attacks on critical race theory, is explicitly aiming "to steal the strategies and principles of the Gramscian left, and then to organize a kind of counterrevolutionary response to 'the long march through the institutions'" (Rufo 2023, 36). Rufo and DeSantis are conducting a top-down restructuring of the New College of Florida as part of their "broader quest to crush any hint of progressivism in public education" (Goldberg 2023). The trend is to make liberal arts colleges more like trade schools, with job preparation first and foremost. Rufo's latest publication is a book-length polemic, first and foremost against Marcuse, but also against Angela Davis, Black Lives Matter, critical race theory, diversity, equality and inclusion, Paulo Freire, and Derrick Bell. Rufo sees himself as the theorist of "the counterrevolution to come" (Rufo 2023, 269).

Rufo is disturbed that for Marcuse "sexual and political liberation were intertwined" (Rufo 2023, 30), and Rufo's work of counterrevolution more viciously articulates a version of the antisemitic "replacement theory" in which cultural Marxism and Marcuse have already supplanted the moderate, formerly established, voices of the *New York Times*. In Rufo's account (2023, 55–56): "Marcuse believed that the university could serve as the 'initial revolutionary institution'...," but the Left's ultimate target was "the prestige media, and the critical theories became the house style of establishment opinion." "Establishment voices at The Times underestimated Marcuse, whose ideas would outlast and eventually supplant the moderate position at the paper of record ... . Marcuse's philosophy would eventually ... consume the newsroom." "Marcuse's 'liberating tolerance,' in which accusations of racism and sexism are wielded to silence dissent, has become the dominant internal culture" (Rufo 2023, 55–56).

Marcuse: No "Pure Tolerance" of Hate Speech Directed at Minoritized Populations

While the conservative free speech fundamentalists have traditionally argued for the free speech rights of racists and fascists, Herbert Marcuse argued that the concept of tolerance, once used in religious and political struggles by marginalized and oppressed groups seeking acceptance from the mainstream society, was instead now even more often used/abused by the rich and powerful, the keepers of the system and protectors of legalized violence and exploitation as a tool to legitimate their oppressive views and oppressive political systems. Reactionary forces presented themselves as aggrieved, apparently because the freedom rights won by minority groups through democratic civil rights struggle were displacing their own oppressive prerogatives. A slogan of the neofascists marching in Charlottesville, Virginia, was "Jews Shall Not Replace Us." This advocacy of genocidal antisemitism was tolerated by Trump[11] and *not* protested by MAGA Republicans.

The essence of "pure tolerance" or free speech absolutism is that it sees *opposition to hate speech* as endangering free speech. Both the reactionaries and the liberals have little understanding that the classical liberalism of John Stuart Mill intended speech protections primarily for the powerless minority voices expressing dissent against the prevailing ideology and its power structure, *not* to protect voices of dominant parties that are already hegemonic as well as often distasteful. The assertion, heard recently, that racist and sexist views contribute necessary components of cultural diversity breaking free of the constraints of liberal political correctness and belonging within an inclusive pluralism is an utterly perverse example of a vicious cultural and political double-speak.

The U.S. "Bill of Rights" included in its first amendment a protection of the rights of minoritized populations from infringement by the majority. If, however, we all have a de jure right to express any opinion in public, the de facto condition is that Left opinions are usually marginalized and often suppressed, while right-wing ones, which benefit the dominant political system, are given free play. "This pure tolerance of sense and nonsense" practiced under the conditions prevailing in the United States today "cannot fulfill the civilizing function attributed to it by the liberal protagonists of democracy, namely protection of dissent" (Marcuse 1965, 94, 117).

10   Herbert Marcuse as Social Justice Educator

Marcuse is adamant that withdrawing democratic tolerance from the Nazi organizers in Germany during the run-up to world war and genocide would have and should have been a necessary decision, yet even so not lightly made.

> Such extreme suspension of the right of free speech and free assembly is indeed justified only if the whole of society is in extreme danger ... . The conditions under which tolerance can again become a liberating force have still to be created.
>
> (Marcuse 1965, 110–111)

Facebook and Twitter, which facilitated a vast expansion of neofascist bigotry and hate speech on their platforms, ultimately realized (though arguably too late) the grave danger and harm it had engendered with no regulation of the racist and neofascist voices of domestic terrorists. After January 6, 2021, they banned Donald Trump in what was an effective action against a grave neofascist threat of force and violence against liberal political leaders and any ordinary citizens who get in their way. This is a kind of censorship to save the traditional liberal order. Today the owner of "X," formerly known as Twitter, is restoring license to racist voices including Donald Trump.

Within the current forms of social unfreedom that are yet called democracies, real crimes by the Right (before 9/11, as well as in its aftermath) are systemically tolerated by the state in practice—such as racist police brutality, the deprivation of millions of Americans from comprehensive health care, treating asylum seekers as criminals, implementing the death penalty in a racially biased manner, supplying arms and training to governments and armed groups around the world that commit torture, political killings, and other human rights abuses (Amnesty International 2023; Bevins 2020; Harcourt 2018; Winter 2020).

How shall we best protect human rights in this era of acrid backlash to antiracist education and anticolonial politics and amid rival redefinitions of freedom? One place to start is critical discourse analysis and to recall Herbert Marcuse's critique of pure tolerance. Both Marcuse and Mill conceived of authentic democracy as requiring a political culture that honors the collision of opposing arguments as a precondition for the pursuit of truth. But it is exactly this authentically democratic educational and cultural context that is lacking even today in the United States. Such a democratic context remains to be created. In terms of the Israel-Gaza War, peace and security for the Israelis and Palestinians is the goal Marcuse, and very likely all of us, would want. The *New York Times* editorial board has just published a lengthy and thoughtful Forum suggesting ten feasible positive futures for the Israelis and Palestinians going forward.[12]

Israelism, Antisemitism, and the U.S. Military Budget

"*Israelism*" is a new word coined to describe "one-sided propaganda about Palestinians that American Jews and others have been indoctrinated with regarding the Israeli occupation, apartheid, and other dehumanizing policies."[13]

Representatives Elisa Stefanik and Virginia Foxx, as well as other MAGA Republicans, recently utilized Israelism to accuse the presidents of Harvard, M.I.T., and the University of Pennsylvania of *antisemitism*. They had ostensibly permitted pro-Palestinian groups to call for a ceasefire in the Israel-Hamas war and allowed them to utilize the slogan "From the river to the sea, Palestine shall be free." This supposedly demonstrated that the students were advocating "genocidal antisemitism." Bizarrely, just weeks before the October 7 Hamas attack on Israel (as reported by *The Jerusalem Post* and the *Times of Israel*) Israeli President Benjamin Netanyahu presented slides to the UN General Assembly on September 22, 2023, using a "Greater Land of Israel" map embracing all the territory—one might say from the river to the sea—with Gaza and the West Bank fully absorbed into Israel. No MAGA Republicans have criticized Netanyahu for the land acquisitions implicit in this re-envisioned geography negating Palestinian self-governance—and which might have been taken to foreshadow the now all-too-real Israeli genocide there—with 34 thousand Palestinians dead (and this number still mounting). Such is the caprice of Israelism. As I write this, Virginia Foxx and her Congressional committee are summoning Harvard back again.[14] The deceptive magic of Israelism is its hypothetical "critique," permitting MAGA supporters to charge antisemitism at any juncture that suits them when defending Israel against accusations of war crimes, while simultaneously allowing right-wingers to cover their own neofascist views—against Jews, liberals, and radicals, whom they tend to demean as cultural Marxists. We have yet to see MAGA Republicans criticize the neo-Nazis marching in Charlottesville, Virginia, in August 2017, chanting "Jews Shall Not Replace Us." When the right-wing charges antisemitism, the accusation is Orwellian.

The Historical Role of U.S. and British Antisemitism

In reality, tens of thousands of Palestinians today have paid with their lives for the history of U.S. and British antisemitism, in which the U.S.A. and Britain both turned away from their shores Jewish refugees from Nazi Germany and refused to resettle Europe's relatively small Jewish population as a group within U.S. borders after World War II. A review of the history of the creation of Israel[15] makes clear that the legally segregated, white supremacist U.S.A. fused its post-war political interests and pressure with the de facto and de jure remnants of British military power (and Soviet acquiescence) to see an Israeli state imposed upon the Palestinian population of the so-called Holy Land. Israeli Defense Minister Moshe Dayan acknowledged this, as we have seen above. U.S. and British policies created a colonial settler state to occupy what had been Palestinian land—catastrophically displacing Palestinians from their homes and property by force of arms.

At the same time, U.S. intelligence agencies were relocating to U.S. shores ex-Nazis who could enhance the military's efforts at rocket building—like former S.S. officer Wernher von Braun, lionized to the nation's youth as the father of the U.S. space program, with buildings and symposia named after him to this day at Marshall Space Flight Center, Huntsville, Alabama. For practical advice

12 Herbert Marcuse as Social Justice Educator

on anti-communist suppression, the C.I.A. protected and paid a notorious Nazi war criminal rather than bring him to justice. This was Klaus Barbie, the butcher of Lyon, who personally participated in the death and deportation of thousands of Jews and resistance fighters in France.[16] The heir to the Imperial German arms-making dynasty, Alfried Krupp, though convicted of war crimes for having used approximately 100,000 forced laborers at Auschwitz as part of his industrial empire, would see his sentence commuted by U.S. authorities only a few years later in 1951.[17] Krupp's property was restored to him. In 1974 the Alfried Krupp von Bohlen und Halbach Foundation established research foundations at Harvard and Stanford.[18]

"Bonanza for Arms Makers As U.S. Military Budget Surges"[19]

Bi-partisan support for a new defense buildup by the U.S.A. in 2021 meant that the Pentagon received $25 billion above what President Biden requested; in 2022 this rose to $45 billion more than the White House's request—$858 billion in all—after Russia invaded Ukraine.[20] This ensured that the military budget had the capacity to extend massive military expenditures beyond the Ukraine War even if it could not have been foreseen that this would come to mean underwriting Israel's colossal act of collective retribution against the people of Gaza in response to the deadly Hamas offensive of October 7, 2023. In our grotesque world, which has now seen the sacrifice of civilians murdered by the tens of thousands and ceasefires vetoed by the U.S.A. in the UN, the fuller cost of war—in terms of lives lost, government lies and illegalities—is regularly suppressed. The U.S. war-makers' budget continues as a bi-partisan mechanism to subsidize owners of the U.S. military-industrial complex.[21] Antisemitism is real. So also is a militarist *Israelism*—supporting the Israeli genocide while falsely charging left-leaning antiwar forces with anti-Jewish bias.

It is well known that MAGA Republicans delayed U.S. military expenditures earmarked for both Ukraine and Israel. This is a policy debate about *where* and *when* to utilize U.S. military resources and power, not about levels of military might at the disposal of government. Let it also be noted here that suicide by active-duty U.S. soldiers and veterans has of late been even deadlier than combat— twenty a day in the six years from 2013–2019.[22] The U.S. military denies that its suicide rates are higher than a non-military population of the same age and gender demographics, and it may be so. The extraordinary self-immolation of active duty Airman Aaron Bushnell February 25, 2024 in front of the White House was an extreme act of protest "to make the point against the indifference of the world in the face of the Israeli genocide in Gaza."[23] It was a protest against Israelism.

Opposing Ecocide with Ecology and Art, the *Bonheur Commun*

A militant defense of the earth and its people occupied much of Herbert Marcuse's final years of life. His late-period writing featured a "green turn," *not* otherwise undertaken in Frankfurt School critical theory (Marcuse 2019).

Campus Opposition to Genocide and Ecocide in Gaza Today   13

Marcuse's work overall stresses that we have it within our power today (despite the obstacles put in our path by the political and economic forces of advanced or neocapitalism) to attain a meaningful and cooperatively productive social life with a politics of peace and love, abundance, racial equality, women's rights, the liberation of labor, the restoration of nature, relaxation, and quietude. Marcuse regarded the environmental movement as the embodiment of life-affirming energy directed toward the protection of earth and the enjoyment of human existence in peace. I call this the goal of EarthCommmonWealth.

> [W]e live in a profoundly immoral and profoundly inhuman society behind the veil of a free democratic process and behind the veil of prosperity.
>
> (Marcuse [1969] 2011, 185)

> To create the subjective conditions for a free society [it is] no longer sufficient to educate individuals to perform more or less happily the functions they are supposed to perform *in this* society or extend "vocational" education to the "masses." Rather ... [we must] ... educate men and women who are incapable of tolerating what is going on, who have really learned what *is* going on, has always been going on, and why, and who are educated to resist and to fight for a new way of life. By its own inner dynamic, education thus *leads beyond the classroom*, beyond the university, *into the political* dimension, and into the *moral*, instinctual dimension.
>
> ([1968] 2009, 35, emphasis in original)

Marcuse's theory of culture pivots on critical social learning linked to an *emancipatory political action* component. Such is the *educative* power in struggle, itself emergent from the political Eros. Marcuse's Marxism theorizes *the militant humanism of* art. For example, socially conscious songs of the U.S. Civil Rights movement were called "freedom songs" in large part because of the visceral sense of freedom and community *in the singing itself*: "Ain't Gonna Let Nobody Turn Me Around, Turn me Around, Turn me Around" or "We Shall Overcome." These expressions of a sublime political Eros were ridiculed by the racist right wing as "kumbaya" moments, but they were moments of *visceral aesthetic protest, communal well-being, and dignity.* Marcuse has an awareness of the struggle with alienation that artists endure, their distance from a flourishing and vibrant life on planet earth, and yet their engagement with art and the aesthetic dimension humanizes their and our earthly sensuous existence. Such singing instantiates the *promesse du bonheur* (promise of happiness, joy, and fulfillment) that art can embody (Marcuse [1945] 1998, 204).

Marcuse stressed back in 1968 that the social dynamics at work in higher education under advanced capitalism have a dialectical character: they require that education must permit (for some) unrestricted access to high-quality knowledge in the humanities, natural sciences, and social sciences to be competitive in the global economic market and to guide the political cultures of nations in a sophisticated manner. Yet education must also shield this

14 Herbert Marcuse as Social Justice Educator

information-based global society against radical change. Marcuse anticipated in *Counterrevolution and Revolt* (1972) the now raging tendencies to insinuate a conservative and patriotic as well as Eurocentric program for the liberal arts in American general education against the critical impulses within it toward multiculturalism, social history, ecological materialism, and critical social theory. Critical education, embodied in a new multicultural approach to the liberal arts and sciences, has in practice disclosed the *real need for* re-humanized and egalitarian forms of 1) productive relations, 2) relations to nature, and 3) interpersonal dynamics; such that these can cultivate the aesthetic and moral worth of civilized life.

Marcuse stresses that the revolts of the '60s and '70s occurred as students responded to an emancipatory political Eros that shaped their striving to reduce society's destructive violence. During the anti-Vietnam War protests and the Civil Rights movement, Herbert Marcuse, like Martin Luther King, Jr., saw such a response as involving "a radical revolution of values."[24] This counteracted the predatory adulation of plutocracy and power that has characterized U.S. American culture. Such adulation, filled with religious zealotry and militarism, continues today to be threatening, pathologically aggressive, sadomasochistic, and punitive. It is also delusional: seeing itself as free and democratic! Racial animosity, anti-immigrant scapegoating, and resurgent nationalism/patriotism are being orchestrated today in the troubled system of American/global capitalism—as neopopulist/neofascist instrumentalities of social control and economic stabilization. Israel on the other hand today has cited the extreme destructiveness of U.S. military operations toward civilians (Falluja, Mosul, Hiroshima) as a defense of its own genocidal policies in Gaza. (Note the front-page article "Israelis Invoking Toll of U.S. Wars as Moral Shield" in *The New York Times*, November 28, 2023.)

The link between the erotic and the political became one of Marcuse's signature notions. Eros ultimately seeks a determined and joyous rebellion against alienation and estrangement, where joy comes from sharing the act of living aligned with ethical and political ideals. This is what Aristotle called our highest happiness, and Marx called our species being; derived from a sense of moral and intellectual accomplishment, humanity finds the stately, noble, logic of gratification, where "the right and true order of the Polis is just as much an Erotic one as the right and true order of love" (Marcuse [1955] 1966, 211). According to Brazilian Marcuse scholar Imaculada Kangussu, Marcuse's hypothesis in this regard is that there is a biological foundation for emancipatory political practice (Kangussu 2021). Eros is an essential element of Marcuse's naturalistic philosophy of liberation and ecological materialism. "Sensual love gives a *promesse du bonheur* which preserves the full materialistic content of freedom … . Sensuality … preserves the goal of political action: liberation" ([1945] 1998, 204). "There is an unbroken ascent in erotic fulfillment from the corporeal love of one to that of others, to the love of beautiful work and play, and ultimately to the love of beautiful knowledge" ([1955] 1966, 211).

Campus Opposition to Genocide and Ecocide in Gaza Today   15

Lauren Langman and George Lundskow (2016) have argued that today's "gods" in the U.S.A. tend to be money, fame, thrills and power, and that this reveals the dominant side of the American character. At its margins, significant historical struggles have occurred: progressive social forces struggling against slavery, for women's suffrage, a populist anti-monopoly radicalism, socialism, co-ops, collectives, communes like New Harmony and Oneida, though even the memory of these struggles has been generally repressed. During the 1960s, "New Sensibilities" of the sort Marcuse described in *An Essay on Liberation* (1969, 23) emerged that prefigure a sane socialist society in 21st-century America. By 1972, Marcuse recognized that even a one-dimensional society could see protest groups emerge among students, women, and civil rights activists, who developed an oppositional philosophy and politics. His essentially hopeful outlook on social justice activism and his lionization as the philosopher of the student revolts of the 1970s were both rooted in the common transvaluation of values accomplished by a political Eros that was shaping the Civil Rights struggles, the Women's Liberation movement, labor militancy, and radical environmentalism.

> The primary *counter-force* to aggressive energy is *erotic* energy: to the degree to which it presses aggression into the service of the Life Instincts— it strives for the unification, pacification, and protection of Life. Here is *the hidden "political" element* in this energy: originating in, but transcending, the personal relationships between individuals—erotic energy *strives to transform* the natural and social environment into one of satisfaction and peace—strives to reduce destructive violence, to undo brutality, cruelty, and ugliness.
>
> (Marcuse [1967] 2017, 23)

The promise of *bonheur* was also heralded decades earlier in European *political* thought: in the first article of the French *Declaration of the Rights of Man* (1793). This is traditionally taken as signifying the well-being of all, the general good: "The aim of society is the common welfare [*bonheur commun*]."[25]

> [T]he development of the productive forces renders possible the material fulfillment of the *promesse du bonheur* expressed in art; political action— the revolution—is to translate this possibility into reality.
>
> (Marcuse [1958] 1961, 115)

Ecosocialism, in Marcuse's view, possesses the potential to bring beauty and sensuous satisfaction to humanity. Ecosocialism delivers on art's promise and nature's promise that we can attain our happiness in common by learning to live with dignity and freedom on planet earth. Marcuse regarded the environmental movement of his day as a critical intervention of Eros against institutional destructiveness and as the embodiment of life-affirming energy.

16   *Herbert Marcuse as Social Justice Educator*

Increasingly, the ecological struggle comes into conflict with the laws which govern the capitalist system: the law of increased accumulation of capital, of the creation of sufficient surplus value, of profit, of the necessity of perpetuating alienated labor and exploitation ... . In the last analysis, the struggle for an expansion of the world of beauty, nonviolence and serenity is a political struggle. The emphasis on these values, on the restoration of the earth as a human environment, is not just a romantic, aesthetic, poetic idea which is a matter of concern only to the privileged; today, it is a matter of survival.

(2019, 3–4)

Following a line of thinking from *Eros and Civilization* ([1955] 1966), he theorizes that the "... mobilization and administration of libido may account for much of the voluntary compliance ... with the established society. Pleasure, thus adjusted, generates submission" (Marcuse 1964, 75). He explains that society's control mechanisms become even more powerful when they integrate sexually suggestive and explicitly erotic and violent content into advertising and the mass media and infuse these into the content of mass entertainment and popular culture. The unrestrained use of sex and violence by large-scale commercial interests accomplishes more effective social manipulation and control in the interest of capital accumulation than has repressive sublimation. *Repressive desublimation* fuels counterrevolution by substituting reactionary emotional release in place of rebellion, and counterrevolutionary illusion in place of freedom.

Marcuse posed the question of whether the ascendency of a neofascist regime in the U.S.A. can be prevented. Among the reasons why he asked this was his conviction that since at least 1972 the U.S.A. had entered a period of masculinist counterrevolution.

According to Freud, the destructive tendency in society will gain momentum as civilization necessitates intensified repression in order to maintain domination in the face of ever more realistic possibilities of liberation, and intensified repression in turn leads to the activation of surplus aggressiveness, and its channeling into socially useful aggression. This total mobilization of aggressiveness is only too familiar to us today: militarization, brutalization of the forces of law and order, fusion of sexuality and violence, direct attack on the Life Instincts in their attempt to save the environment, attack on the legislation against pollution and so on.

([1974] 2005b, 167)

Analogous to the essential extraction of "surplus value" under capitalism according to the Marxist critique, Marcuse theorized that a *surplus* repression of human freedom is exacted from the population in advanced industrial societies ([1955] 1966, 35). Even under egalitarian and partnership conditions, a *basic* repression of instincts and desires is needed to sustain ethical human life and civilization. But the distinction between *basic* and *surplus* repression allows

Campus Opposition to Genocide and Ecocide in Gaza Today 17

him to interpret repression anew: civilization does *not* have to be based *wholly* on repression and sublimation; it can also be based on free libidinous (though predominantly non-genital) relationships within a community. The political sublimation of Eros "*does not repress* or even divert erotic energy, but on the contrary, seeks ways of liberating it ..." ([1967] 2017, 23; emphasis in original). The political Eros seeks to release forces that can produce a *counteroffensive* against the dis-economics of cultural polarization, the destruction of nature, and the dread prospect of extinction. The emancipatory Eros of the environmentalist movement "confronts the concerted power of big capital, whose vital interests the movement threatens ..." (2019, 17). Based on Fourier's philosophy, he concludes that, after socialist transformation, work itself could be liberated from surplus repression and become attractive due to a pleasant togetherness ([1955] 1966, 216–217).

By the end of this volume, we shall be able to conclude that in contrast to Freud's *Unbehagen in der Kultur* (*Civilization and Its Discontents*), Marcuse's militant aesthetic politics and ecosocialism will find a radical *Wohlbehagen* attainable—*a sense of a civilization with a full and rich life.* This would entail the fulfillment of humanity's political potential, our *species being* or *Gattungswesen*. Like Marx, Marcuse sees this future condition as the riddle of human alienation solved:[26] global dehumanization replaced by global re-humanization, and gratitude.

> Can we now speculate, against Freud, that the striving for a state of freedom from pain pertains to Eros, to the life instincts, rather than to the death instinct? If so, this wish for fulfillment would attain its goal not in the beginning of life, but in the flowering and maturity of life. It would serve, not as a wish to return, but as a wish to progress. It would serve to protect and enhance life itself. The drive for painlessness, for the pacification of existence, would then seek fulfillment in protective care for living things. It would find fulfillment in the recapture and restoration of our life environment, and in the restoration of nature, both external and within human beings. This is just the way in which I view today's environmental movement, today's ecology movement.
>
> (2019, 16)

Imaculada Kangussu has written that in Marcuse's view "human beings are determined by social structures, *but not only those presently existing* ..." (Kangussu 2021, 231, emphasis added). Our affective and intellectual capacities (and vulnerabilities) have been developed over time, *within history* socio-ecologically. As a species we have endured because of our sensuous appreciation of our emergent powers: the power to subsist cooperatively; to create, to communicate, and to care communally within that form of society that we may rightly call a commonwealth.

Humanity's Commonwealth Sense of Freedom

A commonwealth sense is present in humanity's first teachings on ethics, which are to be found in ancient Africana philosophy. We work for the good in common because it is through our community that we each flourish. This sense has continued as a moral guide to social behavior up to the present. I argue that a commonwealth ethos is the intercultural core of humanity's historical wisdom traditions and that it is at the heart of a future ecosocialist society (Reitz 2023).

Marcuse sees the necessity of work in society as "ontological" (Reitz 2023). Like Marx, he asserted a radically materialist conception of the essence of socially active human beings: seen from the outside, we are the *ensemble of our social relations*; seen from the inside, we are *sensuous living labor*. Sensuous living labor is the substrate of our being as humans—a topic I shall explore and unfold in several places below. In Marcuse's ecosocialist view, there is the promise of *the radical transformation of the labor process itself* in the future—the liberation of laboring humanity from the surplus repression of commodification and alienation. I am stressing Marcuse's underappreciated insight into the latent power of sensuous living labor to liberate itself from exploitation and to make the commonweal (the CommonWealth) a universal human condition.

Our need for the *bonheur commun* has the power to reclaim our intercultural humanity. Our fundamental desire is to gratify human social needs by freely engaging in a kind of public work for the public good. We know our rights to a commonwealth economy, politics, and culture reside in our commonworks. This involves sensuous living labor authentically actualizing itself through human(ist) activism and creativity—humanity remaking itself through a social labor process in accordance with the commonwealth promise of freedom at the core of our material reality.

Notes

1 Fandos and Otterman, "Inside the Week That Shook Columbia University" (2024).
2 Federman, "The War on Protest" (2024). This panic may be described as *Israelist*. "Israelism" is a new word coined to describe one-sided discourse regarding Palestinians that American Jews and others have been imbued with regarding the Israeli occupation, apartheid, and other dehumanizing policies. See Reitz, "Israelism, Antisemitism, and U.S. Military Spending" (2024a) and Reitz, "The Right-Wing Culture Wars Flare in Support of Israeli War Crimes" (2024b).
3 See also Marcuse, *Eros and Civilization* ([1955] 1966); Marcuse ([1945] 1998, 204; 1978, 64).
4 This action called for the establishment of a Third World Studies program at UCSD to be named Lumumba-Zapata College.
5 Krugman, "The Road from Romney to MAGA" (2023). "For the basic story of the Republican Party, going back to the 1970s, is this: Advocates of right-wing economic policies, which redistributed income from workers to the wealthy, sought to sell their agenda by exploiting social intolerance and animosity... . [T]hey did not pay a big political price ... largely because they were able to offset their economic policies by harnessing the forces of religious conservatism and social illiberalism—hostility toward non-whites, LGBTQ Americans, immigrants and more." Confessore, "Antisemitism on Campus Lets Right Restart a Culture Battle" (2023).

Campus Opposition to Genocide and Ecocide in Gaza Today   19

6 Butler, "There Can Be No Critique" (2023).
7 Corder and Frankel, "Experts Say Hamas and Israel are Committing War Crimes in Their Fight" (2023) and Corder, "After Visiting Israel and Ramallah, the ICC Prosecutor Says He Will Intensify Investigations" (2023). Amnesty International, "Damning Evidence of War Crimes as Israeli Attacks Wipe Out Entire Families in Gaza" (2023). Hu, "UN General Assembly Votes to Demand Immediate Ceasefire in Gaza" (2023).
8 Kershner and Eligon, "Israel to Fight Genocide Claims at World Court" (2024). Al Lawati, "Israel is Facing a Genocide Case in International Court" (2024).
9 Wieczner, "How Bill Ackman's Campaign to Oust Harvard's President Failed" (2023).
10 Wieczner (2023).
11 Henri, "'Jews Will Not Replace Us' – for US-President Trump, the Alt-Right are 'Fine People'" (2017).
12 New York Times Opinion page editors, "What is the Path to Peace in Gaza? Here Are Ten Ideas," *The New York Times*, December 12, 2023: Empower Palestinians; Let NATO Nations Send Troops; Create an Economic Future; The Answer Lies with Biden for a Two State Solution; Establish an International Trusteeship with the UN as an Alternative to Israeli Rule; Grant Gaza Statehood; Consider a Leading Role for the UN; Create a Confederation of Two States, Israel and Palestine; Build a Culture of Peace; Let Palestinians Decide Their Freedom. https://www.nytimes.com/interactive/2023/12/12/opinion/gaza-israel-palestinians-plans.html?searchResultPosition=1
13 See Rampell, "Israelism Bucks Blind Faith in Israeli Occupation, Apartheid, and 'The Jewish Disneyland'" (2024). See also Goodman, "New Film [*Israelism*] Examines US Jews' Growing Rejection of Israel's Occupation" (2024).
14 Hartocollis, "House Committee Subpoenas Harvard for Documents Relating to Antisemitism" (2024).
15 See Bazelon, "The Road to 1948" (2024). See also Tolan, *The Lemon Tree* (2006).
16 Murphy, *The Butcher of Lyon* (1983). Moyers, *The Secret Government* (1990).
17 Golinken, "Stanford, Harvard and NASA Still Honor a Nazi Past" (2022).
18 Golinken, op. cit. NB: MAGA Republican Elisa Stefanik accused Harvard and UPenn of permitting Palestinian protesters to engage in "genocidal antisemitism."
19 Lipton, Crowley and Ismay, "Bonanza for Arms Makers As Military Budget Surges" (2022).
20 Lipton, Crowley and Ismay (2022).
21 Melman, *Pentagon Capitalism* (1970); Melman, *The Permanent War Economy* (1985); Sen. Bernie Sanders' op-ed in *The Atlantic* (2024).
22 Giacomo, "Suicide Has Been Deadlier than Combat for the Military" (2019). See also Reitmann, "Collateral Damage" (2024).
23 De Zayas, "U.S. Airman Aaron Bushnell's Self Immolation Outside the Israeli Embassy in Washington, D.C." (2024).
24 Ransby, "MLK Called for a 'Radical Revolution of Values'" (2017).
25 "Le but de la société est le bonheur commun. Le gouvernement est institué pour garantir à l'homme la jouissance de ses droits naturels et imprescriptibles." *Déclaration Française des Droits de l'Homme et du Citoyen du 24 juin 1793*. http://dcalin.fr/internat/declaration_droits_homme_1793.html I owe this insight to Domenico Losurdo (2021, 46).
26 Marx, "Communism is the Riddle of History Solved, and it Knows Itself to be This Solution" (1982, 135).

References

Al Lawati, Abbas. 2024. "Israel is Facing a Genocide Case in International Court: Could it Halt the War in Gaza?" *CNN*, January 9. https://www.cnn.com/2024/01/09/middleeast/israel-genocide-case-world-court-gaza-mime-intl/index.html

20 *Herbert Marcuse as Social Justice Educator*

Amnesty International. 2023. "Damning Evidence of War Crimes as Israeli Attacks Wipe Out Entire Families in Gaza," October 20. https://www.amnesty.org/en/latest/news/2023/10/damning-evidence-of-war-crimes-as-israeli-attacks-wipe-out-entire-families-in-gaza/

Bazelon, Emily (Ed.). 2024. "The Road to 1948: How the Decisions that Led to the Founding of Israel Left the Region in a State of Eternal Conflict," *The New York Times Magazine*, February 18.

Bevins, Vincent. 2020. *The Jakarta Method: Washington's Anticommunist Crusade & the Mass Murder Program that Shaped our World*. New York: Public Affairs/Perseus/Hachette Book Group.

Butler, Judith. 2023. "There Can Be No Critique," *Boston Review*, December 13. https://www.bostonreview.net/articles/there-can-be-no-critique/

Confessore, Nicholas. 2023. "Antisemitism on Campus Lets Right Restart a Culture Battle," *The New York Times*, December 11, A1.

Corder, Mike. 2023. "After Visiting Israel and Ramallah, the ICC Prosecutor Says He Will Intensify Investigations," *ABC News*, December 3. https://abcnews.go.com/International/wireStory/international-court-prosecutor-intensify-investigations-palestinian-territories-105338386

Corder, Mike and Julia Frankel. 2023. "Experts Say Hamas and Israel are Committing War Crimes in Their Fight," *AP World News*, October 13. https://apnews.com/article/israel-hamas-gaza-war-crimes-icc-1a42212b95a7f6ce54909fb22e0d681d

Davis, Angela. 2016. *Freedom is a Constant Struggle: Ferguson, Palestine, and the Foundations of a Movement*. Chicago: Haymarket Books.

Davis, Angela. 1989. Interview (video). Library of Washington University, St. Louis. http://repository.wustl.edu/concern/videos/p2677092b

De Zayas, Alfred. 2024. "U.S. Airman Aaron Bushnell's Self Immolation Outside the Israeli Embassy in Washington, D.C.," *CounterPunch*, February 27.

Fandos, Nicholas and Sharon Otterman. 2024. "Inside the Week That Shook Columbia University," *The New York Times*, April 23. https://www.nytimes.com/2024/04/23/nyregion/columbia-university-campus-protests.html?searchResultPosition=2

Federman, Adam. 2024. "The War on Protest," *In These Times*, May.

Feenberg, Andrew. 2023. *The Ruthless Critique of Everything Existing: Nature and Revolution in Marcuse's Philosophy of Praxis*. London and Brooklyn: Verso.

Feenberg, Andrew. 2018. "Marcuse: Reason, Imagination, Utopia," *Radical Philosophy Review*, Volume 21, Number 2.

Finan, Christopher M. 2007. *From the Palmer Raids to the Patriot Act: A History of the Fight for Free Speech in America*. Boston: Beacon Press.

Giacomo, Carol. 2019. "Suicide Has Been Deadlier than Combat for the Military," *The New York Times*, November 1.

Goldberg, Michelle. 2023. "DeSantis Allies Plot the Hostile Takeover of a Liberal College," *The New York Times*, January 10, A19.

Golinken, Lev. 2022. "Stanford, Harvard and NASA Still Honor a Nazi Past," *The New York Times*, December 16. A22.

Goodman, Amy. 2024. "New Film [Israelism] Examines US Jews' Growing Rejection of Israel's Occupation," Democracy Now! Reprinted in *Truthout*, January 22. https://truthout.org/video/new-film-examines-us-jews-growing-rejection-of-israels-occupation/

Harcourt, Bernard E. 2018. *The Counterrevolution: How Our Government Went to War Against Its Own Citizens*. New York: Basic Books/Hachette Book Group.

Hartocollis, Anemona. 2024. "House Committee Subpoenas Harvard for Documents Relating to Antisemitism," *The New York Times*, February 16.

Henri, Clemens. 2017. "'Jews Will Not Replace Us' – for US-President Trump, the Alt-Right are 'Fine People'," *The Times of Israel*, August 17. https://blogs.timesofisrael.com/jews-will-not-replace-us-for-us-president-trump-the-alt-right-are-fine-people/

Horowitz, David. 2006. *The Professors: The 101 Most Dangerous Academics in America*. Washington, DC: Regnery Publishing.

Horowitz, David. 2000. *Hating Whitey and Other Progressive Causes*. Dallas, TX: Spence Publishing.

Hu, Caitlin. 2023. "UN General Assembly Votes to Demand Immediate Ceasefire in Gaza," *CNN*, December 12. https://www.cnn.com/2023/12/12/middleeast/ceasefire-vote-gaza-israel-un-intl/index.html

Kangussu, Imaculada. 2021. "Marcuse and the Symbolic Roles of the Father: Someone to Watch Over Me," in Jeremiah Morelock (Ed.), *How to Critique Authoritarian Populism*. Leiden: Brill.

Katsiaficas, George. 2024. *Eros and Revolution*. Los Angeles: Black Rose Press.

Katsiaficas, George. 2013. "Eros and Revolution," *Radical Philosophy Review*, Volume 16, Number 2.

Katsiaficas, George. 1989. "*The Eros Effect*," American Sociological Association, national meeting in San Franscisco.

Kershner, Isabel and John Eligon. 2024. "Israel to Fight Genocide Claims at World Court," *The New York Times*, January 11, A-1.

Kors, Alan C. and Harvey Silverglate. 1998. *The Shadow University: The Betrayal of Liberty on American Campuses*. New York: The Free Press.

Krugman, Paul. 2023. "The Road from Romney to MAGA," *The New York Times*, Sept 19, A27.

Langman, Lauren and George Lundskow. 2016. *God, Guns, Gold, and Glory*. Chicago, IL: Haymarket.

Lipton, Eric, Michael Crowley, and John Ismay. 2022. "Bonanza for Arms Makers As Military Budget Surges," *The New York Times*, December 18, A1.

Losurdo, Domenico. 2021. *Nietzsche the Aristocratic Rebel*. Chicago, IL: Haymarket.

Marcuse, Herbert. 2019. *Ecology and the Critique of Society Today: Five Selected Papers for the Current Context*. Philadelphia, PA: The International Herbert Marcuse Society.

Marcuse, Herbert. [1967] 2017. "Protest and Futility," in Peter-Erwin Jansen, Sarah Surak, and Charles Reitz (Eds.), *Transvaluation of Values and Radical Social Change*. Philadelphia, PA: International Herbert Marcuse Society.

Marcuse, Herbert. [1970] 2014. "Interview with *Street Journal*," in Douglas Kellner and Clayton Pierce (Eds.), *Herbert Marcuse, Marxism, Revolution, and Utopia: Volume 6, Collected Papers of Herbert Marcuse*. New York and London: Routledge.

Marcuse, Herbert. [1971] 2012. "Protocol of the Conversation between Philosopher Herbert Marcuse and Israel's Minister of Defense, Moshe Dayan (December 29, 1971)," *Telos*, Number 158.

Marcuse, Herbert. [1969] 2011. "The Role of Religion in a Changing Society," in Douglas Kellner and Clayton Pierce (Eds.), *Herbert Marcuse, Philosophy, Psychoanalysis and Emancipation: Volume 5, Collected Papers of Herbert Marcuse*. New York and London: Routledge.

Marcuse, Herbert. [1968] 2009. "Lecture on Education, Brooklyn College. 1968," in Douglas Kellner, Tyson Lewis, Clayton Pierce, and K. Daniel Cho (Eds.), *Marcuse's Challenge to Education*. Lanham, MD: Rowman & Littlefield.

Marcuse, Herbert. [1972, 1977] 2005a. "Thoughts on Judaism, Israel, etc.," in Douglas Kellner (Ed.), *Herbert Marcuse, The New Left and the 1960s: Volume 3, Collected*

22   *Herbert Marcuse as Social Justice Educator*

Papers of Herbert Marcuse. New York and London: Routledge. The 1977 material repeats many of Marcuse's 1972 statements from: "Isreal is Strong Enough to Concede" same volume.

Marcuse, Herbert. [1974] 2005b. "Marxism and Feminism," in Douglas Kellner (Ed.), *Herbert Marcuse, The New Left and the 1960s: Volume 3, Collected Papers of Herbert Marcuse.* New York and London: Routledge.

Marcuse, Herbert. [1945] 1998. "Some Remarks on Aragon: Art and Politics in the Totalitarian Era," in Douglas Kellner (Ed.), *Herbert Marcuse, Technology, War, and Fascism: Volume 1, Collected Papers of Herbert Marcuse.* New York and London: Routledge.

Marcuse, Herbert. 1978. *The Aesthetic Dimension, Toward a Critique of Marxist Aesthetics.* Boston, MA: Beacon Press.

Marcuse, Herbert. 1972. *Counterrevolution and Revolt.* Boston, MA: Beacon Press.

Marcuse, Herbert. 1969. *An Essay on Liberation.* Boston, MA: Beacon Press.

Marcuse, Herbert. [1955] 1966. *Eros and Civilization: A Philosophical Inquiry into Freud.* Boston, MA: Beacon Press.

Marcuse, Herbert. 1965. "Repressive Tolerance," in R.P. Wolff, B. Moore, and H. Marcuse (Eds.), *Critique of Pure Tolerance.* Boston, MA: Beacon Press.

Marcuse, Herbert. 1964. *One-Dimensional Man, Studies in the Ideology of Advanced Industrial Society.* Boston, MA: Beacon Press.

Marcuse, Herbert. [1958] 1961. *Soviet Marxism, A Critical Analysis.* New York: Vintage.

Marx, Karl. 1982. "Communism is the Riddle of History Solved, and it Knows Itself to be This Solution," in Dirk J. Struik (Ed.), *The Economic and Political Manuscripts of 1844.* New York: International Publishers.

Melman, Seymour. 1985. *The Permanent War Economy.* New York: Simon & Schuster.

Melman, Seymour. 1970. *Pentagon Capitalism: The Political-Economy of War.* New York: McGraw-Hill.

Moyers, Bill. 1990. *The Secret Government: Constitution in Crisis.* Santa Ana, CA: Seven Locks Press.

Murphy, Brendan. 1983. *The Butcher of Lyon: The Story of Infamous Nazi Klaus Barbie.* New York: Empire Books.

Rampell, Ed. 2024. "Israelism Bucks Blind Faith in Israeli Occupation, Apartheid, and 'The Jewish Disneyland'," *CounterPunch*, February 11. https://www.counterpunch.org/2024/02/11/israelism-bucks-blind-faith-in-israeli-occupation-apartheid-and-the-jewish-disneyland/

Ransby, Barbara. 2017. "MLK Called for a 'Radical Revolution of Values.' The Movement for Black Lives Delivers One," *In These Times*, April 4. https://inthesetimes.com/article/mlk-called-for-a-radical-revolution-of-values-the-movement-for-black-lives

Reitmann, Janet. 2024. "Collateral Damage," *The New York Times Magazine*, June 23.

Reitz, Charles. 2024a. "Israelism, Antisemitism, and U.S. Military Spending," *CounterPunch*, March 1.

Reitz, Charles. 2024b. "The Right-Wing Culture Wars Flare in Support of Israeli War Crimes," *CounterPunch*, January 14.

Reitz, Charles. 2023. *The Revolutionary Ecological Legacy of Herbert Marcuse: Ecosocialism and the EarthCommonWealth Project.* Cantley, Quebec: Daraja Press.

Rufo, Christopher F. 2023. *America's Cultural Revolution: How the Radical Left Conquered Everything.* New York: Broadside Books.

Sanders, Bernie. 2024. "Defense Contractors are Bilking the American People," *The Atlantic*, February 27.

Sethness Castro, Javier. 2018. *Eros and Revolution*. Chicago, IL: Haymarket Press.

Tauber, Zvi. 2013. "Herbert Marcuse on Jewish Identity, the Holocaust, and Israel," *Telos*, Number 165.

Tauber, Zvi. 2012. "Herbert Marcuse on the Arab-Israeli Conflict: His Conversation with Moshe Dayan," *Telos*, Number 158.

Tolan, Sandy. 2006. *The Lemon Tree: An Arab, A Jew, and the Heart of the Middle East*. New York: Bloomsbury.

Volpe, John Della. 2022. *Fight: How Gen Z is Channeling Their Fear and Passion to Save America*. New York: St. Martin's Press.

Wieczner, Jen. 2023. "How Bill Ackman's Campaign to Oust Harvard's President Failed," *New York Magazine*, The Intelligencer, December 12. https://nymag.com/intelligencer/2023/12/how-bill-ackmans-plan-to-oust-harvards-president-failed.html

Winter, Rainer. 2020. "Review: Bernard E. Harcourt, The Counterrevolution," *Theory, Culture & Society*, Volume 37, Number 7–8, December.

2 Herbert Marcuse as Social Justice Educator

The Liberal Arts and Sciences, Critical Political Economy, Ecopedagogy

Herbert Marcuse stood in solidarity with the movements against the Vietnam War and ecological destruction and for women's rights and civil rights for oppressed social groups. As we have seen, a similar spirit of revolt is resurgent today, especially among young people, as phenomena of protest have appeared globally against genocide and ecocide in Gaza, the ecological crisis, militarism, gender oppression, police violence, racist and masculinist marketing of automatic weapons to civilians, and labor force precarity. Herbert Marcuse's critical social theory is intended to serve as a countervailing force to conventional intellectual and political theory. It seeks to apprehend the dialectic of the historical and material world and the changing social condition of humanity within it. It is permeated with a multifaceted concern for educational issues and radical action for our political future. It may function thereby as the general theory of social justice education.

Marcuse was a philosophical advocate of revolutionary social change in pursuit of the imperatives of freedom—moral and political imperatives arrested and repressed in advanced industrial society but ultimately understood as real and attainable. His study of the "and" in *Reason and Revolution* ([1941] 1960) turned to both Hegel's philosophy and to Marx's *Economic and Philosophical Manuscripts of 1844* for help in understanding humanity's historical condition of alienation and the rationale and prospect of fulfilling the highest political promise of liberated human beings within a new social order. Marcuse noted that, for Marx, communism is "the real appropriation of the essence of man by man and for man, therefore it is man's complete conscious ... return to himself as a social, that is human, being" (Marx in Marcuse [1941] 1960, 286).

Marcuse furnished his readers with a theoretical orientation otherwise largely untaught in the U.S. educational system. By introducing students in the social sciences and humanities to the Frankfurt School's view of critical social theory, Marxism, and classical German philosophy, he highlighted an appreciation for much of the conflict in our lives, which he contended were unduly stressed, repressed, and torn. The essential connection of education to a comprehension of these social tensions and their conceivable resolution is an integral part of his general theoretical discourse, consistent with the classical goal of the liberal arts and sciences in higher education—the liberation of the full social potential of humanity.

DOI: 10.4324/9781003571582-2

When World War I ended in 1918, Marcuse was witness to the ensuing political tumult in Berlin. A revolutionary uprising of soldiers and striking workers, with whom he empathized, sought to establish self-governing socialist republics in Berlin and Munich. These efforts ended in defeat, and Marcuse became politically demoralized by what he understood as the complicity of the conservatively Marxist German social democrats, whom he had supported, in the assassination of the revolutionary communist leaders Karl Liebknecht and Rosa Luxemburg. Disillusioned with his own political activism, Marcuse turned in his twenties to university study to reflect upon the troubled condition of the world and the very limited possibilities he saw for a truly socialist revolution. The dissertation he was then preparing would not look to economic analyses or party-oriented political action, but rather to works of art from the history of German literature for advice in the struggle against the alienating conditions of social life.

Higher Culture as Humanization: *Bildung*

Marcuse's 1922 PhD dissertation was ultimately published (though not in English) as *The German Artist-Novel* [in 19th and 20th-century literature], by Suhrkamp in *Schriften 1*, in 1978, long after he had established his renowned academic career. Its focus is on the recurrent issues addressed in modern German fiction and deals with the artist's stress and frustration at the incompatibility of an aesthetic life with the painful exigencies of everyday existence. Marcuse's approach was consistent with that of historian Wilhelm Dilthey, foremost representative of the then-prevailing *Geisteswissenschaftliche Bewegung*. This was a reform movement in German higher education emphasizing a renewal of German culture after the war. It sought this renewal through study of the humanities and social sciences, the *Geisteswissenschaften*, rather than through the *Naturwissenschaften* or what in the U.S.A. today are called STEM disciplines, Science, Technology, Engineering, and Mathematics. The ostensibly neutral logical positivism and empiricism of the latter fields were thought to have left unchallenged the technocratic and dangerously imperial leadership mentality of Germany's recent militarist past. Dilthey proposed that the *Geisteswissenschaften* served as an organon (standard collection of works) for critical reflection on historical human reality and that human existence in society could best be understood out of historical works of literature. The concluding sentence of Marcuse's dissertation highlights this same conviction: "Above and beyond the literary-historical problems, a piece of human history becomes visible: the struggle of the German people for a new commonwealth [*Gemeinschaft*]" (Marcuse [1922] 1978, 333, my translation).

According to Dilthey, literary art discloses that internal, human domain where ideals and realities are thought to meet, in a conflicted and enigmatic totality that is true to "Life." Literary art, epic and lyrical poetry, drama, and the novel become the foundation of philosophical and historical understanding. Great literary art is educative and builds empathy. Through self-reflection and

26 *Herbert Marcuse as Social Justice Educator*

introspection (and a modicum of resignation) it forms a dis-alienating strength of character, a seasoned maturity, a self-assuredness and sense of personal worth. Great literary art reveals wisdom and discloses a ground of reason with a "second dimension" beyond superficial, meaningless, and "one-dimensional" appearances.

Marcuse's study of the German artist-novel finds that the social life of the artist is entangled in the ontological paradox of the human condition. Yet the lives of artists differ qualitatively from the lives of non-artists, their experiences often having greater sensory awareness, (excessive) emotionality, the Romantic drama of erotic passions with unrequited love, and/or a religiosity of inwardness and sadness. The artist's personal concern with the problems of being an artist, the alienated quality of their life and activity vis à vis the general forms of social existence emergent from advancing civilization, leads to intellectual and emotional pain, often with pathetic-ecstatic illusions of freedom which are not viable as a form of life. This becomes dissipated artistic and social failure: ethereal "beautiful souls" want to act but recoil from acting. To Marcuse, the testimony of the German artist-novel leads beyond this and shows that a person's self-confidence and aplomb require a certain distance from any uncritical surrender to empty convention, immersion in a subjectively Romantic aestheticism, or engagement in radical mass organizations and social movements.

Goethe as Educator

In Goethe's writing Marcuse sees a search for a *viable form of artistic life in society*. Education as *Bildung* implies the passage from youthful naivete and subjective excess to active and practical adulthood, a process of seasoning and artistic maturation allowing for perfection of one's social self. In Goethe's *Wilhelm Meister's Apprenticeship*, the artist sees in Shakespeare how the theater may have profoundly dis-alienating and educative effects, highlighting, yet ultimately reconciling, inner conflicts. Wilhelm Meister undertakes a "theatrical mission," producing Shakespeare and playing Hamlet himself. To Goethe this is only possible through forms of discipline and self-control (*Entsagung*, resignation and repression) that will permit the harmonious development of his innermost creative impulses and powers within an active life in the real world. Wilhelm realizes that only by voluntarily renouncing his boundless yearnings entangled in life's *Sturm und Drang* for the measure and proportion of an artwork itself can he attain a meaningful social life. The artist must be measured and tempered and fit into the established order, not as capitulation but as an extension of the concept of an effectual and educated ripeness and maturity (*Bildung*). To be *gebildet* (educated) means to be seasoned and hardened, i.e. no longer "green." It means being in control of oneself; repressed yes, but also duly gratified in a sublimated fashion. This does not mean that social and political dimensions of discontent are simply resolved back into the *psychological* domain as *personal* responsibility; rather for Goethe's character, Wilhelm Meister, they are taken up as a theatrical (political and educative) mission: to reform and elevate the theater into a dis-alienating educative agency, a *Bildungsanstalt*. Goethe's fundamental desire is artistry with impact; art against alienation. One must understand one's central intellectual and political task as compatible with the "harmonious regularity of the universe, the world art-work." Marcuse will fifty years later (1972) also emphasize "nature as an ally"! In Goethe he found the epical-realistic or objectivist/Enlightenment mode of the artist-novel.

The Literary Young Germans as Educators

Marcuse's dissertation notes importantly that artist-novels sometimes also convert to novels of contemporary social and political events. Here one sees the artist's experimentation with socially engaged art and with radical/democratic politics as a further mode of social existence that could help resolve the problem of aesthetic alienation and assist in the attainment of new forms of community and solidarity. But the radical cultural goals of the artists, as portrayed by the *Young German* writers, were essentially depicted as being destroyed in the context of revolutionary practice. Subsequent artist-novels drew away from explicit engagement with current events.

Thomas Mann as Educator

Mann's novel, *Buddenbrooks*, is not an artist-novel as such but one with an "artistic-human foundation." It's about the decline of a bourgeois family whose capacity for life has been killed by knowledge and compulsion to perform. Escape comes through aesthetic forms of existence: decadence. Mann's redemptive vision is to reconstitute familial social existence at the level of the high-serious German burgher, who overcomes decadence and aestheticism through an admittedly ironic appreciation of the "joys of the usual." The artist needs to be linked to organic historical (i.e. bourgeois) roots, not to a purely potential utopian vision of reality. In *Death in Venice*, the main character is a music educator who has transformed his subjective yearning into a socially prestigious bourgeois profession, so he is no longer stigmatized as an outsider. The lifestyle of the master artist/professor is only maintained through strict discipline bordering on heroism. Yet this character knows it is ridiculous that he should be *an educator*! He sensed he would fall back into the abyss of self-destructive aesthetic subjectivity, which is of course his tragedy. But Mann is emphasizing also that this is the tragedy not just of an individual but the tragedy of the modern day.

In what ways did this dissertation prepare the way for the Marcuse we are familiar with today? It certainly undergirds his paeans to the value of great art and art's *promesse du bonheur* in his chapters on "The Aesthetic Dimension" in *Eros and Civilization* as well as his final book *Die Permanenz der Kunst* (*The Aesthetic Dimension*). He refers to the aesthetic dimension as the "second dimension," illumining reality beyond the single dimension that is otherwise

28 Herbert Marcuse as Social Justice Educator

everywhere in *One-Dimensional Man*. These valedictions also contribute to the formation of a determined sense of rebellion in pursuit of a just social community and joy—that is to say, to the signature concepts dealing with what he later develops as a critique of ecological destruction, neofascism, white supremacy, hate speech, racist police killings, and the radical goals of socialism.

Émigré as Educator: The Humanities as "Affirmative" Culture

A Jewish-German academic émigré fleeing for his life from the Nazi *Gleichschaltung*[1] (enforced political conformity) (and worse, during the German Third Reich), Herbert Marcuse was, in 1934, the first member of the staff of the Frankfurt Institute to arrive in New York City and represent it at Columbia University. The work of Horkheimer, Adorno, Marcuse and their collaborators will always be rightfully known as the work of the Frankfurt School, but the very concept of "critical theory" is a product of the New York period of the Institute in exile. Critical theory for Marcuse was not an alternative or substitute for Marxism. He sought to raise the philosophy of Marx to its highest level. Marxism furnished new norms for understanding and for justice that enable us to constructively imagine the partnership perspectives, policies, and organizations of the future that might make possible new ways of holding resources and real opportunities for all persons to reclaim the full social power of labor, leadership, and learning. The need to understand and transform the ever-developing human material condition was urgent for Marcuse. Therefore, his social and political theory was perpetually *creative* as well as critical.

As we have seen, Marcuse's 1922 dissertation examined the value of the education afforded by a study of the German artist-novel and Germany's literary art more broadly. In 1937 writing in German from the U.S.A., Marcuse published "The Affirmative Character of Culture," in the *Zeitschrift für Sozialforschung*, an essay outstanding in its use of dialectical method to advance philosophical understanding of education. It demonstrates a profound appreciation and critique of classical German idealism and its venerable *Erziehungsphilosophie*, from Herder to Dilthey. Marcuse employs an explicitly Marxist analysis of bourgeois culture (derived from *Capital* as well as the 1844 *Manuscripts*), yet this examination is also clearly on the way toward the aesthetic vision of liberation (grounded also in Schiller and Nietzsche) to be more fully developed in *Eros and Civilization* ([1955] 1966). This essay—a statement of Marcuse's new aesthetic direction and of the political program of his maturing philosophy emphasizing the practical value of the arts and education against alienation—was first translated into English and published in *Negations* in 1968.

In a careful reading of "The Affirmative Character of Culture," one is confronted by both the immense breadth and intricate sophistication of Marcuse's theorizing. The piece is long and stylistically difficult. It begins with a lengthy consideration of the classical metaphysical separation of practice from theory in the philosophies of Plato and Aristotle and the concomitant "break between the necessary and useful on the one hand and the 'beautiful' on the other" (Marcuse

Herbert Marcuse as Social Justice Educator   29

[1937] 1968, 88; all page numbers in parentheses that follow refer to this). Likewise, Marcuse calls to mind the ancient and hierarchical division of the human psyche into "lower" and "higher" spheres: "The history of the human soul transpires between the poles of sensuality and reason" (90). Neither Plato nor Aristotle was thought to have questioned these separations or the accompanying devaluation of the material and "appetitive" realms. Both consigned happiness to the activities of "pure theory" and "higher culture." In Marcuse's analysis this was, in itself, not a fundamental problem because the philosophies of Plato and Aristotle did not ignore the social ills or the historical realities of commercial Athens in classical Greece. In Marcuse's opinion, these philosophies took up a critical stance to their social situation *precisely in their idealism.*

> Plato's idealism is interlaced with motifs of social criticism ... . And the authentic, basic demand of idealism is that this material world be transformed and improved in accordance with the truths yielded by knowledge of the Ideas. Plato's answer to this demand is his program for the reorganization of society.
>
> (91–92)

Aristotelian theories were less idealistic or more realistic than their Platonic counterparts; therefore, "the reorganization of society no longer occupies a central role" in Aristotle's *Politics* (92). Marcuse described a process at work here in which what he considered to be the *genuine intent of idealism*—that is, the *actualization of its goals*—had decayed and subsided: "The history of idealism is also the history of its coming to terms with the established order" (92). In his estimation, idealism ultimately came to "exonerate" (92) the inadequacies and injustices experienced in the practical realm by promoting an acquiescence to them at the same time as it became abstractly preoccupied with the concepts of the good, the true, and the beautiful that were thought to belong to a "higher" or "finer" world. In this sense, Marcuse maintained that idealism became "tranquilized" (93) sedated, quietist. In a term he apparently coined for this essay, idealism became *affirmative.* Art, education, and culture are considered affirmative in so far as *they confine ideals to a transcendent realm and leave the social world unaltered.*

> When the reproduction of material life takes place under the rule of the commodity form and continually renews the poverty of class society, then the good, the beautiful, and the true are transcendent to this life.
>
> (90)

> The abstract equality of men realizes itself in capitalist production as concrete inequality.
>
> (97)

> The organization of this world by the capitalist labor process has turned the development of the individual into economic competition and left the

30 Herbert Marcuse as Social Justice Educator

satisfaction of his needs to the commodity market ... . The soul is sheltered as the only area of life that has not been drawn into the social labor process.

(108)

Marcuse recognized that the affirmative tradition in culture also included an affirmative *educational component*. His essay presents a philosophical critique of the cultural education propounded by such figures as the 18th-century German romantic Johann Gottfried Herder. Marcuse felt that Herder's positions constituted poetizing approaches to reality revolving around "man's noble education to reason and freedom" (101). Herder's educational scheme stressed an understanding of the human spirit through a nation's art (that is, its folksongs and legends). In Marcuse's estimation, this Romantic educational approach actually betrayed the ideals of human progress and the development of critical intelligence and became instead regressive or apologetic. While freedom and reason were "supposed to be effected through the cultural education of individuals" (103), the real meaning of these notions became fatally sublimated and spiritualized, and represented "a world to be brought about not through the overthrow of the material order of life, but through events in the individual's soul" (103). In their affirmative modes, education and culture belonged "not to him who comprehends the truths of humanity as a battle cry, but to him in whom they have become a posture which leads to the proper mode of behavior" (103). Herder's aesthetic and educational philosophy was seen as part and parcel of the history of affirmation that had attended the idea of beauty as a "noble ideal" in conventional cultural and educational theory and practice, and that has traditionally led to political quietism and social tranquilization. Where Marcuse's dissertation had interpreted the political detachment of the Young German literary artists in their own terms, here he emphasizes acerbically that "in the struggle for a better human future, profound and refined souls may stand aside, or on the wrong side" (113).

Marcuse criticizes the repressive and ideological function of affirmative culture's continual *poetization* (110) of the soul and sublime beauty. The education of "the soul has a tranquilizing effect" (112). Marcuse was aware of the paradoxical circumstance in which the aesthetic treatment of social realities could actually lead to an *anesthetization* of perception and thought. He was intently concerned with emancipating aesthetic theory from this tradition of affirmation. It was thus necessary for him to formulate alternative norms of art and culture that might enable humanity to intervene and transform social reality in the direction of an ideal or utopian conception of social justice. This became clear in *Reason and Revolution* ([1941] 1960) and *One-Dimensional Man* (1964). Marcuse's effort toward socio-aesthetic activism begun in 1937 was generally sustained throughout *An Essay on Liberation* (1969) and *Counterrevolution and Revolt* (1972). He wanted to develop an alternative aesthetic and educational philosophy that could be integrated with emancipatory socio-political action. He was convinced that one could construct a synoptic theory building upon the intention of the Platonic program for the reorganization of society and a critical appreciation of Friedrich Schiller's utopian and humanist declaration of the emancipatory political potential of aesthetic education. Yet he recognized that even these potentially liberating theories would have to be revised in the direction of a social materialism and human sensuality. While acknowledging, on the one hand, that great bourgeois art had a progressive character in its earlier phases, when it represented unattained and utopian goals, Marcuse claims that it nonetheless "entered increasingly into the service of the suppression of the discontented masses" (98). He pointed out that the heroic form of German affirmative culture paved the way for the subservience of the individual to a "total mobilization" (127) in the 1933 German authoritarian state, where "inner freedom abolishes itself by turning into outer unfreedom" (127).

Marcuse wanted to restore a militant concern for material social improvement and striving for sensual (rather than purely intellectual) happiness to the philosophies of art, education, and culture.

> When all links to the affirmative ideal have been dissolved, when in the context of an existence marked by knowledge, it becomes possible to have real enjoyment without any rationalization, and without the least puritanical guilt feelings, when sensuality, in other words, is entirely released by the soul, then the first glimmer of a new culture emerges.
>
> (116–117)

It was clearly Marcuse's intention to revive the tendencies toward utopianism present in even affirmative aesthetic activity. This meant restoring the political dimension to the philosophies of art and education. Marcuse praises, in this regard, the 19th-century cultural historian Jakob Burckhardt for his notion of the Renaissance man as a model for "a life as expansive and full of deeds as possible" (123), noting that affirmative culture has drained the life from this model of expansive activism. Affirmative culture in contrast promoted an ideal of "the person who renounces his instincts and places himself under the categorical imperative of duty" (119). Affirmative culture represented a conservative, Protestant, and neo-Kantian ethical asceticism, which Marcuse sought to redeem by stressing the sensualist aspect of Kant's own doctrines of fantasy and imagination (Marcuse [1955] 1966, 177–178; 1969, 30–31). As a result of the affirmative tendencies toward instinctual renunciation and contempt for the "lower" pleasures of the human body, Marcuse claimed that the potentially liberating countertendencies present in the aesthetic dimension were forced underground. Marcuse wanted to develop an aesthetic and educational philosophy that could *abolish* rather than affirm these repressive and alienating conditions. His search aimed at a theory that could demonstrate the practical value of art, culture, and education for the full elimination of alienation from the material life process. He desired a theory of art and beauty that would be fundamentally incompatible with a bad present. "The Affirmative Character of Culture" represented only the very beginning of his revised aesthetic and educational thinking. It did not yet adequately demonstrate how a philosophy of

32 Herbert Marcuse as Social Justice Educator

art or philosophy of education could negate or transform or perfect the processes of material life in the direction of their fullness and concreteness—toward an actualized ideal. His shift in emphasis from the soul to human sensuousness was clear, as was the shift from the contemplation of Utopia to its realization. Yet he had not been able to depict in detail the sources of power that might enable art and education to accomplish the new cultural goals he thought the contemporary world required. Marcuse was convinced that culture *could be* purged of its affirmative character— that is, of its compatibility with and subservience to the established society—if it could become a countermovement to the social and ideological conditions that alienated the human spirit. A genuinely utopian and humanist form of aesthetic education was considered necessary (though not fully adequate) to cultivate and illumine the emancipatory faculties in humanity's sensuous practical activity, i.e. social labor in accordance with the "New Sensibility" and the radical goals of our political Eros.

Marcuse's Re-definition of Culture

The artist's alienation from the humdrum of ordinary routines in daily life has been a situation that poets and writers have long addressed. Art acts against this alienation. It can be a protest that brings consolation, a sense of sorrow that brings peace, a sense of joy that brings determined rebellion. Marcuse's aesthetic philosophy becomes an earthly one, grounded in human sensuality and social criticism. His aesthetic ethos is *not* some unattainable ideal but a force for change in the real world, inseparable from utopian social practice and the human interest in social justice. In the aesthetic form, the sensuous power of beauty is thought able to imaginatively subordinate death and destructiveness to the non-aggressive life instincts and to herald a logic of gratification that is required precisely by its societal absence. Yet, even the Great Books require a dialectical approach melding liberation and learning.

Multidimensionality and intersectionality function as a restorative presence within Marcuse's philosophizing, as they should for all educators, but they often do not for those trained primarily in the dominant habits of thought in 20th-century U.S. academic routines (business-oriented economics, functionalist and empiricist sociology, instrumentalist educational theory). Marcuse's *One-Dimensional Man* sought to break through the "pre-established harmony between scholarship and national purpose" (Marcuse 1964, 19). Marcuse's philosophy of education synthesizes the emancipatory elements of the liberal arts and sciences tradition with also his emphasis on critical political economy, its attendant intercultural socialist/humanist ethics, radical political activism, and his deep affinity for what today is called ecopedagogy. Rickard Kahn (2009) was among the first to elaborate Herbert Marcuse's value to environmental education.

Conservative reform approaches to the humanities and a liberal arts education (Dinesh D'Souza, William Bennett, E.D. Hirsch, and Allan Bloom) traditionally see them as serving universal aims and goals but fail to acknowledge that a discriminatory politics of race, gender, and class have distorted not only the curriculum but also patterns of faculty hiring and student recruitment and

Herbert Marcuse as Social Justice Educator   33

support. To this degree, the humanities have incorporated the false universalisms of Eurocentrism and Anglo-conformity. Marcuse's Marxism enabled him to assess critically the behaviorism, empiricism, and logical positivism, as well as the racist and colonialist elements still prevalent in the monocultural norms of Anglo-American higher education. Marcuse thus reclaimed the critical elements of the classical philosophical tradition to confront the conventional political theorizing and culture of corporate capitalism with an immanent critique of its own philistinism and provincialism. Critical social theory reexamined advanced industrial society's standards of rationality, i.e. self-interest and private accumulation. It developed a social, philosophical, and historical context for informed judgment critical of exploitation, inequality, alienation, and mindful of possibilities for social transformation. Its criteria were meant to enable humanity to build from within the realities of the present partnership organizations and institutions for the future to permit new ways of holding resources and real opportunities for all persons to reclaim the full social power of labor.

Marcuse's 1965 essay, "Remarks on a Re-definition of Culture" confronted the then-contemporary conventional wisdom about higher education and culture with its reality in the U.S.A.

> Looking at the professed goals of Western Civilization and at the claims of their realization, we should define culture as a process of *humanization*, characterized by the collective effort to protect human life, to pacify the struggle for existence by keeping it within manageable bounds, to stabilize a productive organization of society, to develop the intellectual faculties of man, to reduce and sublimate aggressions, violence, and misery ... . It is only the exclusion of cruelty, fanaticism, and unsublimated violence which allows the definition of culture as the process of humanization.
>
> (1965a, 190–191)

This is a reformulation of his 1937 perspective in "The Affirmative Character of Culture," which perhaps led to that essay's 1968 translation and publication. Marcuse's re-definition sought to contextualize culture's high-sounding goals, noting critically that these are often accomplished "*through* the practice of cruelty and violence" (1965a, 191), and that this practice was rooted in social structure. This was of course a major refrain of Horkheimer and Adorno's *Dialectic of Enlightenment* ([1944] 1972).

Marcuse's *One-Dimensional Man* (1964) had an immense critical cultural impact in the U.S.A. This was in no small measure related also to questions of science and research in service to the "logic of domination" (1964, 144) attendant upon advanced industrial society's systems of social control and warmaking, regulated by a "total administration" (1964, 7). *One-Dimensional Man* examined the "ideology" rather than the "culture" of the epoch, in a further redefinition, as its subtitle made clear: *Studies in the Ideology of Advanced Industrial Society*. The volume expressed and explained Marcuse's revulsion at

34   *Herbert Marcuse as Social Justice Educator*

what he saw as the displacement of higher education's traditional emphasis on the liberal arts and basic scientific research in favor of scholarship explicitly serving capitalism's corporate, military, scientific, and governmental priorities. Marcuse contends that capitalism is obsessed with efficiency, standardization, mechanization, and specialization (all proxies for profit growth), and that this accumulation fetish involves aspects of repression, fragmentation, and domination that impede real education and preclude the development of real awareness of ourselves and our world. Alienation, in Marcuse's estimation, was thought to be the result of students having been "trained to forget" (1964, 104) their authentic human potentials—by educationally eradicating the realm where this knowledge was best preserved, i.e. in the humanities. In *Eros and Civilization*, he had emphasized "The individual does not really know what is going on; the overpowering machine of education and entertainment unites him with all others in a state of anesthesia ..." ([1955] 1966, 103–104). Alienation was seen in large part as the result of miseducation or half-education.

At the same time, Marcuse criticized the many recreational as well as routine activities that had been seductively commercialized by integrating explicitly erotic and violent content into the mass media, mass entertainment, popular culture, and advertising. He coined the term "repressive desublimation" (1964, 75) to characterize what had become one of the culture's most formidable social control mechanisms. Repressive desublimation substituted reactionary emotional release in place of rebellion—an illusion of freedom and satisfaction consistent with the commodity form.

In both his earliest and latest writings, Marcuse directs special attention to discerning an emancipatory power of the intelligence gained through a proper study of the humanities. Marcuse's understanding of the cognitive value of art and philosophy, particularly the great literatures of classical Greece and modern Europe, thus needs also to be appreciated in its dialectical complexity. It is within this context that we may perceive a central theme in his philosophy—its several interconnected attempts to extract critical reason from art and the aesthetic dimension.

Marcuse regards classical learning by means of discourse and reflection on philosophy, literature, drama, music, painting, sculpture, etc. as liberating insofar as this form of learning impels humanity beyond the "first dimension," the realm of mere appearance, to the world of significance and meaning. As Marcuse proposes in *Eros and Civilization*, the very form of beauty is dialectical, uniting the *order of sensuousness* and *the order of reason* ([1955] 1966, 181). It unites the opposites of gratification and pain, death and love, repression and need, and therefore can authentically represent what he takes to be the conflicted, tragic, and paradoxical substance of human life. In Marcuse's view, the insights provided by these liberal studies are transhistorical and are considered the precondition to any political transformation of alienated human existence into authentic human existence.

Marcuse's philosophy of protest within higher education was an emphatic criticism of the corporate liberal vision of Clark Kerr, yet Kerr was never

Herbert Marcuse as Social Justice Educator   35

explicitly named. As head of the University of California, Kerr was a major liberal spokesperson who thereafter became chairperson of the Carnegie Commission on Higher Education. Kerr's view of the pragmatic political *Uses of the University* (1963) represented a decisive departure from the traditional collegiate self-conception as an autonomous ivory tower or grove of academe, one step removed from the practical realm, and stressed instead a logic of corporate and government involvement in higher education. Institutionalized during the '60s at Columbia, Harvard, Berkeley, and at the State Universities of Wisconsin and New York among other places, Kerr called for the transformation of higher education into the "multiversity" having the function of extended service to business, the government, and the military. This quickly came to be implemented almost everywhere in the U.S. system of higher education, as well as now in Europe, where the U.S. model is now displacing traditional higher education structures at an ever-accelerating pace since the events of 1989. As far back as the post-Sputnik, early-Vietnam era, radical critics of U.S. higher education pointed out that the phenomenal growth of these conglomerate systems was heavily subsidized by grants from the federal government and corporations for research into areas such as aerospace, intelligence, and weapons. A massive expansion of Reserve Officer Training Corps programs also occurred during that time. What today would be called neoliberal or market interests characteristically came to influence higher educational policy, giving priority to the needs of the business and military establishments. Many objected also to the dehumanization displayed in an increasing commitment to behavioral objectives in teaching and learning and performance-based criteria for intellectual competence, as well as the growing predominance of managerial language and thinking in the organization of higher education.

Herbert Marcuse's critical philosophy, in contrast to the corporate mentality of Kerr, was permeated with a multifaceted concern for the liberal arts and sciences as educative processes linked to humanization goals as well as radical engagement for the future political actualization of our sense of commonwealth. Art was thought to preserve a liberating memory that our social and cultural worlds are *not* the inevitable products of the gods or of time or of nature; *nor* are they fixed or static. Social forces and social structure are factors derived from the creative and productive acts of human labor and objectification. Reification is said to occur when this human creative action is forgotten. By the time of his final book, *The Aesthetic Dimension* (1978), Marcuse claimed (echoing Horkheimer and Adorno's statement in *Dialectic of Enlightenment*): "'All reification is a forgetting,' Art fights reification by making the petrified world speak, sing, perhaps dance" (1978, 73). Marcuse theorized that art and philosophy provided a deeper kind of remembrance and cognition by recalling *the species-essence of the human race* from philosophical oblivion ([1955] 1966, 232). He contended that the reality of death and human suffering assert themselves as pivotal phenomena in the educative process of recollection, even where the artist and the work of art draw away from them in pursuit of an eternity of joy and gratification. He stressed the emancipatory potential of a renascent

36 Herbert Marcuse as Social Justice Educator

sensuality under the guidance of the most rational and legitimate goals of art. In this way a renewed form of liberal arts education could act against one-dimensionality and cultural alienation, re-humanizing political life.

In addition to "The Affirmative Character of Culture" ([1937] 1968) and "Remarks on a Re-definition of Culture" (1965a), there are two documents in particular in which educational philosophy becomes Marcuse's primary focus. These are the "Lecture on Education, Brooklyn College, 1968" (2009a), as well as the "Lecture on Higher Education and Politics, Berkeley, 1975" (2009b). These were unpublished lectures located in the Frankfurt Marcuse archive subsequently brought out by Douglas Kellner, Tyson Lewis, Clayton Pierce, and K. Daniel Cho in *Marcuse's Challenge to Education* (2009). While comparatively unknown even today, they can be taken to undergird a valuable contemporary approach to the critical theory and practice of education.

Marcuse's immense respect for theoretical education and its power to enhance human life was clearly reflected in the central tenets of the Brooklyn lecture, which stresses that our future and our freedom hinge on a new and expanded cultural emphasis on general education. He also understood that there needs to be a key unity in educational philosophy linking critical thought to radical action. This means students *and teachers* must "become partisan against oppression, militarization, brutalization" ([1968] 2009a, 38). While Marcuse has elsewhere pointed to the philosophies of Kant (1972, 27) and Schiller ([1955] 1966, 187) with regard to the critical rationality of art in higher learning, most educators in the U.S.A. have been unfamiliar with these German pedagogical perspectives. Of course, certain outstanding figures in the history of education in the U.S.A.—like John Dewey, Charles W. Eliot, and W.E.B. Du Bois—had studied in Germany or otherwise knew well the value of its high culture. Nonetheless, Marcuse is right about the regrettable fact that general education in the United States is really "a very recent concept" ([1968] 2009a, 33). While he does not elaborate the historical detail in this regard, much effort toward general education was made in the U.S. A. during the 1940s, largely after World War II. This was rooted primarily in the Great Books movement and the work of Robert M. Hutchins, Chancellor of the University of Chicago, as well as in the Harvard Report on General Education (1945). In this context, general education via the liberal arts and sciences was a conservative Cold War phenomenon hostile to social criticism and directed against progressive reform efforts in education. Marcuse had in 1964 already commented on the tendencies in U.S. education to flatten out and surrender the critical potential of higher learning to single-dimensionality (1964, 64–65). His 1968 lecture at Brooklyn College in contrast elaborates education's emancipatory (though rigorously constrained) *potential*. "General education," is a kind of education previously "restricted to the ruling class ... , [but] education is *not* general even today" (2009a, 33, emphasis in original). Access to the Great Books and general education, he says, remains confined to the privileged few and is an upper-class phenomenon, not only because it is an expression of underlying structures of social inequality but because it contains a potentially dangerous critical dimension.

General education tends to be socially and institutionally controlled, he emphasizes, because of "the *subversive* element" in this education. Theoretical education involves "... knowledge, intelligence, reason as catalysts of social change—projection of the possibilities of a 'better' order; violation of socially useful taboos, illusions" ([1968] 2009a, 33–34). Opposition to this general theoretical education arises from below and from above, due to a deeply seated vocationalist anti-intellectualism in U.S. history and culture. Still, Marcuse stresses that wider reform efforts toward general education are gaining momentum "on a very material basis," namely ... the need for industrial society to increase the supply of skilled workers and employees, especially scientists, technicians, etc. for the efficient development of the productive forces and their apparatus and, more recently, the need for psychologists and sociologists for analyzing, projecting and stimulating economic and political demand ([1968] 2009a, 34).

The world has witnessed in the intervening years since Marcuse addressed the material forces impelling U.S. education toward the general and the theoretical the full-scale ascent of the information age, the rise of electronic technologies for information processing, the Internet, artificial intelligence and now the postdigital realm of teaching and learning. Marcuse's 1968 insights also retain a contemporary relevance given the neoliberal culture wars that started in the mid-1980s and continue up to the present day. In the '80s era of Reagan, conservative authors William Bennett and Lynne Cheney attempted to revivify an elitist, Eurocentric program for the liberal arts. Today Christopher Rufo (2023) is doing much the same as Allan Bloom (1987) did, railing against Marcuse, multiculturalism, and critical social/race theory.

The political imperatives of neoliberalism today are more openly vicious than the "comfortable, smooth, reasonable, democratic unfreedom" (1964, 1) that Marcuse condemned in the '60s. Global polarization and growing immiseration have brought an end to what he once described as the harmoniously integrated and totally administered political universe of the liberal welfare/warfare state. A resurgence of reactionary rhetoric and racist tendencies on the right is occurring today; for example, in the right wing's attacks on critical race theory and curriculum reform efforts like *The 1619 Project* led by Nikole Hannah-Jones (2021).

Marcuse's *Counterrevolution and Revolt* (1972) warned of the emergence of an assault (usually more stealthy than Rufo and DeSantis) by an increasingly predatory capitalist system against *liberal democratic change*, and *not only against the radical* opposition (1972; also [1974] 1987, 172, emphasis added). Marcuse emphasized:

> The Western world has reached a new stage of development: now, the defense of the capitalist system requires the organization of counter-revolution at home and abroad. ... Torture has become a normal instrument of "interrogation" around the world ... even Liberals are not safe if they appear as too liberal.
>
> (1972, 1)

38 *Herbert Marcuse as Social Justice Educator*

These regressive developments render Marcuse's educational and political insights ever more relevant. Marcuse's educational philosophy emphasizes that if democracy means the institutionalization of freedom and equality and the abolition of domination and exploitation, then democracy remains "to be created" ([1968] 2009a, 38).

For Marcuse, educational work is a form of democratic activism. In his estimation, critical educators and students need to continue to take risks and struggle to infuse the curriculum with analysis of the "critical, radical movements and theories in history, literature, philosophy" ([1968] 2009a, 37). The curriculum must afford a world-historical, international, and multicultural perspective that examines the pivotal social struggles that have led to the emergence of key standards of criticism in ethics, in logic, in the worlds of art, physical science, production and technology. These standards constitute the criteria of judgment which intelligence requires.

Marcuse's publications broke through the Cold War paralysis of criticism in the U.S.A., making it possible for many *students* to reframe social circumstances theoretically. Marcuse was *educating the educator*, consistent with Marx's admonition in *Theses on Feuerbach* (1845), and presaging contemporary educational theorists like Henry Giroux, Douglas Kellner, and Peter McLaren. Critical education, for Marcuse, is education that by its own inner dynamic "leads beyond the classroom"... and may define action and behavior patterns "*against the Establishment*" ([1968] 2009a, 35, emphasis in original).

> The voice of the Establishment is heard day and night over the media of mass communication—program as well as commercials, information as well as advertisement—and it is heard through the machine of each of the two parties. The voice of the radical opposition is sometimes heard [but] through no machine. It has no promising jobs to give, *no money* to buy adherents and friends. Within this structure of basic inequality, the radical opposition can be tolerated *up to the point* where it tries to break through the limits of its weakness, through the illusion of democracy, and then it meets the reality of democracy, as the police, the National Guard, and the courts ... . Institutionalized violence ... confronts any action by the opposition which transcends the limits set by, and enforced by, established Law and Order.
>
> ([1968] 2009a, 36)

Marcuse knew that the crisis of educational theory required a transformation of the frayed academic credo of liberation through the arts into a more philosophically and sociologically advanced and radical form of critical theory ([1937] 1968). According to Marcuse's 1975 "Lecture on Higher Education and Politics" at Berkeley:

> To attain our goal, we need *knowledge*. It is still true that *theory* is the guide of radical practice. *We need history* because we need to know how it came about that civilization is what it is today: where it went wrong. And

we need the history not only of the victors, but also of the victims. *We need a sociology* which can show us where the real power is that shapes the social structure. *We need economics* which are not "sublimated" to mathematics. *We need science* in order to reduce toil, pain, disease, and to restore nature.

([1975] 2009b, 43)

Marcuse's focus is on social transformation: "*The alternative* is not a free-wheeling emotionalism, intolerance, but another concept and another practice of objectivity, another interpretation of facts, namely in terms of the given possibilities to build a better society through radically changing the established one" ([1975] 2009b, 42). Technology and education tend to facilitate forces of domination, but Marcuse makes clear that they also have the capacity to overcome alienated labor and bring qualitative change to our lives with generous amounts of leisure and free time if propelled by ecosocialist politics as we build a new world system.

> Radical social change requires men and women who *not only* want productive relations without exploitation—that is a planned economy, the equal distribution of the social wealth—but also a life that is no longer spent in making a living—that is an end-in-itself, to be enjoyed in solidarity with other free human beings, and nature.
>
> ([1975] 2009b, 40)

> Warning! This is not the relaxing of scholarship, not the reduction of learning, not the abandonment of scientific attitude, but their redirection, their emancipation.
>
> ([1975] 2009b, 41)

> The restructuring of the university, and the *new concept of learning and teaching* will be the reintroduction of ethics, passion, "existential commitment and involvement," into learning and teaching.
>
> ([1975] 2009b, 42)

We need science, philosophy and religion that function in a humane, critical, and creative manner, such that our scholarly works are consecrated in service to the qualitative improvement of human life on earth. It is necessary to theorize our society critically if we are to have a vehicle for correctly informed transformative practice.

Ecofeminists like Silvia Federici (2020), Ariel Salleh ([1997] 2017), and Maria Mies and Vandana Shiva ([1993] 2021) criticize the "warrior science" of the sort practiced at Los Alamos (where the Manhattan Project's research was tethered to atomic bomb making), or at Monsanto (where research aimed at altering and patenting genetic life into GMO seed for profit maximization in spite of ecological destruction). Ecofeminism urges instead a science of degrowth, wealth in

40 Herbert Marcuse as Social Justice Educator

common, and *buen vivir*. Likewise, critical naturalist philosopher Roy Bhaskar called for an advanced level of our understanding of science and nature outside those traditionally taught in graduate school or utilized in business: a new critical naturalism that includes a restructuring of science and social science: such that we can *"love" them* (Bhaskar, Singh, and Hartwig [2001] 2020, 35). In Bhaskar's estimation, the dynamic realities of nature and society operate independently of any human mind, but *without love*, philosophical accounts of nature, science, and society do not present a cogent explanation of the full secular and material reality. In his view, we must re-purpose teaching and research in accordance with principles of compassion, mercy, and love, in order to care adequately and effectively for our societal and planetary futures.

As we have seen, general education in the liberal arts and humanities for Marcuse was linked essentially to *practical efforts at cultural transformation*, something I have elsewhere characterized as Edu*Action* (Reitz 2002). Edu*Action* is my term for innovative teaching strategies grounded in critical materialist analysis of society and its prospects. I draw both on Marcuse and Paulo Freire, who offers an active learning process focusing on three areas of inquiry in *Pedagogy of the Oppressed* ([1970] 1993). Students should be given the opportunity to identify on their own: 1) the most serious and disturbing "limit situations" (obstacles, contradictions, negations) that they (and by extension, all of us) need to know more about as challenges to their (and our) fulfillment and humanization; 2) student action(s) in response to these limit situations, both actual and possible; and 3) structures of society and institutional realities that require transformation in order to free us from these limit situations in the future (Freire [1970] 1993). Embedded within these questions we see Freire's fundamental commitment to the subtle, yet foundational, critique of political economy. As did Socrates, Freire called for "directed dialogue" with students. Marcuse concurs that it is absolutely indispensable to bring the theoretical analysis of problems and prospects deftly and appropriately to bear in conversation and to guide the dialogue in a manner consistent with critical political economic insights. The teacher's own analysis must be informed by philosophy and social science and the critical materialist sociological insights. It is only a mastery of scholarship and knowledge that gives one the capacity to be a critical intellectual.

Despite Marcuse's valuable attention to issues of class, race and gender, he does from time to time continue to view literary-aesthetic education as standing apart from sociological and historical methods as well as from the philosophical categories generally associated with a dialectical or historical materialism. Political, historical, and educational issues are at times considered best understood *out of art itself and out of art alone*. This aspect of Marcuse's approach, drawn from Dilthey, as well as the cultural radicalism of Nietzsche and the depth psychology of Freud, occasionally asserts a logical and political-philosophical priority over his treatment of the thought of Hegel and Marx, and appears to define Marcuse's understanding of aesthetic education as a foundation of a critical theory.

Herbert Marcuse as Social Justice Educator   41

Viewing Marcuse's life's work as a whole, I stress that he is an immensely complex and sometimes contradictory thinker. He both juxtaposes and attempts to reconcile two robust paradigms in philosophy. These are intertwined, yet they both have distinctive criteria for critical insight. The *ontological/hermeneutic/aesthetic paradigm* considers meaning primarily in terms of a human core of subjectivity and experience. Thus his 1932 volume written for Heidegger was titled *Hegel's Ontology*, not "Hegel's Dialectic." Likewise, in 1955 he wrote about the human condition in terms of the internal turmoil and distress held to be inherent in the depth dimension of human existence (with Eros and Thanatos as the core sensual forces), i.e. what is often termed his Freudian Marxism. Here conflict is theorized as revealed, enclosed, preserved and transformed by the aesthetic form, and its truth is elevated above societal and historical particulars.

But there is, in my view, an *historical materialist side* of Marcuse's critical social theory that ultimately gains greater explanatory power because it retains external referentiality implicating knowledge and art in the context of a structural and historical analysis of social life. This affords a malleability and freedom from a priori essentialist presuppositions. This side of his theorizing possesses a capacity to intervene against material structures of oppression in ways beyond the reach of the ontological/hermeneutical/aesthetic approach. As this volume progresses, I shall attempt to harmonize these tendencies within what I have come to call Marcuse's *ecological materialism*. But it is essential to show that Marcuse undertook a strong, critical examination of political economy—especially the social dynamics of economic inequality, militarism, and racism—and this is a vital part of his social justice approach to education and to the de-humanizing processes of commodity culture. Today we must still inquire, as he did, into strategies of cultural transformation.

Critical Political Economy

The conventional educational wisdom in the U.S.A. generally offers an account of our social order and our history *without critical political economy, without an examination of the structural drivers of unequal life chances, without a materialist theory of power* that can hold accountable the predatory enforcement of extractive and exploitative economic relations grounded in the substantive differentials between propertied and non-propertied segments of the population. Without critical political economy, one does not come to understand that inequality is *not* simply a matter of the gap between rich and poor but of the structural relationships in the economic arena between propertied and non-propertied segments of populations.

As we have seen, Marcuse utilized classical Marxist concepts from *Capital* in "The Affirmative Character of Culture." Later, he systematically outlined his critical political economy of a U.S.-led, global capitalist world in his *Paris Lectures at Vincennes University, 1974*, published posthumously by the International Herbert Marcuse Society (Jansen and Reitz 2015). Marcuse finds that

42 Herbert Marcuse as Social Justice Educator

the very development of "capitalism invalidates its own production relations, that capitalism invalidates its own way of life, its own existence" ([1974] 2015, 48). Most importantly, in this and other works, he shows that there are attainable and realistic economic alternatives—including those that have emancipatory political dimensions once derided as utopian.

In 1974 Marcuse saw American society as having attained the "highest stage in the development of monopoly capitalism" (2015, 21):

- Economic power is more highly concentrated in the U.S.A. than among other advanced capitalist countries. U.S.-dominated multinational corporations have penetrated in a neo-imperialist fashion into the developed as well as undeveloped countries. The U.S.A. is exporting *production itself* from the metropolitan countries to other capitalist and pre-capitalist countries with lower production costs.
- There is a fusion of *political, economic,* and *military power* in which the representatives of particular corporate interests have shaped the key leadership in government and administration.
- "You know too well, I suppose, the progress which by virtue of the electronic industry has been made in surveilling an entire population secretly, if desired" ([1974] 2015, 23).
- The population, generally managed without overt force through advanced forms of political economic manipulation, is now controlled through *the systematic and methodical increase in the power of the police*. This enforcement keeps itself within the framework, although reduced framework, of the patterns of unfreedom that pass for American democracy.

([1974] 2015, 23)

This fourth point, especially, was quite perceptive given the nation's recently awakened awareness of the regularity of police killings of unarmed black men in the U.S.A. after incidents such as Ferguson and Minneapolis and Edward Snowden's revelations fifty years after Marcuse's lectures, not to mention the aggressive police actions against campus encampments protesting genocide in Gaza in 2024.

To a large degree in these lectures, Marcuse's overall perspective valorizes a classical Marxian analysis of political economy of the U.S.A. and its sphere globally. This analysis has today won wide acceptance among a range of anti-globalization activists and in the more radical circles of the Occupy movement and Black Lives Matter. We can see that it was Marcuse who, fifty years ago, warned of the global economic and cultural developments that are now much more obvious given capitalism's crescendo of economic failures since 2008. Political and philosophical tendencies that are often referred to as "neoliberalism" and/or "neoconservatism" in much analytical work today are treated in depth by Marcuse in these lectures. One significant insight is that

Herbert Marcuse as Social Justice Educator   43

At the highest stage of its development, capitalism reproduces itself by devoting a growing portion of socially-necessary labor time to labor outside of the material production of goods and to the work of commercial and financial operators, professional supervisors, and so on.

([1974] 2015, 43)

He thus recognized the incipient tendencies toward the growth of the financialization of the economy. Speculation on fluctuations in asset prices is displacing the production of goods or services as a source of capital accumulation, and this has come to dominate what passes for "investment" in the U.S. political economy today.

Marcuse discerned in these Paris lectures a dialectic of the *ripening and rotting* ([1974] 2015, 13) of the productive forces.

Capitalism retains [its] stabilizing power in a reorganized form, reorganized on the national as well as global scale. A few indications of this reorganization: On the national scale, in the recent years we have witnessed a considerable and still growing restriction on civil rights and liberties by the courts, by administrative decree, by legislation. We have observed a continued and a growing manipulation of the still-existing democratic process, as if it would not have been manipulated enough already before. If it is impossible to become a candidate in the elections without disposing of a fortune of around a million dollars, this is in any case a strange form of democracy.

([1974] 2015, 5)

The development of U.S. capitalism involved advancing economic and political dysfunction. Marcuse continues:

I suggest to analyze this problem in the classical Marxian terms, namely, that the very forces which make for the preservation and for the growth of the capitalist system are also the forces which make for its decline and eventual collapse. This is the classical dialectical conception, and I've found that it is the only one that gives, or may give us, an adequate understanding of what is going on.

([1974] 2015, 37)

In *One-Dimensional Man* (1964), Marcuse had stressed the nearly total absorption of the populations of advanced industrial societies within a completely administered welfare/warfare state. Ten years later, in a "stage of unprecedented social wealth and unprecedented growth capacity ... this contradiction [capitalist productivity and continued alienated labor—CR] threatens to explode" ([1974] 2015, 48). Marcuse's unique analytical perspective stressed that

44 *Herbert Marcuse as Social Justice Educator*

it is not the threat of impoverishment, it is not dire material privation and need, but on the contrary, it is the reproduction and re-creation of increasing social wealth, it is the high standard of living on an enlarged scale, which ushers in the end of capitalism.

([1974] 2015, 48)

This is the Twentieth Century form of the contradiction: On the one hand, the increasing production of goods which could constitute a realm of freedom, joy, and creative work. And on the other hand, the perpetuation of toil and alienated labor in order to be able to purchase and sell these goods to be enjoyed in a realm of freedom.

([1974] 2015, 52)

Marcuse believed he could discern a societal disintegration in the U.S.A. from what was actually happening in the process of production itself. First, there was the "increasing unproductivity of those who control the destructive and wasteful productive forces today" ([1974] 2015, 33). He pointed out that in 1974 the Pentagon was the nation's largest industrial enterprise with 14.2 million workers directly or indirectly dependent on military spending.

[I]f you throw together—which as an orthodox Marxist you might well do—unemployment and employment for the military services, you arrive at the following figures: a total of over 25% of the labor force, i.e. 22.3 million, were either unemployed or dependent on military spending directly or indirectly.

([1974] 2015, 42)

This is a capitalism of a different stripe, one in which living labor is overshadowed by the preponderance of congealed labor (capital goods), intensifying the classic tendency of the rate of profit to fall. This is a capitalism with a frantic bourgeoisie that has become more and more militarist and predatory; super profits are generated by wasteful war production, and any limited prosperity among war production workers eludes the masses of working people whose conditions of life become more and more precarious.

Marcuse saw that the composition of the workforce was also changing and its opposition was still not organized on a mass scale. Yet within the labor force there were in 1974 evident forms of unorthodox opposition: absenteeism, sabotage, unauthorized strike action by militant autoworkers, etc. Labor's recognition of the obsolescence of alienated toil has become more and more palpable, even if workforce rebellion was noticeably dampened until the eruption of a nationwide strike wave in 2023, epitomized by the UAW's successful strike against the big three automakers. Rehabilitating the concept "proletariat," Marcuse wrote in one of his last publications: "Can there still be any mystification of who is governing and in whose interests, of what is the base of their power?" ([1979] 2014). This was an echo of his 1974 statement: "No specific group can substitute, can replace the working class as the subject and agent of radical social change" ([1974] 2015, 60).

Marcuse's 1974 *Paris Lectures* articulates a broad view of labor and the Left, seeing it globally and locally as the opposition posed by workforce militants of all sorts, the opposition posed by the intelligentsia, and the opposition posed by the women's liberation movement. The question he considers key is whether these oppositional forces are or are not gaining power. In his estimation, increasing numbers of individuals are no longer adhering to the operational values that essentially help keep the system going. He believes there are warranted prospects for radical change and that there is the "possible advent of a free socialist society" ([1974] 2015, 69).

On the question of "who is or could be the avant-garde today" ([1974] 2015, 11), Marcuse discusses the *historical agents and subjects of social change* under three headings, each of which he sees as having now a *primarily preparatory, educational function*:

The Working Class

> What is actually happening at this stage of capitalist development is not the emergence of a new working class but a vast extension of the working class, an extension of the working class to strata of the middle classes which at previous stages of capitalism have been independent.
>
> ([1974] 2015, 46)

Within this, in 1974, wildcat strikers and small groups of black people and Chicanos were the most radical. "This small minority may very well be the beginning of a process which may well threaten the system as a whole" ([1974] 2015, 67). Working class for Marx and Marcuse meant all those, whether employed or unemployed, whose income is dependent upon wages and salaries in exchange for labor, rather than those whose income flows primarily from property holdings, in the form of dividends, interest, profit, or rent, i.e. as returns on capital. Despite attempts by "capital to intensify and enlarge the division within the working class itself," ([1974] 2015, 67) ... "a potentially revolutionary attitude expresses itself outside and against the trade union bureaucracy" ([1974] 2015, 62–63). "In the place of a still not actually revolutionary working class, the preparatory educational political work of such groups as students assumes all-important significance" ([1974] 2015, 8).

The Intelligentsia

The intelligentsia has a political potential much admired by Marcuse, but he states: "I have never said that ... students could be a replacement" ([1974] 2015, 8) for the working class. In fact, Marcuse recognizes that the student movement of the '60s and '70s had quite subsided; that it needed to regroup after disappointment and prepare for the long haul. Yet movement students and public intellectuals as independent and critical thinkers could educate the nation! Marcuse warned against the theory that "knowledge workers" were becoming a new class. While knowledge was becoming a decisive productive force,

46 *Herbert Marcuse as Social Justice Educator*

the application of knowledge in the process of production remains dependent on the actually ruling class. The vast majority of these so-called knowledge workers do not by themselves make decisions which actually would control the development of the economy. Their knowledge and at least the application of their knowledge remains subordinated to this interest ...

([1974] 2015, 15)

The Women's Liberation Movement

Marcuse also underscores his belief that the women's movement is potentially one of the most important political movements. This movement is seen as key in the transformation of civilization's traditionally patriarchal values, and this is central to what he sees as the "context of the enlarged depth and scope of the revolution, of the new goals and possibilities of the revolution" ([1974] 2015, 60) such that the movement for the liberation of women finds proper political significance.

Intellectuals and students in the late 1970s increasingly saw their task as political education as well as radical opposition to oppressive educational and political realities. This was also the period of the most intense and successful reform movement in education, especially higher education: the multicultural education reform movement.

The multicultural education reform movement that developed during the 1980s was international in scope and a response to the racial tension that often confronted newer waves of immigrants coming into England, Germany, France, the U.S.A., Canada, Australia, and elsewhere. The movement exhibits a variety of political perspectives ranging from liberal to radical to revolutionary forms, and its overarching goal was (is) to help students and teachers develop more positive attitudes toward ethnic (and linguistic) minorities, to help them oppose discrimination, and to pursue goals of social justice and fuller equality. One area of broad agreement has been that the voices of oppressed minorities must be allowed to speak for themselves and thus be granted entry into the canonical curriculum (Banks and Banks 1997). Henry Giroux and Peter McLaren were prominent voices in this regard, with revolutionary multiculturalism a major feature of revolutionary critical pedagogy.

The New Sensibility—Discontent from the Left: A Transvaluation of Values

Marcuse argued that the spirit of rebelliousness during the '60s expressed a visceral repugnance at the totality of the efficiently functioning social order of advanced industrial society. He finds crucial "the emergence in the individual of needs and satisfactions which can no longer be fulfilled within the framework of the capitalist system, although they were generated by the capitalist system itself" ([1974] 2015, 53). These include the struggle for the restoration of nature, women's equality, racial equality, reduction in profitable waste. Here he is developing the perspective presented two years earlier in *Counterrevolution and Revolt*.

> [W]hat is at stake in the socialist revolution is not merely the extension of satisfaction within the existing universe of needs, nor the shift of satisfaction from one (lower) level to a higher one, but the rupture with this universe, the *qualitative leap*. The revolution involves a radical transformation of the needs and aspirations themselves, cultural as well as material; of consciousness and sensibility; of the work process as well as leisure.
>
> (1972, 16–17)

The final paragraphs of Marcuse's *Paris Lectures* conclude with a question that appears to refine the form of radical opposition that he had previously termed the "Great Refusal" (1969, viii–ix; 10)—with his revolutionary admonition to work for the *radical* rather than the *minimal* goals of socialism, consistent with Kohei Saito's (2024) emphasis on degrowth in Marxism.

> Is this opposition in any demonstrable way really tending towards a revolution which would not only do away with capitalism but also bring about, perhaps, a new form of socialism, namely socialism as in any and every respect qualitatively different and a break with capitalism, again the radical transformation of values of which I spoke? And it seems to me that only a decisive redirection of production itself would in this sense be a revolutionary development. A total redirection of production, first of all, of course, towards the abolition of poverty and scarcity wherever it exists in the world today. Secondly, a total reconstruction of the environment and the creation of space and time for creative work; space and time for creative work instead of alienated labor as a full-time occupation.
>
> One only has to formulate these goals in this way in order to see what is involved here, namely, such a revolution, which would truly replace the capitalist system with a true socialist system, may well, and perhaps with necessity, mean a lower standard of living for the privileged population in the metropolitan countries. The abolition of waste, luxury, planned obsolescence, unnecessary services and commodities of all kinds may well mean a lower standard of living, which may not be a price too high to pay for the possible advent of a free socialist society.
>
> ([1974] 2015, 69)

Marcuse was attracted to the New Left during this period because the radicals were conscious not only of what they were *against* but also what they were *for*. They were against capitalism because it represented the waste and the degradation of the earth; profitable plastic litter, air pollution, trash (planned obsolescence), toxic dumping, air and water pollution, resource depletion, etc. The "Great Refusal" (1969. viii–ix; 10) constituted a multidimensional expression of *system negation*. In his estimation, the New Left was *radical* and not merely negative: it projected the potentialities in the objective conditions; it anticipated possibilities not yet realized including the economy's potential to

48   Herbert Marcuse as Social Justice Educator

eliminate want and misery, making feasible a new emphasis on quality of life not just a secure subsistence. Their subjective and radical consciousness was way ahead of the objective conditions and pointed the way forward.

In a statement that he ironically characterized as "off the record," given the fact that "all of these things [recording devices in the Vincennes lecture hall] are on," Marcuse made a clear declaration:

> I do believe, as I said, there will be a socialist revolution. I do believe that in order to be really global and successful it will have to occur, as Marx foresaw, in the most highly developed industrial country in the world, and in order to come about it will take a time of at least 75 to 150 years. Now there you have it.
>
> ([1974] 2015, 34)

Socialism's minimum standards required the provision of adequate social needs-oriented programs and services such as housing, health care, childcare, and education, to everyone, as well as government policy, law enforcement, and public media that ensure the optimization of the human material condition. But for Marcuse, the *radical* goals of socialism went beyond the elimination of want and poverty through efficient production and distribution of use-values: they involved a "qualitative leap" in needs and values—not only against

> the fragmentation of work, the necessity and productivity of stupid performances and stupid merchandise, against the acquisitive bourgeois individual, against the servitude in the guise of technology, deprivation in the guise of the good life, against pollution as a way of life.
>
> (1972, 16–17)

The *fullest development of socialism/communism reaches farther*: to labor that is freed from its commodity form (as wages or salaries), becoming common *work* for the common *wealth*. Labor's liberation from and sublation to the new *common-wealth form* allows human life to be infused with beauty from its foundation up—ultimately for the entire society to express itself as a work of art.

Ecopedagogy and the EarthCommonWealth Alternative

Marcuse is the only figure of the Frankfurt School who developed writings addressing ecological problems and strategies as such. His final published essay, "Ecology and the Critique of Modern Society," addresses "the destruction of nature in the context of the general destructiveness which characterizes our society" (Marcuse 2019, 7; [1979] 2011).

> Under the conditions of advanced industrial society, satisfaction is always tied to destruction. The domination of nature is tied to the violation of nature. The search for new sources of energy is tied to the poisoning of the life environment.
>
> (Marcuse 2019, 12; [1979] 2011, 209)

Herbert Marcuse as Social Justice Educator 49

Marcuse's earlier essay "Ecology and Revolution" (2019; [1972] 2005) emphasized that the North Vietnamese fighters were engaging in "revolutionary ecological liberation." "U.S. bombs are meant to prevent the people of North Vietnam from undertaking the economic and social rehabilitation of the land" (2019, 2; [1972] 2005, 174). The ecology movement joined the women's movement and student anti-war protests in opposing the capitalist "violation of the Earth" (2019, 1; [1972] 2005, 174).

> [T]he demands on ever more intense exploitation come into conflict with nature itself ... and the demands of exploitation progressively reduce and exhaust resources: the more capitalist productivity increases, the more destructive it becomes. This is one sign of the internal contradictions of capitalism.
>
> (Marcuse 2019, 2; [1972] 2005, 174)

EarthCommonWealth is my term for a Marcusean vision of an *ecosocialist system-alternative*. Its environmental vision sees all living things and their non-living earthly surroundings as a global community capable of a dignified, deliberate coexistence. This is an earth-friendly economic perspective. The EarthCommonWealth Alternative seeks the restoration of nature's bounty and beauty by opposing the profitable misuse of limited natural resources, in large measure by negating planned obsolescence and its attendant wasted abundance. EarthCommonWealth envisions the displacement and transcendence of capitalist oligarchy as such, not simply the removal of its most bestial and destructive components. This is a concept explored in preliminary form in my *Ecology and Revolution* (Reitz 2019), negating the capitalist fetish of exchange value, and liberating commonwealth labor through the elimination of its commodity form or wage. In addition to being an earth-friendly alternative, this is a *common-wealth alternative* because 1) it opts for a new system of ecological production, egalitarian distribution, partnership/humanist values, shared ownership, liberated (i.e. non-alienated) labor, and democratized governance, having its foundation in the ethics of partnership labor and partnership productivity, and 2) because of its ecosocialist and humanist commitment to living our lives on the planet consistent with the most honorable and aesthetic forms of human social and political fulfillment. The EarthCommonWealth Alternative hinges on key political economic changes: what Marxism has traditionally called the "expropriation of the expropriators," the abolition of rent-seeking and the for-profit financial industry, and the elimination of universal commodity dependency through the decommodification/socialization of the economy. It would decouple income both from individual labor activity and from property ownership through an ecosocialist form of universal guaranteed income. Human needs require that 1) income be distributed without reference to individual productivity and as equally as feasible; 2) hours of labor be substantially reduced; 3) the well-rounded scientific and philosophical development of the young be made possible through 4) a system of multicultural general education

50 *Herbert Marcuse as Social Justice Educator*

privileging no single culture, religion, or language. Following both Marx and Marcuse, the concept of *EarthCommonWealth* aspires to connote a social-political philosophy with the potential to fulfill humanity's "species being"— our latent and hitherto repressed capacity to be humane.

Science and technology must be enlisted in the service of humanity, *not capital accumulation*. The violations of the earth entailed in its commercialized exploitation must be halted and corrected. Marcuse says that in a sense we must recognize nature as "a subject with which to live in a common universe" (1972, 60). From this perspective, nature must be made whole where it has been damaged. The 2008 Preamble to the Constitution of Ecuador includes a recognition of nature's rights in an explicit provision: "We hereby decide to build a new form of public coexistence, in diversity and harmony with nature, to achieve the good way of living [*buen vivir, sumac kawsay*]." Marcuse's ecosocialism is likeminded: "The Marxian conception understands nature as a universe which becomes the congenial medium for human gratification to the degree to which nature's *own* gratifying qualities and forces are recovered and released" (1972, 67).

The methodologies of ecology, critical philosophy, and sociology take interconnected *systems* to be the focus of analysis (in terms of statics and dynamics, structures and processes), rather than primarily on isolated particular units, individuals, experiences, or inert machinery. Georg Lukács thematized these approaches in his treatment of totality and reification, the whole being greater than the sum of the parts (Lukács [1924] 1971). Hegel and Marx studied the systemic interconnectivities in nature and the social world in terms of reciprocities and mutualities, as well as tensions, conflicts, and antagonisms, where opposition can lead to contradiction as well as qualitative transformation, progress or regress, as the case may be.

In 1972 Marcuse understood that advanced industrial society was also a threat to nature. He regarded the environmental movement of his time as the embodiment of a life-affirming energy directed toward the protection of earth and the pacification of our human existence overall. Both are linked through the political Eros into a campaign for "revolutionary ecological liberation" (2019, 2; [1972] 2005, 174).

It is extraordinary that Marcuse sees nature as an *ally* in the struggle for liberation! Marcuse rejects the theology implied if one holds that nature can be a "manifestation of subjectivity" (1972, 65). Nature is in motion; it is dynamic, and it is because humanity and nature are *dialectically interdependent* that the "liberation of nature" can be a "vehicle for the liberation of man" (1972, 59).

A Marcusean ecosocialism seeks a genuine association of free people: 1) within a democratic society that satisfies universal human needs; 2) based on our communal work; and 3) having a determination to restore nature. Further, it wishes to establish 4) a realm where Eros can be embodied within the material and sensual human condition in aesthetic form. This calls for the elimination of capitalism's fetish with exchange value and the commodity form in the capitalist economy. Instead of the sovereignty of the rich, the military-industrial

Herbert Marcuse as Social Justice Educator

complex, and Wall Street, revolutionary ecological liberation fights for socio-cultural equality and sustainable political-economic wealth. It requires the transformation from oligarchic capital to a new world system of partnership and multicultural democratic equality.

Great Refusal: A Global Alliance of Transformational Forces

Marcuse's description of the Great Refusal during the '60s meant that he saw a *universalization of resistance* underway. He saw the Great Refusal as envisaging "a new culture which fulfills the humanistic promises betrayed by the old culture" (1969, 10). Refusal "takes a variety of forms" (1969, vii), particularly in *la contestation permanente* of the 1968 French student movement, but also of the guerrilla forces in Latin America, and the revolutions "being defended and driven forward" while struggling to "eschew the bureaucratic administration of socialism" in Vietnam and Cuba and China (1969, viii–ix). All forms were geared toward liberation. As *a collective project*, it constituted a multi-dimensional expression of negation against systems of domination—and represented the new *general interests* of humanity.

Marcuse was aware that the development of the women's movement and the intensification of the student anti-war protests were in harmony with ecosoci-alism and that they could protest together against the capitalist "violation of the earth." The extraordinary value of Marcuse's strategy is that of a "united front," against today's sociopathic political disregard for our future—and for our common humanity. The multiplicity of possible refusals could and should become a *systemic negation*. System negation in this sense has the appeal of a new *general interest*, and Marcuse called upon us to actualize the *promesse du bonheur* (promise of happiness associated with dignified political fulfillment) of ecosocialism through a *global alliance of transformational forces*.

In terms of activist approaches to educational theory and practice, catalyst groups within higher education institutions quite remarkably advanced educa-tional philosophy in the U.S.A. during the '70s, '80s, and '90s, especially through the anti-racist and anti-sexist multicultural education reform movements. Critical education, embodied in a new multicultural/intercultural approach, disclosed the *real need for* and *revolutionary possibility of* re-humanized and egalitarian forms of productive relations, relations to nature, and interpersonal dynamics, such that these might cultivate the aesthetic and moral worth of civilized life. What have been called the civilizing forces of our age, the organized social struggles against racism, sexism, poverty, war, and imperialism, have educated this nation about alienation, oppression, power, and empowerment. BLM (Black Lives Matter) has effectively educated the nation about the real nature of undemocratic governance (in municipalities and higher education institutions) and the cavalier use of racist deadly force (on and off the campus). The professoriate, as such, certainly was not always in the lead in these educational efforts, although many individual college teachers, like Marcuse, played key roles.

52 *Herbert Marcuse as Social Justice Educator*

Key to an emancipatory universalization of resistance is the revolt of youth as a global phenomenon: today against guns, war, and weaponry, women's oppression, racial animosity, labor force precarity and exploitation, LGBTQ stigmatization, and the devastation of the earth—and increasingly for solidarity with immigrants and for socialism. A convergence of these forces forms the core of my proposal for a *CommonWealth Counter-Offensive* (Reitz 2019, 2023) to unleash all of the latent power of the Left.

Peter McLaren's *Pedagogy of Insurrection* (2015) takes a visionary turn, breaking new ground with his emphasis on several key new themes arising from radical struggles around the world. He is one of the rarest of critical theorists of education engaged with pedagogical issues developed in the Global South. McLaren contends:

> *Comunalidad* is a Oaxacan concept that serves as a type of cosmovision, and it deals with "the complex intertwining of history, morality, spirituality, kinship and communal practices" [derived from] "[t]he concept of reciprocity ... that requires the other or others to make ... equivalent response[s], and it is meant to be a permanent relation and inclusive of all members of the community."
>
> (McLaren 2015, 328)

McLaren highlights the concepts of *planetary comunalidad* and the *revolutionary ecopedagogy*, which are commensurate with the above.

> Critical educators, who have addressed for decades and with firm commitment topics of race, class, gender, sexuality, disability and other social justice issues are now casting their eyes to the antagonism between capitalism and nature to ask themselves how we can rationally regulate the human metabolic relation with nature. In our struggle for a "transformed economy founded on the nonmonetary values of social justice and ecological balance" we don't follow a productivist socialism or capitalist market ecology. We emphasize use value, not exchange value and "a liberation from the alienating economic 'laws' of the growth-oriented capitalist system." .... [Vandana] Shiva's general principle of "earth democracy" is congruent with the idea that the foundations of the means of production in land, seed, water and so on, need to be kept in perpetuity by an arranged social commons.
>
> (McLaren 2015, 301, 316)

Education's most venerable goal is knowing who we are as beings-for-ourselves. We have seen that one of the central purposes of Marcuse's critical theorizing has been our political education, helping each of us to grasp intellectually and politically the being that is our own. Yet a proper education is not really possible under capitalism, because the abolition of wage labor is impossible under capitalism. By collectively struggling to overcome the commodification and deformation of our lives, we can critically inform our teaching and learning in the liberal arts and sciences, general education, and ecopeda-gogy. The theory of our alienation must analyze, as did Marx in the 1844 *Manuscripts*, the dynamics of capital accumulation involving the seizure of surplus value during the social production process, which separates productive individuals from the product of their labor, from control of the labor process, from solidarity with other members of the workforce, and from the political potential of the human species itself. Humanity's educational task is the authentic search for philosophical and scientific wisdom. Our educational work can pre-figure, within the realm of necessity, a new re-humanized world order with an intercultural architecture of equality, ecological balance, abundance, leisure, freedom, and peace.

One further Marcuse statement on education has astonishing relevance and must be appreciated in bringing this chapter to a close. Its pertinence hangs on his understanding (and critique) of the explicitly educational views of John Stuart Mill. I bring this to mind through several excerpts from Marcuse's famous "Repressive Tolerance" essay (1965b, 121–122) that are less well known—

> The radical critics of the existing political process are thus readily denounced as advocating an elitism, a dictatorship of intellectuals as an alternative. What we have in fact is a government, representative govern-ment by a non-intellectual minority of politicians, generals, and business-men. The record of this "elite" is not very promising ... .

> In any case, John Stuart Mill, not exactly an enemy of liberal and repre-sentative government, was not so allergic to the political leadership of the intelligentsia as the contemporary guardians of semi-democracy are ... .

> [Mill's advocacy of] "distinction in favor of education, right in itself" was also supposed to preserve "the educated from the class legislation of the uneducated," without enabling the former to practice a class legislation of their own.

> Today, these words have understandably an antidemocratic, "elitist" sound—understandably, because of their dangerously radical implications. For if "education" is more and other than training, learning, preparing for the existing society, it means not only enabling man to know and under-stand the facts which make up reality but also to know and understand the factors that establish the facts so that he can change their inhuman reality. And such humanistic education would involve the "hard" sciences, ("hard" as in the hardware bought by the Pentagon?), would free them from their destructive direction. In other words, such education would badly serve the Establishment, and to give prerogatives to the men and women thus edu-cated would indeed be anti-democratic in the terms of the Establishment. But these are not the only terms.

54 *Herbert Marcuse as Social Justice Educator*

However, the alternative to the established semi-democratic process is *not* a dictatorship or elite, no matter how intellectual, but the struggle for real democracy.

(1965b, 121–122)

Plato's *Republic* had asked us to what extent we are enlightened or unenlightened (educated or uneducated) about our being. Hegel's *Phenomenology* likewise asked (in its sections on the mind alienated from itself and mind assured of itself) how our being can be known to us as our own being. Reason appeared to him as an acquisition of mind, won through struggle against not only error, illusion, deception, and self-deception but also against oppressive social forces. "[T]he notion of an education within the existing society for a better future society is a contradiction, but a contradiction that must be solved for progress to take place" (Marcuse 1965a, 207). In our epoch, humanity may come into possession of itself by struggling to learn inside institutions of domination—as well as outside of and in spite of them.

Note

1 On the *Gleichschaltung* as the attempt to absolutely control public political discourse and legitimate the totalitarian rule of the Nazi state, see, Franz Neumann, Chapter 1.3, "Die Gleichschaltung des politischen Lebens" in his *Behemoth: Struktur und Praxis des Nationalsozialismus, 1933–1944* (1988, 79–85). Alfred Schmidt, German translator of *One-Dimensional Man*, notably chooses *Gleichschaltung* to render Marcuse's word, *coordination*, in the first paragraph of ODM. "Dass diese technische Ordnung eine politische und geistige Gleichschaltung mit sich bringt ..." Marcuse, *Schriften 7, Der eindimensionale Mensch* (1989, 21).

References

Banks, James A. and Cherry A. McGee Banks (Eds.). 1997. *Multicultural Education*. Boston, MA: Allyn and Bacon.

Bhaskar, Roy, Savita Singh, and Mervyn Hartwig. [2001] 2020. *Reality and Its Depths: A Conversation Between Savita Singh and Roy Bhaskar*. Singapore: Springer.

Bloom, Allan. 1987. *The Closing of the American Mind*. New York: Simon & Schuster.

Federici, Silvia. 2020. *Revolution at Point Zero: Housework, Reproduction, and Feminist Struggle*. Oakland, CA: PM Press.

Freire, Paulo. [1970] 1993. *Pedagogy of the Oppressed*. New York: Continuum.

Hannah-Jones, Nikole. 2021. *The 1619 Project: A New Origin Story*. New York: One World.

Harvard University Committee Report on the Objective of General Education in a Free Society. 1945. *General Education in a Free Society*. Cambridge, MA: Harvard University Press.

Horkheimer, Max and Theodor W. Adorno. [1944] 1972. *Dialectic of Enlightenment*. New York: Herder & Herder.

Jansen, Peter-Erwin and Charles Reitz (Eds.). 2015. *Herbert Marcuse's 1974 Paris Lectures at Vincennes University*. Philadelphia, PA: The International Herbert Marcuse Society.

Herbert Marcuse as Social Justice Educator   55

Kahn, Richard. 2010. *Critical Pedagogy, Ecoliteracy, and Planetary Crisis*. Bern: Peter Lang.

Kellner, Douglas, Tyson Lewis, Clayton Pierce, and K. Daniel Cho (Eds.). 2009. *Marcuse's Challenge to Education*. Lanham, MD: Rowman & Littlefield.

Kerr, Clark. 1963. *The Uses of the University*. New York: Harper & Row.

Lukács, George. [1924] 1971. *History and Class Consciousness*. Cambridge, MA: MIT Press.

Marcuse, Herbert. 2019. *Ecology and the Critique of Society Today: Five Selected Papers for the Current Context*. Philadelphia, PA: International Herbert Marcuse Society.

Marcuse, Herbert. [1974] 2015. *Paris Lectures at Vincennes University, 1974*. Peter-Erwin Jansen and Charles Reitz (Eds.). Philadelphia, PA: International Herbert Marcuse Society.

Marcuse, Herbert. [1979] 2014. "The Reification of the Proletariat," in Douglas Kellner and Clayton Pierce (Eds.), *Herbert Marcuse, Marxism, Revolution, and Utopia: Volume 6, Collected Papers of Herbert Marcuse*. New York and London: Routledge.

Marcuse, Herbert. [1979] 2011. "Ecology and the Critique of Modern Society," in Douglas Kellner and Clayton Pierce (Eds.), *Herbert Marcuse, Philosophy, Psychoanalysis and Emancipation: Volume 5, Collected Papers of Herbert Marcuse*. New York and London: Routledge.

Marcuse, Herbert. [1968] 2009a. "Lecture on Education, Brooklyn College. 1968," in Douglas Kellner, Tyson Lewis, Clayton Pierce, and K. Daniel Cho (Eds.), *Marcuse's Challenge to Education*. Lanham, MD: Rowman & Littlefield.

Marcuse, Herbert. [1975] 2009b. "Lecture on Higher Education and Politics, Berkeley, 1975," in Douglas Kellner, Tyson Lewis, Clayton Pierce, and K. Daniel Cho (Eds.), *Marcuse's Challenge to Education*. Lanham, MD: Rowman & Littlefield.

Marcuse, Herbert. [1972] 2005. "Ecology and Revolution," in Douglas Kellner (Ed.), *Herbert Marcuse, The New Left and the 1960s: Volume 3, Collected Papers of Herbert Marcuse*. New York and London: Routledge.

Marcuse, Herbert. 1989. *Schriften 7, Der eindimensionale Mensch*. Frankfurt: Suhrkamp.

Marcuse, Herbert. [1974] 1987. "Zeit-Messungen," in *Schriften 9*. Frankfurt: Suhrkamp.

Marcuse, Herbert. [1922] 1978. "Der deutsche Künstlerroman," in *Schriften 1*. Frankfurt: Suhrkamp.

Marcuse, Herbert. 1978. *The Aesthetic Dimension: Toward a Critique of Marxist Aesthetics*. Boston, MA: Beacon Press.

Marcuse, Herbert. 1972. *Counterrevolution and Revolt*. Boston, MA: Beacon Press.

Marcuse, Herbert. 1969. *An Essay on Liberation*. Boston, MA: Beacon Press.

Marcuse, Herbert. [1937] 1968. "The Affirmative Character of Culture," in *Negations: Essays in Critical Theory*. Boston, MA: Beacon Press.

Marcuse, Herbert. [1955] 1966. *Eros and Civilization*. Boston, MA: Beacon Press.

Marcuse, Herbert. 1965a. "Remarks on a Re-definition of Culture," *Daedalus, The Proceedings of the American Academy of Arts and Sciences*, Volume 94, Number 1. Winter.

Marcuse, Herbert. 1965b. "Repressive Tolerance," in R.P. Wolff, B. Moore, and H. Marcuse (Eds.), *A Critique of Pure Tolerance*. Boston, MA: Beacon Press.

Marcuse, Herbert. 1964. *One-Dimensional Man: Studies in the Ideology of Advanced Industrial Society*. Boston, MA: Beacon Press.

Marcuse, Herbert. [1941] 1960. *Reason and Revolution*. Boston, MA: Beacon Press.

McLaren, Peter. 2015. *Pedagogy of Insurrection*. New York and Bern: Peter Lang.

Mies, Maria and Vandana Shiva. [1993] 2021. *Ecofeminism, With a Foreword by Ariel Salleh*. New York and London: Bloomsbury.

56 Herbert Marcuse as Social Justice Educator

Neumann, Franz. 1988. "Die Gleichschaltung des politischen Lebens," in *Behemoth: Struktur und Praxis des Nationalsozialismus, 1933–1944*. Frankfurt: Fischer Taschenbuch Verlag.

Reitz, Charles. 2023. *The Revolutionary Ecological Legacy of Herbert Marcuse*. Cantley, Quebec: Daraja Press.

Reitz, Charles. 2019. *Ecology and Revolution: Herbert Marcuse and the Challenge of a New World System Today*. New York and London: Routledge.

Reitz, Charles. 2002. "Elements of EduAction; Critical Pedagogy and the Community College," in Judith J. Slater, Stephen M. Fain, and Cesar A. Rossatto (Eds.), *The Freirean Legacy: Educating for Social Justice*. New York and Bern: Peter Lang.

Rufo, Christopher F. 2023. *America's Cultural Revolution: How the Radical Left Conquered Everything*. New York: Broadside Books.

Saito, Kohei. 2024. *Slow Down: The Degrowth Manifesto*. New York: Astra House.

Salleh, Ariel. [1997] 2017. *Ecofeminism as Politics: Nature, Marx and the Postmodern*. London: Zed Books.

3 Marcuse as Antifascist Social Critic

Immigrants have been an important and creative force in U.S. history, as they are also today. Such is the case with Herbert Marcuse, whose role as a German exile intellectual in the U.S.A. became that of antifascist social critic and social justice educator. Marcuse's *Reason and Revolution* ([1941] 1960) is widely recognized as having brought the critical social theory of the 20th-century Frankfurt School to the U.S.A., and with it the spark that would become the New Left and student movements here during the 1960s and 1970s.[1] Key aspects of the development of Marcuse's critical theory, hitherto quite under-appreciated, can be illumined by stressing Marcuse's impact as a radical intellectual outsider.

By 1941, the Institute's self-funded budget was brutally stressed, and Horkheimer strongly encouraged Marcuse to find additional employment and to reduce his reliance on Institute resources. According to Rolf Wiggershaus (1988, 295, 331–332, 338), Horkheimer lowered Marcuse's salary as a means of pressuring him into finding other sources of income and ultimately into separating himself monetarily from the Institute and its foundation while continuing to identify intellectually with it.[2] In this way, Marcuse came to serve with U.S. military intelligence in the Office of Strategic Services (OSS) during World War II, where he did assiduous intellectual work against fascism. Marcuse's unpublished wartime papers and publications have uncanny currency given the rise of neofascism in the U.S.A. today.

Marcuse wrote not only of German fascism in "The New German Mentality" (Marcuse [1942] 1998c) but also of the future threat of *neofascism* in the U.S.A. This latter was in an essay titled "33 Theses toward the Military Defeat of Hitler-Fascism" ([1947] 1998a, 215). It theorizes neofascism as the emergent political expression of totalitarian governance in the advanced industrial countries of the *anti-Soviet post-war West*.

> [T]he world is dividing into a neofascist and a Soviet camp. ... [T]here is only one alternative for revolutionary theory: to ruthlessly and openly criticize both systems and to uphold without compromise orthodox Marxist theory against both.
>
> (Marcuse [1947] 1998a, 217)

DOI: 10.4324/9781003571582-3

58 Herbert Marcuse as Social Justice Educator

Marcuse's essay stressed that the structural economic forces of corporate capitalism ultimately undergirded counterrevolutionary interests. *Studies in Prejudice* was a series of volumes undertaken by members of the Frankfurt School in the U.S. in partnership with the American Jewish Committee in California. Volume 5 in the series, *Prophets of Deceit*, written by Leo Löwenthal and Norbert Guterman ([1949] 1970), emphasized that any individual antisemitic or racist demagogue must be understood concretely in the social context of the contradictory economic and political conditions of the historical time period. This was stressed by Herbert Marcuse in his "Foreword," added to the 1970 paperback edition of this volume of *Studies*. Racism, involving hate speech and hate crime, thus always needs to be seen in connection with the institutional structures that support and promote it.

Following the war, Marcuse continued to do intelligence research with the U.S. State Department for several years (Kellner 1998a; Reitz 2000). In an interview with Jürgen Habermas (1978b), Marcuse described his experience in U.S. government service:

> MARCUSE: At first I was in the political division of the OSS and then in the Division of Research and Intelligence of the State Department. My main task was to identify groups in Germany with which one could work toward reconstruction after the war, and to identify groups which were to be taken to task as Nazis. There was a major de-Nazification program at the time. Based on exact research, reports, newspaper reading, and whatever, lists were made up of those Nazis who were supposed to assume responsibility for their activity ...

> HABERMAS: Are you of the impression that what you did was of any consequence?

> MARCUSE: On the contrary. Those whom we had listed first as "economic war criminals" were very quickly back in the decisive positions of responsibility in the German economy. It would be very easy to name names here.
>
> (1978b, 130–131)

Unlike Brecht, Eisler, and several academic leftists in America, the central proponents of critical theory, Horkheimer, Adorno, and Marcuse, were not called before the House UnAmerican Activities Committee (HUAC) during the McCarthy period. An outer circle Institute associate, Karl August Wittfogel, actually became a friendly informant to HUAC. Leo Löwenthal became research director for the patriotic Voice of America (1949–1953). Marcuse was, however, the subject of several FBI background investigations. The earliest was in 1943 in connection with his work of the sort discussed above with Habermas for the Office of Strategic Services.

A second wave of inquiries, about his loyalty to the U.S.A. during his 1950s employment by the State Department, discloses that the FBI consulted with

Marcuse as Antifascist Social Critic 59

HUAC concerning his case. During the 1960s, he was also under surveillance in connection with his ties to the New Left and international student movements.[3]

Marcuse's *Soviet Marxism* ([1958] 1961) was written while working at the Russian Institute of Columbia University and the Russian Research Center at Harvard. It depicted Soviet philosophy and politics as one-dimensional expressions of an untenable bureaucratism, a technological rationality, and an aesthetic realism, etc. Marcuse did something unique and unexpected in Cold War-fueled political writing: he fearlessly risked censure in the U.S.A. by comparing U.S. and Soviet culture, finding them both wanting. He saw both the U.S. and Soviet systems as worthy of fundamental social critique. "It has been noted ... how much the present 'communist spirit' resembles the 'capitalist spirit' which Max Weber attributed to the rising capitalist civilization" (Marcuse [1958] 1961, 169).

Secure in his anti-fascist and anti-Soviet credentials, Marcuse in 1958 did not back away from profound criticisms of U.S. culture in *Soviet Marxism* that might clearly have led him to be branded as "anti-American." This was a major departure from the much more cautious politics of the Horkheimer inner circle as well as from the conventional wisdom in the U.S. academic sphere. Marcuse felt confident enough to develop a clearly dialectical perspective in *Soviet Marxism*, and in this manner this volume was crucial in the development of critical theory. Marcuse's *Eros and Civilization* ([1955] 1966) and *One-Dimensional Man* (1964) would likewise proclaim an incisive new type of criticism of U.S. culture, and Marcuse gradually became a proponent of an activist politics against U.S. war-making and imperialism.[4]

Marcuse's most militant and lengthy critique of fascism/neofascism is in a 1972 piece, "The Historical Fate of Bourgeois Democracy"—never published until Kellner's 2001 volume 2 of Marcuse's archival papers. In the context of the Vietnam war and the Nixon presidency, Marcuse concluded that "bourgeois democracy no longer presents an effective barrier to fascism ... ."

> Law and morality no longer stand in the way. It is as if capitalism now feels safe enough to throw off the brakes on its productive destruction— legal, moral, political brakes ... Its own behavior demonstrates daily the truth of Marxian theory. Engels' Third Part of *Anti-Dühring*,[5] Lenin's analysis of imperialism are tame and restrained in comparison with reality.
> ([1972] 2001, 176)

It is a "regressive development of bourgeois democracy, its self transformation into a police and warfare state" ([1972] 2001, 165) supported by the sadomasochistic tolerance of a "free" people—"tolerance of the crooks and maniacs who govern them" ([1972] 2001, 171). The ongoing relevance of Marcuse's Vietnam era analysis to contemporary conditions is vividly revealed in the following comment:

> In free elections with universal suffrage, the people have elected (not for the first time!) a warfare government, engaged for long years in a war which is

60 Herbert Marcuse as Social Justice Educator

but a series of unprecedented crimes against humanity—a government of the representatives of the big corporation (and big labor!), a government unable (or unwilling) to halt inflation and eliminate unemployment, a government cutting down welfare and education, a government permeated with corruption, propped up by a Congress which has reduced itself to a yes-machine.

(Marcuse [1972] 2001, 168)

Marcuse emphasizes the role racism has played in U.S. elections, especially that of Nixon, and the reactionary segregationist ideology of the antibusing movement.

On the road to fascism, advanced capitalism draws largely on primary aggressiveness ... cruelty, injustice, and vice are invariably rewarded.

(Marcuse [1972] 2001, 172–173)

He proposes on the other hand that a socialist morality can become a political force. Here the student anti-war movement and the women's movement, as well as the rank-and-file opposition within the union movement, become key; weaving them together is the future strategic challenge—i.e. as a New Sensibility, discussed more fully below—culminating in the Great Refusal as a unifying project.

By the late 1960s, Marcuse had become the philosopher of the student revolts and the most prominent intellectual leader of the student movement in the U.S. A. This German-born intellectual, seventy years old, was communicating deftly with disaffected American youth. According to Douglas Kellner (1984, 1), at that time "Herbert Marcuse was more widely discussed than any other living philosopher." During the events of May 1968, Marcuse spoke to a UNESCO conference in Paris and lent qualified support to the student-worker uprising there. When he returned home to California, he was attacked by the American Legion and conservative politicians, notably then-Governor Ronald Reagan and the Regents of the California System of Higher Education, who opposed the renewal of Marcuse's contract, though they did not succeed in rescinding it (Kellner 2005; Kātz 1982, 174–175; 186).

Since its journal was published exclusively in German in 1940, it could be argued that it was never intended that critical theory should take effect in the U.S.A. Habermas and Marcuse seem to concede this (Marcuse 1978b, 130). The term "critical theory" was not utilized at all in Frankfurt, however, but was first coined in the U.S.A. in essays devoted specifically to this concept written by Horkheimer and Marcuse, which appeared in the *Zeitschrift* in 1937. Wiggershaus (1988, 432) has emphasized that Horkheimer, especially, saw himself as a guest in this country and that he was naturally sensitive about being seen as promoting "unamerican ideas." Their creative revision of Marxist social science critical theory in some ways represented a substantive philosophical shift from economics-based dialectical materialism. Horkheimer and Adorno would also see the U.S. and German student movements as "anti-American," so they were careful to distance themselves from activist students, and from Marcuse.

Marcuse developed in the post-World War II era the most radical and advanced critical theory, and he does this in the U.S. context. We must credit it to Marcuse that the work of the Frankfurt Institute ultimately became an indispensable part of American academia. Wiggershaus (1988, 676) has pointed out that in Marcuse one encountered what was lacking in other members of the Frankfurt School: an analysis of advanced industrial society. While the Institute was housed at Columbia University during the '30s and '40s (through the good graces of Nicholas Murray Butler and Robert S. Lynd), Marcuse wrote several essays developing his version of critical theory (first published in the *Zeitschrift für Sozialforschung* but republished in 1968 as *Negations*). So too *Reason and Revolution* was written there, which heralded the need for a transformed revolutionary philosophy where "economic theory would turn into critical theory" (Marcuse [1941] 1960, 281). Marcuse's subsequent work at Brandeis and UC-San Diego, *Eros and Civilization, One-Dimensional Man, An Essay on Liberation, and Counterrevolution and Revolt* were each published first in the U.S.A. and first in English language versions. Marcuse's American books represented to the world the Frankfurt School's critical social theory. Also, Marcuse developed the most political version of critical theory, reformulating his critical theory in relation to the activism of the New Left and other radical movements of the time.[6]

While Marcuse's social philosophy has become quite widely known in the U.S.A., his philosophy of education has not. This circumstance is being countered through recent contributions of my own (Reitz 2000, 2009a, 2009b) and Douglas Kellner, Tyson E. Lewis, and Clayton Pierce's book *On Marcuse: Critique, Liberation, and Reschooling in the Radical Pedagogy of Herbert Marcuse* (2009), and an edited collection *Marcuse's Challenge to Education* (Kellner, Lewis, Pierce, and Cho 2009). Quite early on Marcuse specifically criticized American schooling, opposing "... the overpowering machine of education and entertainment ... [which unites us all] ... in a state of anesthesia ... " ([1955] 1966, 104). In both his earliest and latest writings, Marcuse directs special attention to the emancipatory power of the intelligence gained through a study of the humanities.

Art, Alienation, and Education

The failure to address significant issues in educational theory has meant that the current status of scholarship on Marcuse's general philosophical orientation is incomplete. A vindication of Marcuse's theory and the future of critical theorizing hinge upon this educational philosophical effort. Marcuse's last book, *The Aesthetic Dimension* (1978a), deals importantly with the aesthetic sources of our wisdom and learning and once again with the theory of literary art. *The German Artist-Novel*, as we saw above, was concerned with the education of the artist as this is depicted in modern German fiction. Marcuse's continuing merit and appeal stem precisely from his work on the problems of knowledge and the political impacts of education. I find his critique of the prevailing mode of enculturation in the United States as education to alienation and to single-

62 Herbert Marcuse as Social Justice Educator

dimensionality to be immensely relevant today. So too his emphasis on the emancipatory and dis-alienating potential of art and the humanities.

Marcuse stresses the educational value of the arts because of the qualitative difference he finds between the multi-dimensional kind of knowledge thought to be produced by the aesthetic imagination and the uni-dimensional kind of knowledge attributed to what he describes as the controlled and repressive rationalities of achievement, performance, and domination. Marcuse theorizes that art provides a kind of deeper cognition, not through mimesis or by replicating worldly objects, but by retrieving the species-essence of the human race from philosophical erasure. He contends that the reality of death and human suffering assert themselves as pivotal phenomena in the educative process of recollection, even where the artist and the work of art "draw away" from them in pursuit of an eternity of joy and gratification. Alienation, in his estimation, is thought to be the result of training people to forget their authentic human nature—its essential internal turmoil and social potential—by educationally eradicating the realm where this knowledge is considered to be best preserved, i.e. the humanities. Marcuse was appalled at what he saw as the displacement of the humanities in the 1970s by a form of higher education that had become mainly scientific and technical and that primarily stood in service to the needs of commerce, industry, and the military. Marcuse's theory contends that our society is obsessed with efficiency, standardization, mechanization, and specialization, and that this fetish involves aspects of repression, fragmentation, and domination that impede real education and preclude the development of real awareness of ourselves and our world. Alienation is seen as the result of a miseducation or half-education that leads people to accept sensual anaesthetization and social amnesia as normal. Conditioned to a repressive pursuit of affluence, making a living becomes more important than making a life.

This aspect of Marcuse's approach to alienation is explicitly drawn from Schiller's arguments in favor of art and against crass utilitarianism in *Letters on the Aesthetic Education of Man* (1793). During his most militant period, Marcuse, like Schiller, urges education and art as countermovements to alienation: an aesthetic rationality is thought to transcend the prevailing logic of performance and achievement in the one-dimensional society and to teach radical action toward social justice and human fulfillment. He even sees a possible reconciliation of the humanistic and technological perspectives via the hypothesis that art may become a social and productive force for material improvement, re-constructing the economy in accordance with aesthetic goals and thus reducing alienation in the future. There is, however, also a "turn" in Marcuse's theorizing. He finds that the best education (to art through the humanities) can itself be alienating, even if it is also in an essential sense emancipatory. The artistic and cultured individual remains rather permanently separated from the broader social community and is stigmatized as an outsider in a way that precludes close identification with any group. Art, then, may respond to alienation with a more extreme, and higher, form of alienation.

Marcuse as Antifascist Social Critic 63

Allan Bloom sought to "rescue" the humanities from the perils of political protest and value relativism in *The Closing of the American Mind* (1987). While higher education in the humanities is traditionally thought of as pursuing universally human aims and goals, Bloom is unwilling to admit that a cultural politics of class, a cultural politics of race, and a cultural politics of gender have set very definite constraints upon the actualization of the humane concerns of a liberal arts education. Instead, Bloom attributes a decline of the humanities and U.S. culture in general to the supposedly inane popularization of German philosophy in the United States since the 1960s, especially the ideas of Nietzsche, Heidegger, and Marcuse, which are regarded as nihilistic and demoralizing. Bloom argued against Marcuse, multicultural education reform, and the Frankfurt School, asserting that we are importing "… a clothing of German fabrication for our souls, which … cast doubt upon the Americanization of the world on which we had embarked …" (Bloom 1987, 152). In a typically facile remark, Bloom says of Marcuse: "He ended up here writing trashy culture criticism with a heavy sex interest …" (Bloom 1987, 226). No hint from him that one of Marcuse's prime contributions to the critical analysis of American popular culture, as explained above, is his notion of "repressive desublimation"—how the unrestrained use of sex and violence by the corporate mass media and other large-scale commercial interests accomplishes social manipulation and control in the interest of capital accumulation. Or that Marcuse (in some ways very much like Bloom) valued high art and the humanities precisely because they teach the sublimation of the powerful urge for pleasure which in other contexts threatens destruction. Marcuse was no uncritical advocate of a Liberal Arts humanism. As we have seen, he had pointed out the traditionally conservative and politically apologetic or affirmative quality of much high-serious German art and education in his 1937 *Zeitschrift* piece, "The Affirmative Character of Culture" (1968), but he did also hold that there was a critical dimension embedded within even the most conservative approach to a traditional *Bildungshumanismus*.

Marcuse back in 1964, even as a relatively recent immigrant intellectual, had the fortitude to speak out in *One-Dimensional Man* against the congenital defects of U.S. culture—"The fact that the vast majority of the population accepts, and is made to accept, this society does not render it less irrational and less reprehensible" (1964, xiii). Of course, 1963–1964 also marked the culmination of the U.S. civil rights movement with its black-led (i.e. SCLC, CORE, and SNCC) bus boycotts, lunchcounter sit-ins, freedom rides, and voter registration campaigns, which also involved the support of many progressive whites, especially students. Marcuse would make an explicit contribution to the movement against racism with the 1965 publication of his critique of pure tolerance, "Repressive Tolerance," an essay still a factor in the ferment surrounding issues of race in contemporary political and moral philosophy, though admittedly an underappreciated and often misinterpreted one.[7]

Marcuse's Signature Concepts

Savita Singh is a much-published feminist poet and is currently professor in the School of Gender and Development Studies at the Indira Gandhi National Open

64   *Herbert Marcuse as Social Justice Educator*

University in New Delhi. She also serves on the Board of the International Herbert Marcuse Society. One of the key interests she brings to Marcuse studies concerns the nature of creativity in critical social theory. She has also had the opportunity to discuss the nature of the creative process in science and philosophy with Roy Bhaskar (Bhaskar, Singh, and Hartwig [2001] 2020), whose immense recent contributions to critical realism and naturalism we have mentioned in the previous chapter.

In Bhaskar's view,

> Creative model building in science ... is an intuitive *non*-algorithmic process ... . [C]reativity always comes from total absorption ... inner creativity always requires that you are totally immersed and absorbed in the subject matter ... we can be creative because we build in a knowledge of our field into our innermost being ... .
>
> (Bhaskar, Singh, and Hartwig [2001] 2020, 66–67)

As he sees it, our serious critical absorption in the subject under study makes a eureka moment possible.

Marcuse's familiarity with both the history of German philosophy and literary art, as well as the history of freedom movements in Europe and modern-day America, facilitated his most creative strategic efforts at the theory and practice of liberation. His appreciation of the student anti-war protesters, rank and file auto militants, and the women's movement of his own time all shed light on his critical Marxism in a new and creative way. Marcuse sought to disclose truths encompassing our human condition and our human potential that are factually *absent* from established patterns of academic and political discourse yet *there* at a deeper level in an analysis of reality.

In addition to the *affirmative character of culture*, the following concepts are among his signature contributions: the New Sensibility, the Great Refusal, the Critique of Pure Tolerance, and the link between the erotic and the political—this latter expressed on the one hand as *Repressive Desublimation* and on the other hand as art's *promesse du bonheur*, which we have already touched upon above. These are among the most prominent of Marcuse's creative elaborations of critical Marxism and constitute the hallmarks of his philosophical ingenuity. *One-Dimensional Man* lives in a manner oblivious to the problematic nature of prevailing social and economic relations and gets detailed attention in the chapter 4.

The New Sensibility

This represented discontent with existing conditions from the left, with determinate and joyous rebellion. Science and technology are increasingly recognized as being socially and politically implicated in systems of oppression. The new sensibility

> is emerging today in the women's movement against patriarchal domination, which came of age socially only under capitalism; in the protests

against the nuclear power industry and the destruction of nature as an ecological space that cuts across all fixed class boundaries; and in the student movement, which despite being declared dead, still lives on in struggles against the degradation of teaching and learning into activities that reproduce the system.

(Marcuse 2019, 48)

Marcuse wrote of

the steady growth among the youth of the New Sensibility—new needs, generated under capitalism, but which capitalism cannot fulfill, for gender equality, ecological economics, and anti-racism ... . [the capitalist system's] blatant irrationality has not only penetrated the consciousness of a large part of the population, it has also caused, mainly among the young people, a radical transformation of needs and values which may prove to be incompatible with the capitalist system, its hierarchy, priorities, morality, symbols (the counter-culture, ecology).

([1975] 2015a, 304–307)

For Marcuse, the new sensibility is characterized by an *aesthetic ethos* of partnership, racial and gender equality, satisfaction from work, earth admiration, and ecological responsibility. This transvaluation of values prefigures a sane socialist society, a *new socialist rationality* freed from exploitation, race and gender discrimination, spurring militant direct action for radical (rather than minimal) social change, culminating in the Great Refusal as a unifying project. Science, technology, and production are released from service to exploitation when mobilized by this *vision of the political Eros of socialism* (1969, 23, 26).

The Great Refusal

This was his designation of a multidimensional, militant, activist expression of *system negation* against all forms of domination. *Refusal* and negation having become the unifying principles of a *new general interest*. I bring to the reader's attention again Marcuse's hallmark statement:

This society is obscene in producing and indecently exposing a stifling abundance of wares while depriving its victims abroad of the necessities of life; obscene in stuffing itself and its garbage cans while poisoning and burning the scarce foodstuffs in the fields of its aggression; obscene in the words and smiles of its politicians and entertainers; its prayers, in its ignorance, and in the wisdom of its kept intellectuals.

(1969, 7–8)

66 *Herbert Marcuse as Social Justice Educator*

[O]pposition is [now being] directed against the totality of a well-functioning, prosperous society—a protest against its Form—the commodity form of men and things.

(1972, 49, 51)

Marcuse's Great Refusal was and is meant to be our collective project, bringing radicals together powerfully today; much more on this below.

The Critique of Pure Tolerance

Marcuse combatted institutional racism by arguing there should be *No Pure Tolerance of hate speech, racism, antisemitism, or fascist rhetoric.* "To treat the great crusades *against* humanity (like that against the Albigensians) with the same impartiality as the desperate struggles *for* humanity means neutralizing their opposite historical function, reconciling the executioners with their victims, distorting the record" (1965, 113).

Reactionary and liberal forces systematically utilized the doctrine of pure tolerance to derail or destroy the possibility of democratic egalitarianism. It was a fallacy to call for "free speech" rather than *limiting the hate speech* of white supremacists and antisemites because speech freedom was intended by its classical advocates (like John Stuart Mill) as protection for relatively powerless minoritized voices—i.e. to have the "civilizing function of protecting dissent"—not to promote the established and discriminatory powers that be. The Critique of Pure Tolerance expressed Marcuse's Marxist opposition to fascism as well as his critique of the liberal doctrines of tolerance that made the Third Reich possible.

The link between the erotic and the political was expressed by Marcuse in two major new propositions on the nature of Repressive Desublimation and the *promesse du bonheur of art.*

Repressive Desublimation

Predatory capitalism stabilizes its system of economic inequality through political stratagems as the normalization of pornography and in the venting of the race- and gender-based prejudices that furnish a repressive gratification. Following a line of thinking from *Eros and Civilization* ([1955] 1966), Marcuse theorized that the "... mobilization and administration of libido may account for much of the voluntary compliance ... with the established society. Pleasure, thus adjusted, generates submission" (1964, 75). He explains that capitalism's social control mechanisms become even more powerful when they integrate sexually suggestive and explicitly erotic and violent content into advertising and the mass media and infuse these into the content of mass entertainment and popular culture. In this manner the unrestrained use of sex and violence by large-scale commercial interests accomplishes more effective social manipulation and control in the interest of capital accumulation than had repressive sublimation. Repressive *de*sublimation fuels counterrevolution by substituting reactionary emotional release in place of rebellion, and counterrevolutionary illusion (often a sadistic mix of toxic masculinity and gun violence) in place of freedom, while leaving the established repressive political order unchallenged.

The Promesse du Bonheur *of Art*

Aesthetics for Marcuse is understood not primarily in terms of "works of art" (paintings, architecture, literature) but in terms of *human sensuality and love of life, love of knowledge, love of justice*, i.e. art is viewed through an emotion-laden and emancipatory political lens. As I have noted above, "sensual love gives a *promesse du bonheur* which preserves the full materialistic content of freedom. ... Sensuality ... preserves the goal of political action: liberation" ([1945] 1998b, 204). Marcuse connected the *promesse du bonheur* to the capacity of art and beauty to convey a sense of a future of *political* gratification and serenity for humankind. In *One-Dimensional Man* (1964, 210), the *promesse du bonheur* is a token of a fully liberated human future. Art and beauty proclaim the possibility of our communal gratification and encourage us to work to fulfill our natural and political needs as non-alienated social beings. "[T]he development of the productive forces renders possible the material fulfillment of the *promesse du bonheur* expressed in art; political action—the revolution—is to translate this possibility into reality" ([1958] 1961, 115).

In terms of creativity, Marcuse also knew that an array of artists is needed to assist any culture in the transvaluation of values. Great Art, including tragedy, has the power to engender an elevated sense of calm and love of life and enhance our desire to abide in a serene (*erhaben*—Schiller) state of being on the surface of planet earth. Art can help human beings transform a society. It brings us to a knowledge of ourselves as sensuous living labor and to the beauty of consecrated effort (as in the latter life stages of Buddhism and Hinduism), offering, in the fullest composure, key abilities in service to the community. As shall be explained below, *Commonwealth* is humanity's (that is, sensuous living labor's) aesthetic form: workmanship and artistry, emancipated from repression, taking place "in accordance with the laws of beauty" (Marx's tribute to Schiller [1844] 1982, 114).

Revolutionary Ecological Liberation

To the five points I have made above I add a sixth signature concept that is too little recognized. Marcuse's critical Marxism demonstrates a "Green Turn" consistent with a thoroughly dialectical materialist philosophy. Chapter 2 above has discussed the notable environmentalist essays by Marcuse that are rarely appreciated even by readers most familiar with his work in general. His final published piece, "Ecology and the Critique of Modern Society" (2019; [1979] 2011), addresses "the destruction of nature in the context of the general destructiveness which characterizes our society." What had been the symbiotic, metabolic relationship between humanity and nature was now socially

68   *Herbert Marcuse as Social Justice Educator*

perverted through monopoly-stage capitalism into extractive violations of nature and oppressive violations of human dignity.

> Under the conditions of advanced industrial society, satisfaction is always tied to destruction. The domination of nature is tied to the violation of nature. The search for new sources of energy is tied to the poisoning of the life environment.
>
> (2019, 12; [1979] 2011, 209)

Both the earth and humanity itself require the protection of a movement for revolutionary ecological liberation that I shall sketch out as this book progresses. Marcuse proposes a program of global action against capitalism's wasted abundance and climate change, revolving around what he considered to be the *radical* rather than minimum goals of socialism. *Radical* here meaning an *ecosocialism* informed by the New Sensibility and the full circle of creative contributions outlined above.

Marxism Needs Feminism

Marcuse was also one of the only members of the Frankfurt School to write creatively and critically about the relationship of Marxism to women's issues in his 1974 essay "Marxism and Feminism." This was at about the same time he wrote his most militant essays on ecology, global opposition to capitalism, and the essential potential of art to reclaim our common humanity. Marcuse appreciated the *strength of the movement for women's equality* as pushing beyond the immediate goal of selling one's labor on terms equal with men in the capitalist market. He lauded the feminist critique of toxic masculinity, the indictment of the male propensity toward violence against women and toward male domination in society. What had in the past been the virtue of bravery in terms of self-defense had long ago been twisted into overarching male aggressiveness and menacing hostility.

He saw the women's movement as key in the transformation of civilization's traditionally patriarchal values, and this as *central* to what he saw as the "context of the enlarged depth and scope of the revolution, of the new goals and possibilities of the revolution" ([1974] 2015b) such that the feminist movement supplies a creative impulse of momentous significance in what remains the ongoing struggle for human emancipation.

Because Marcuse's essay "Marxism and Feminism" is so little known and was relatively inaccessible until it appeared in Douglas Kellner's Volume 3 of Marcuse's posthumous publications ([1974] 2005), I include several excerpts here that might aid it in being more justly acknowledged:

> I believe the Women's Liberation Movement today is, perhaps, the most important and potentially the most radical political movement that we have, even if the consciousness of this fact has not yet penetrated the Movement as a whole.
>
> ([1974] 2005, 165)

But the very goals of this Movement require changes of such enormity in the material as well as intellectual culture that they can be attained only by a change in the entire social system.

([1974] 2005, 166)

[L]iberation implies the construction of a society governed by a different Reality Principle, a society where the established dichotomy between masculine and feminine is overcome in the social and individual relationships between human beings.

([1974] 2005, 166)

It means not only a commitment to socialism (full equality of women has always been a basic socialist demand), but a commitment to a specific form of socialism, which has been called "feminist socialism."

([1974] 2005, 167)

Socialism, as a *qualitatively* different society, must embody the *antithesis*, the definite negation of the aggressive and repressive needs and values of capitalism as a form of male-dominated culture.

([1974] 2005, 167–168)

[In] a qualitatively different way of life, [we] would not only use the productive forces for the reduction of alienated labor and labor time but also for making life an end in itself, for the development of the senses and the intellect, for pacification of aggressiveness, for the enjoyment of being, for the emancipation of the senses and the intellect from the rationality of domination: creative receptivity versus repressive productivity.

([1974] 2005, 170)

Feminine characteristics would cease to be specifically feminine to the degree to which they would be universalized in socialist culture, material and intellectual.

([1974] 2005, 170)

They would operate as needs and eventual goals in the socialist organization of production, in the social division of labor, in the setting of priorities once scarcity has been conquered. And thus, entering the reconstruction of society as a whole … .

([1974] 2005, 170)

Alexandra Kollontai, Nadezhda Krupskaya, Clara Zetkin, and Rosa Luxemburg were early Marxist leaders and feminists in Europe in the 1920s who influenced Marcuse. Marcuse's protégé Angela Davis recounts the history of women and black people within the U.S. communist movement during that historical period in *Women, Race, and Class* (1981, 148–171). She highlights the

70 Herbert Marcuse as Social Justice Educator

struggles and voices of Lucy Parsons, Ella Bloor, Anita Whitney, Elizabeth Gurley Flynn, and Claudia Jones to bring a feminist and an antiracist perspective to early 20th-century Marxism. These radical women pioneered an intersectional Marxism, chiding male-dominated Marxist organizations that had been neglectful of the needs of women and minorities.

Charnie Guettel's *Marxism and Feminism* (1974) discusses the special oppression of women—as women and as workers—arguing that economic insecurity is at the heart of male chauvinism. She also discusses Juliet Mitchell's Althussarian structuralist perspective, which raises a critique of traditional Marxism that Marxism would have to meet, but Mitchell's critique nowhere mentions *class* as a structure impacting the condition of women (Guettel 1974, 33). Likewise, Guettel sees Shulamith Firestone's *Dialectic of Sex* as de-centering the fundamental processes of economic exploitation from her analysis of women's inequality (Guettel 1974, 41). Marcuse came to understand that Marxism must not involve the subordination of women's issues or those of racism to those of the capitalist infrastructure. Interpersonal dynamics as well as institutional structures must be understood in terms of a complex whole, a dialectical humanism.

As an escapee from German fascism and an outsider critic of American philosophical conventions and neofascist tendencies, Marcuse's intellectual and political resourcefulness challenged this nation's illusions of democracy and the surrender of its "kept intellectuals" to business protocols and priorities. His theoretical works modeled an elaboration of critical Marxism that monopoly capitalism's single-dimensional thought patterns and predatory political-economic tendencies. Today, we have an urgent need to consider global strategies for emancipatory change and for creative visions of system alternatives embodying the pursuit of social freedom. Hence also my own creative attempts below to extend—on the basis of Marcuse's views of the *higher* aims of education and most *radical* goals of socialism—a way forward to the social justice strategies and the foundations for critical teaching that I call the Earth-CommonWealth Alternative and the Ecosocialist EarthCommonWealth Project.

Notes

1 See also Kellner, "Introduction" to *Herbert Marcuse, Technology, War, and Fascism: Volume One* (1998b).
2 Franz Neumann had even earlier been cut off from institute funding and completed his massive study of the Nazi system, *Behemoth*, in 1942 while working for the OSS. See also Kellner (1998a).
3 See especially Gennaro and Kellner, "Under Surveillance: Herbert Marcuse and the FBI" (2009).
4 For an overview of Marcuse's postwar politics, see Kellner, *The New Left and the 1960s: Volume Three* (2005).
5 Later published separately as *Socialism, Utopian and Scientific*.
6 Marcuse gives credit to Horkheimer and Adorno for developing critical theory in their work *The Authoritarian Personality* (1950). Fromm's U.S. publications *Escape From Freedom* (1941) and *Marx's Concept of Man* (1961) might also be considered seminal in this regard. See Kellner, *The New Left and the 1960s: Volume Three* (2005).

7 See the inclusion of this essay in Boss, *Analyzing Moral Issues* (1999, 607–615). See also Bloom, op. cit., and Kors and Silverglate, *The Shadow University* (1998). In addition: Reitz, "Herbert Marcuse and the New Culture Wars" (2009a).

References

Bhaskar, Roy, Savita Singh, Mervyn Hartwig. [2001] 2020. *Reality and Its Depths: A Conversation Between Savita Singh and Roy Bhaskar*. Singapore: Springer.

Bloom, Allan. 1987. *The Closing of the American Mind*. New York: Simon & Schuster.

Boss, Judith A. 1999. *Analyzing Moral Issues*. Mountain View, CA: Mayfield Publishing Company.

Davis, Angela. 1981. *Women, Race, and Class*. New York: Vintage.

Gennaro, Stephen and Douglas Kellner. 2009. "Under Surveillance: Herbert Marcuse and the FBI," *Fast Capitalism*, Volume 5, Issue 2.

Guettel, Charnie. 1974. *Marxism and Feminism*. Toronto: Canadian Scholars Press.

Kātz, Barry. 1982. *Herbert Marcuse & the Art of Liberation*. London: Verso.

Kellner, Douglas. 1984. *Herbert Marcuse and the Crisis of Marxism*. Berkeley, CA: University of California Press.

Kellner, Douglas (Ed.). 2005. *Herbert Marcuse, The New Left and the 1960s: Volume 3, Collected Papers of Herbert Marcuse*. London and New York: Routledge.

Kellner, Douglas (Ed.). 1998a. *Herbert Marcuse, Technology, War, and Fascism: Volume 1, Collected Papers of Herbert Marcuse*. London and New York: Routledge.

Kellner, Douglas (Ed.). 1998b. "Introduction," in *Herbert Marcuse, Technology, War, and Fascism: Volume 1, Collected Papers of Herbert Marcuse*. London and New York: Routledge.

Kellner, Douglas, Tyson E. Lewis, and Clayton Pierce. 2009. *On Marcuse: Critique, Liberation, and Reschooling in the Radical Pedagogy of Herbert Marcuse*. Rotterdam: Sense Publishers.

Kellner, Douglas, Tyson Lewis, Clayton Pierce, and K. Daniel Cho (Eds.). 2009. *Marcuse's Challenge to Education*. Lanham, MD: Rowman & Littlefield.

Kors, Alan C. and Harvey Silverglate. 1998. *The Shadow University: The Betrayal of Liberty on American Campuses*. New York: Free Press.

Löwenthal, Leo and Norbert Guterman. [1949] 1970. *Prophets of Deceit, Studies in Prejudice Series*, Volume 5. New York: Harper & Brothers, Copyright American Jewish Committee, Palo Alto, CA: Pacific Books.

Marcuse, Herbert. 2019. *Ecology and the Critique of Society Today: Five Selected Papers for the Current Context*. Philadelphia, PA: International Herbert Marcuse Society.

Marcuse, Herbert. [1975] 2015a. "Why Talk on Socialism?" in Charles Reitz (Ed.). *Crisis and Commonwealth: Marcuse, Marx, McLaren*. Lanham, MD: Lexington Books.

Marcuse, Herbert. [1974] 2015b. *Paris Lectures at Vincennes University, 1974*. Peter-Erwin Jansen and Charles Reitz (Eds.). Philadelphia, PA: International Herbert Marcuse Society.

Marcuse, Herbert. [1979] 2011. "Ecology and the Critique of Modern Society," in Douglas Kellner and Clayton Pierce (Eds.), *Herbert Marcuse, Philosophy, Psychoanalysis and Emancipation: Volume 5, Collected Papers of Herbert Marcuse*. New York and London: Routledge.

Marcuse, Herbert. [1974] 2005. "Marxism and Feminism," in Douglas Kellner (Ed.), *Herbert Marcuse, The New Left and the 1960s: Volume 3, Collected Papers of Herbert Marcuse*. New York and London: Routledge.

72 Herbert Marcuse as Social Justice Educator

Marcuse, Herbert. [1972] 2001. "The Historical Fate of Bourgeois Democracy," in Douglas Kellner (Ed.), *Herbert Marcuse, Towards a Critical Theory of Society: Volume 2, Collected Papers of Herbert Marcuse*. New York: Routledge.

Marcuse, Herbert. [1947] 1998a. "33 Theses toward the Military Defeat of Hitler Fascism," in Douglas Kellner (Ed.), *Herbert Marcuse, Technology, War, and Fascism: Volume 1, Collected Papers of Herbert Marcuse*. New York: Routledge.

Marcuse, Herbert. [1945] 1998b. "Some Remarks on Aragon: Art and Politics in the Totalitarian Era," in Douglas Kellner (Ed.), *Herbert Marcuse, Technology War, and Fascism: Volume 1, Collected Papers of Herbert Marcuse*. New York and London: Routledge.

Marcuse, Herbert. [1942] 1998c. "The New German Mentality," in Douglas Kellner (Ed.), *Herbert Marcuse, Technology War, and Fascism: Volume 1, Collected Papers of Herbert Marcuse*. New York and London: Routledge.

Marcuse, Herbert. 1978a. *The Aesthetic Dimension: Toward a Critique of Marxist Aesthetics*. Boston, MA: Beacon Press.

Marcuse, Herbert. 1978b. "Theory and Politics: A Discussion with Herbert Marcuse, Jürgen Habermas, Heinz Lubasz, and Tilman Spengler," *Telos*, Number 38.

Marcuse, Herbert. 1972. *Counterrevolution and Revolt*. Boston, MA: Beacon Press.

Marcuse, Herbert. 1969. *An Essay on Liberation*. Boston, MA: Beacon Press.

Marcuse, Herbert. [1937] 1968. "The Affirmative Character of Culture," in *Negations: Essays in Critical Theory*. Boston, MA: Beacon Press.

Marcuse, Herbert. [1955] 1966. *Eros and Civilization*. Boston, MA: Beacon Press.

Marcuse, Herbert. 1965. "Repressive Tolerance," in R.P. Wolff, B. Moore, and H. Marcuse (Eds.), *A Critique of Pure Tolerance*. Boston, MA: Beacon Press.

Marcuse, Herbert. 1964. *One-Dimensional Man: Studies in the Ideology of Advanced Industrial Society*. Boston, MA: Beacon Press.

Marcuse, Herbert. [1958] 1961. *Soviet Marxism: A Critical Analysis*. New York: Vintage.

Marcuse, Herbert. [1941] 1960. *Reason and Revolution: Hegel and the Rise of Social Theory*. Boston, MA: Beacon Press.

Marx, Karl. [1844] 1982. *The Economic & Philosophical Manuscripts of 1844*. Dirk Struik (Ed.). New York: International Publishers.

Reitz, Charles. 2009a. "Herbert Marcuse and the New Culture Wars," in Douglas Kellner, Tyson Lewis, Clayton Pierce, and K. Daniel Cho (Eds.), *Marcuse's Challenge to Education*. Lanham, MD: Rowman & Littlefield.

Reitz, Charles. 2009b. "Herbert Marcuse and the Humanities: Emancipatory Education and Predatory Culture," in Douglas Kellner, *et al.Marcuse's Challenge to Education*. Lanham, MD: Rowman & Littlefield.

Reitz, Charles. 2000. *Art, Alienation, and the Humanities: A Critical Engagement with Herbert Marcuse*. Albany, NY: SUNY Press.

Wiggershaus, Rolf. 1988. *Die Frankfurter Schule*. München: Deutscher Taschenbuch Verlag.

4 The Activist Legacy of *One-Dimensional Man*

Marcuse's *One-Dimensional Man*[1] (ODM) addressed the problems of alienation and social control in advanced industrial societies as well as the closed universe of discourse and thought in modern ways of life. It continues today as his most influential work (Maley 2017; Lamas 2016 and Radical Philosophy Review 2016). Marcuse believed alienation theory required revision because advanced capitalism had become a society of plenty rather than scarcity and because the condition of the working class had fundamentally altered. ODM is centrally concerned with the new aspects of alienation resulting from the increasingly sophisticated exercise of the social control apparatus of corporate capitalism. According to its famous first sentence: "A comfortable, smooth, reasonable, democratic unfreedom prevails in advanced industrial civilization, a token of technical progress" (Marcuse 1964, 1).

Marcuse argues the wholesale integration of the individual into mass society. Alienation consists in the total absorption of the personality into the processes and systems of capitalist commodity production. This gives rise to a new kind of totalitarianism, unlike that formerly characteristic of fascist societies. With this work in 1964, Marcuse consolidated his key and characteristic argument that U.S. *culture* is politically and economically *unfree*.

> By virtue of the way it has organized its technological base, contemporary industrial society tends to be totalitarian. For "totalitarian" is not only a terroristic *political coordination* [in Alfred Schmidt's German translation[2]— *Gleichschaltung*] of society, but also a non-terroristic political coordination which operates through the manipulation of needs by vested interests. It thus precludes the emergence of an effective opposition against the whole. Not only a specific form of government or party rule makes for totalitarianism, but also a specific system of production and distribution which may well be compatible with a "pluralism" of parties, newspapers, "countervailing powers," etc.
>
> (ODM, 3)

Thus emerges a pattern of *one-dimensional thought and behavior* in which ideas, aspirations and objectives that, by their content, transcend the

DOI: 10.4324/9781003571582-4

74   *Herbert Marcuse as Social Justice Educator*

established universe of discourse and action are either repelled or reduced to terms of this universe.

(ODM, 12)

ODM thus contributed vitally to a new way of understanding U.S. culture, by bringing in insights from Marcuse's experience with fascism in Germany. But what's more, ODM widened what has sometimes been criticized as critical theory's Eurocentric focus[3] through Marcuse's effort to deepen intellectually certain, broadly critical projects already underway in the U.S.A.—perhaps most importantly the demystification of the vaunted myths of affluence and melting pot assimilation in American life. "In the contemporary era, the conquest of scarcity is still confined to small areas of advanced industrial society. Their prosperity covers up the Inferno inside and outside their borders ... ." (ODM, 241). Marcuse understood how the notion of the "affluent society" masked "New Forms of Social Control" (ODM, 1), i.e. the gravely unequal, patriarchal, and monocultural forms of Anglo-conformity (an exclusively WASP-controlled oligarchy and patriarchy).[4] The conventional wisdom within the nation itself was largely oblivious to its own intellectual and political limits (and in many ways it continues to be).

The year 1963, just before ODM's publication, also marked the culmination of the U.S. civil rights movement with its black-led (i.e. SCLC, CORE, and SNCC) bus boycotts, lunch-counter sit-ins, freedom rides, and voter registration campaigns, and the March on Washington. These also involved the support of many radical and progressive whites, especially students. Marcuse would make an explicit contribution to the movement against racism with the publication of his critique of pure tolerance, "Repressive Tolerance" (1965), an essay still contributing to the ferment surrounding issues of race in contemporary political and moral philosophy.[5]

In 1964 in ODM, perhaps thinking of some of the recent and high profile lynchings, bombings, and murders of black people in the U.S.A. (Emmett Till, Medgar Evers, and the four girls in Birmingham's 16th Street Baptist church, where Angela Davis had grown up), Marcuse wrote: "Those whose life is the hell of the Affluent Society are kept in line by a brutality which revives medieval and early modern practices" (ODM, 23). As Nina Simone was singing "Mississippi Goddamn" and castigating the "United Snakes of America," ODM famously concluded:

> ... underneath the conservative popular base is the substratum of the outcasts and outsiders, the exploited and persecuted of other races and other colors ... . Their opposition hits the system from without ... it is an elementary force which violates the rules of the game. When they get together and go out into the streets, without arms, without protection, in order to ask for the most primitive civil rights, they know that they face dogs, stones, and bombs, jail, concentration camps, even death ... . The critical theory of society ... wants to remain loyal to those who, without hope, have given and give their life to the Great Refusal.

(ODM, 257)

The *Activist Legacy of* One-Dimensional Man   75

Marcuse called out this nation's tendencies toward the control and coordination of the population through a *total administration* (85) that operationalized "the manipulation of needs by vested interests" (3) and an indoctrination of the public mind that closed its cultural and political worlds (19).

> At nodal points of the universe of public discourse, self-validating, analytical propositions appear which function like magic-ritual formulas. Hammered and re-hammered into the recipient's mind, they produce the effect of enclosing it within the circle of the conditions prescribed by the formula.
>
> (88)

In this type of one-dimensional thinking: "The meaning is fixed, doctored, loaded" (94). Today we might think of examples of this rhetoric in which the political cards are already stacked through the familiar phraseology of "No Child Left Behind," "Equal Opportunity Employer," "Job Creators," etc.

As a critical philosophical work, ODM foregrounded and combated the empiricism, behaviorism, and the British perspective on linguistic analysis that framed the functionalist schools of social and political thought in this country.[6] It revealed the built-in theoretical blinders, silences, repressiveness, and false concreteness of our prevailing ways of thinking and acting. Marcuse understood our reigning WASP patriotism and militarism, our economic instrumentalism, as single-dimensional.

One-dimensional living is living in a manner *oblivious to the problematic nature of prevailing social and economic relations.*

> If mass communications blend together harmoniously, and often unnoticeably, art, politics, religion and philosophy with commercials, they bring these realms of culture to their common denominator—the commodity form. Exchange value, not truth value counts. On it centers the rationality of the status quo, and all alien rationality is bent to it.
>
> (57)

In his view, one-dimensional modes of thinking conformed to and were coordinated with the general commodification and commercialization of social life. In politics, science, and education in the U.S.A., this meant an acritical culture that generally tended to *reject theory as useless.*

Perhaps reflecting on an experience of his own, Marcuse wrote:

> The intellectual is called on the carpet. What do you mean when you say ... ? Don't you conceal something? You talk a language which is suspect. You don't talk like the rest of us, like the man on the street, but rather like a foreigner who does not belong here.
>
> (192)[7]

76 Herbert Marcuse as Social Justice Educator

Marcuse nonetheless had the civic courage and also philosophical means—due to his association with the traditions of classical German philosophy, Marxism, and the Frankfurt School—to break through the "pre-established harmony between scholarship and the national purpose" (19) and the paralysis of critique characteristic of our mid-century U.S. triumphalism and parochialism.

In 1987, conservative culture warrior Allan Bloom's *The Closing of the American Mind* was a bizarre attempt to turn the political tables and attack Herbert Marcuse's critical and cosmopolitan perspective. Bloom attributed a general decline in U.S. culture to what he considered the illegitimate popularization of German philosophy in the U.S.A. in the 1960s, especially Nietzsche, Heidegger, and Marcuse. Bloom argued that U.S. culture, entertainment, and education have imported "... a clothing of German fabrication for [our] souls, which ... casts doubt on the Americanization of the world upon which we had embarked ... ."[8]

The life and theory of Herbert Marcuse led to the *deprovincialization* of American life because he counterposed a profoundly multidimensional,[9] proto-multicultural, and Marxist social analysis to the essentially single-dimensional Anglo-American view of the world. I define deprovincialization as a philosophical counter-current to the logical fallacy and obstacle to critical thinking of *provincialism*. It is a concept I borrow from Egon Schwarz's (1992) autobiography about emigration to the Americas during the Nazi period.[10] According to Howard Kahane's and Nancy Cavender's *Logic and Contemporary Rhetoric* (2006, 121), provincialism is the tendency to see things only from the point of view of those in charge of our immediate in-groups.[11] This generates an easy (if in many respects ultimately specious) loyalty to the local.

Hegel likewise has some pertinent observations on provincialism:

> What is familiar is not known simply because it is familiar ... . God, nature, the understanding, the sensibility, etc., are presupposed as familiar and valid foundations without having been scrutinized, and they are accepted as fixed points of departure and return. [T]he spirit that educates itself matures slowly and quietly ... dissolving one particle of the edifice of its previous world after the other ... .[12]

Kahane and Cavender note that provincialism can operate at various levels, in terms of individuals, families, towns, nations, and institutions such as the corporate media. They emphasize that we Americans, for instance, pay relatively little attention to the peoples of the rest of the world and misconstrue what is happening there. Thus we fail to notice how the U.S. government has toppled several democratically elected governments around the world (Iran, Guatemala, and Chile come to mind), yet we believe that we are a nation founded upon principles of democracy and fair play. According to the poet and critical educationist Lloyd Daniel,

The Activist Legacy of One-Dimensional Man   77

From the beginning when we murdered the people who were here first, the Native people, we were sure it was a democracy. When we enslaved African people to pimp their backs for profit, we were sure it was a democracy. When half the Americans had no right to vote, for over 100 years after the beginning of the nation, we knew it was a democracy ... . And now that we engage in a genocidal air war against the people of Iraq, we are sure that it is in the name of democracy.[13]

So deprovincialization, for me, carries with it a notion of the demythologization of a range of American myths that taken together in their unreconstructed form comprise a hagiography of the "American Pageant:" Horatio Alger on meritocratic individualism and limitless opportunities, Manifest Destiny and American moral supremacy, and the racial superiority of white people. In short, deprovincialization counteracts the dominant order's necessary illusions about class, race, and gender. One especially vibrant and critical multicultural anthology for English literature confronts the mythology of the "model family;" education as "empowerment;" "true women" and "real men;" the "melting pot," "land of liberty," etc.[14]

In addition to his own dialectical resources from Hegel, Marx, and German critical philosophy, Marcuse brings to bear in ODM insights from such critical and subaltern sources as the black auto-worker and Marxist-Humanist Charles Denby; labor activist and journalist Charles R. Walker; criticism of the U.S. militarism from the American Friends Service Committee; as well as lengthy quotations *in the original French* of material from Gilbert Simondon, Jean-Paul Sartre, Serge Mallet, and Francois Perroux (in ODM, chapter 2) and *in the original German* from Adorno (69–70, 99), Bertolt Brecht (70), and Walter Benjamin (257). Some of Brecht's German language quotations are *not* translated for the reader even in editorial footnotes.

For Marcuse, American cultural kitsch is grounded in the pleasant sanitization and repression of life's internal inconsistencies and contradictions, which facilitates adjustment and compliance to the established social order. Brecht's lyrics, on the other hand, as Marcuse points out, might contain sentimental and nostalgic references to the blue sea, the moon, whisky, etc., but these do not go unrecognized as illusions of happiness: "The deceived sing of their deception, but they learn (or have learned) its causes, and it is only in learning the causes (and how to cope with them) that they regain the truth of their dream" (70). Art must employ an estrangement effect. Marcuse's explicitly challenging discourse in ODM models the new multi-dimensional sensibility he is seeking to convey.

As is well-known, Marcuse describes in ODM the triumph of a "happy consciousness" in U.S. cultural life as characteristic of its one-dimensionality. This and especially Marcuse's analysis in ODM's chapter 3 of a *controlled and repressive desublimation* figure prominently in Marcuse's continuing relevance. Marcuse warned, in this signature notion, against popular entertainment and consumerist pleasures that deliver a superficial sense of satisfaction. The prolific use of sex and violence by the corporate mass media and other large-scale commercial interests accomplishes a broadened manipulation and

78   Herbert Marcuse as Social Justice Educator

control in the interest of capital accumulation, and may devolve into the grotesque. Repressive desublimation substitutes reactionary emotional release in place of rebellion. The personality remains totally absorbed in the system of commodity production.

In contrast to the happy consciousness and its repressive desublimations, Marcuse proposes that critical education must develop a mentality more sensitive to questions of complex causality and more skeptical of simplistic visions of the good life or good society. Such education must confront "the power of positive thinking" (which he holds to be *destructive of philosophy*) with "the power of negative thinking," which illumines "the facts" in terms of the *real possibilities* which the facts deny. Critical pedagogy, as he sees it, is thus essentially always dialectical, realistic, and normative—i.e. philosophical and generative of fuller cultural freedom.

The technological achievements of advanced industrial systems are thought to have contributed to the establishment of one-dimensional social realities and social philosophies from which all contradiction has been eliminated. "Technology has become the great vehicle of reification—reification in its most mature and effective form" (Marcuse 1964, 168). This reification, as a reduction of rationality to calculative and operationalist modes, is the epistemological phenomenon characteristic of the oppressive tendencies in advanced technological cultures, wherever practice and theory have forsaken the human dimension of experience and reason in favor of a strictly instrumentalist or functionalist logic of discourse and action. Reason alienated in this manner may assume even the most inhuman tasks through the technological rationalization of methods of domination directed against society and nature. Andrew Feenberg argues that Marcuse's critical theory

> seized on Lukács' concept of reification, which ... became the basis of [his] critique of positivism and its dialectical reformulation of Marxist theory ... . [His] aim is the establishment of a dialectical paradigm of rationality suited to the task of social self understanding and human liberation.
> (Feenberg 1981, xii–xiii; see also 1991, 2014, and 2023)

The critique of advanced industrial society's technological rationality becomes the revolutionary task of reason.

Marcuse's efforts to examine critically the nature of U.S. culture and education actually led to a *recovery of philosophy* in the post-'60s academic context in the United States. This was especially the case among a new generation of scholars in the humanities and social sciences, who became more conscious than ever of issues arising from conflicts involved in the context of our political, moral, and academic culture. Philosophy has never been wholly in the possession of any single school of thought; instead, it has developed out of a clash of opposing views.

After World War II, empiricism, logical positivism, and ordinary language philosophy generally prevailed as the underlying social science and philosophical methodology in U.S. graduate schools and within the undergraduate curricula as well. European approaches such as phenomenology, existentialism, Marxism, and critical theory tended to be marginalized, even at the largest universities. Although Marcuse died in 1979, the philosophical upheavals which developed throughout the 1980s in the American Philosophical Association (APA)—for example, those splitting "analysts" and "pluralists"—reflected the influence of ODM.

Critics of the APA's leadership argued that the association was administered by an entrenched set of philosophers for whom a narrowly conceived technical analysis of logic and language is taken to define the most valuable approach to the discipline.[15] The dissenters argued that the Deweyian heritage of looking at philosophical issues in the context of actual social, political, and cultural conflict had been driven underground. Continental European influences and venerable non-Western approaches were too often relegated to the margins of the profession. Today, the pluralists have gained entry to APA circles and are influential in programming and leadership, but these issues are far from being fully resolved. Letters in the APA *Proceedings* have contended that this debate was exaggerated and unfruitful, and some even deny that there is such a thing as an analytic school. In an account published in the *Chronicle of Higher Education*, Bruce Wilshire commented: "Analysts tend to believe that there is a single right method or technique for attacking all philosophical problems." Wilfred Sellars recalled as well that: "When I was a student at Harvard in the late '50s and early '60s, it never occurred to me to study Hegel. It was an axiom that it didn't amount to anything."[16]

I take the phrase "recovery of philosophy" from Yale professor and Dewey scholar John E. Smith, who adopted it from Dewey himself.[17] Dewey had characterized this recovery as an attempt to liberate philosophy from its customary treatment in the American academy and to orient it anew to genuine societal problems, assessing complex questions of causality and the amelioration of human suffering. Smith was a leading advocate for the pluralists. His ally in this regard, Charles M. Sherover, was quoted with reference to these controversies in a page one article in the *New York Times*. It was his contention that the gatekeepers of the philosophy profession in the U.S.A. have admitted for the most part only persons with little philosophical inclination and interest. According to Sherover: "You're much more likely to find philosophically inclined people outside of philosophy, because if you're philosophically inclined, you've probably been excluded."[18] The APA's own kind of *Positivistenstreit* was underway at the end of 1989.

Of course, during the last three decades of the *culture wars* in the American academy, some forms of postmodernism (especially in their a-sociological and anti-foundationalist aspects) have again brought the categories of essence, ontology, so-called grand narratives, even science into disrepute in favor of the social and linguistic gaming profoundly criticized by Marcuse in ODM. Even as postmodernism was making sizable academic inroads however, ODM was republished in 1991 with a new introduction by Douglas Kellner—further testimony to its ongoing pertinence to continuing controversies.[19]

80 Herbert Marcuse as Social Justice Educator

Marcuse's 1969 APA address, "The Relevance of Reality," vividly demonstrated his radical and heretical stance vis à vis U.S. academic orthodoxy. Marcuse called for a rethinking of the relevance of reality in four key areas of philosophy: 1) linguistic analysis, emphasizing a new, more *political* linguistics; 2) aesthetics, emphasizing the nexus of artwork and *society*; 3) epistemology, moving toward an *historical* understanding of transcendent knowledge; and 4) the history of philosophy itself, emphasizing the internal relationships *linking theory of education to the theory of politics since Plato*: "authentic democracy presupposes equality in the ways, means, and time necessary for acquiring the highest level of knowledge."[20]

As discussed earlier, the general framework of Marcuse's critical social theory dialectically transformed (through negation, preservation, and elevation) a central assumption of classical European philosophy: higher education may cultivate the political Eros to help us accomplish our humanization. Philosophy, art, and social theory (i.e. the humanities and social and political history) can, by virtue of their admittedly elitist critical distance, oppose an oppressive status quo and furnish a proto-revolutionary *telos* by which to guide personal growth and emancipatory social practice.[21]

Marcuse, as discussed above, is attracted to the humanities, social philosophy, and political theory because their subject matter and methodology are thought to focus upon questions of the meaning of human experience, rather than on the sheer description of conditions (this latter procedure being rejected as the non-philosophical approach of behaviorism and empiricism). He regards classical learning by means of discourse and reflection on history, philosophy, literature, drama, music, painting, sculpture, etc. as liberating insofar as this is thought to propel humanity beyond the "first dimension" (the realm of conformity to what is). Here his Marxism encompasses not only Brecht's theatrical estrangement effect but widens to Rilke and Wilhelm von Humboldt: "The substantive universal intends qualities which surpass all particular experience, but persist in the mind, not as a figment of the imagination nor as mere logical possibilities, but as the 'stuff' of which our world consists" (213). Learning involves insight into the multidimensional world of significance and meaning that allows us to re-create life in accordance with the highest potentials of human beings. The rational work of man is man, to become who we are (24).

Let's focus for a moment on our work to become who we are. Marcuse's theory contends that advanced capitalism is obsessed with efficiency, standardization, mechanization, and specialization, and that this fetish involves aspects of domination that impede real education and preclude the development of real awareness of ourselves and our world. "At this stage, it becomes clear that something must be wrong with the rationality of the system itself. What is wrong is the way in which men have organized their societal labor" (144).

This society is fully capable of abundance as Marcuse recognized in ODM, yet the material foundation for the persistence of economic want and political unfreedom persists. Corporate globalization is intensifying social inequality and cultural polarization worldwide. Increasing globalization correlates directly

The Activist Legacy of One-Dimensional Man 81

with growing inequality both within and between nations.[22] This global polarization and growing immiseration have brought to an end what Herbert Marcuse originally characterized in ODM as the totally integrated and completely administered political universe of the liberal welfare/warfare state.

Chapter 2 above emphasized that neoliberalism has today replaced the "comfortable, smooth, democratic unfreedom" of the U.S.A. with something more openly vicious. Marcuse called this new stage *counterrevolution* in his 1972 volume *Counterrevolution and Revolt*, and stressed the necessity of addressing anew the radical goals of socialism. Marcuse envisaged liberation and human flourishing via the revolutionary passage from work for wages and salaries to what I call common*work* for the common*wealth.* [23]

On the educational front, as we also noted, Marcuse advised critical educators and students to continue to take risks and struggle to infuse the curriculum with analysis of the "critical, radical movements and theories in history, literature, philosophy."[24] He believed that education *could* act against our one-dimensional culture and our economic oppression.

The social sciences and liberal arts help us reclaim our common humanity. Yet, as Herbert Marcuse's stepson Osha Neumann correctly observes: "Our myriad histories and endlessly varied bodies are the medium through which, and only through which, our common humanity emerges. This common humanity exists inextricably bonded to our diversity."[25] As mentioned earlier, for Marcuse the curriculum must afford a world-historical, international, and multicultural perspective that examines the pivotal social struggles that have led to the emergence of various standards of criticism in ethics, in logic, in the worlds of art, physical science, production, technology, and politics. These standards constitute the *historical* and *material* (i.e. not merely abstract) philosophical *criteria* of judgment which intelligent action requires.

Marcuse found within the classical liberal arts philosophy critical impulses toward multiculturalism, social history, and critical social theory. Educational activity can and must become the *negation* of exploitation, inequality, alienation. Marcuse stressed that traditional liberal arts education must be renewed with an aesthetic sensibility and multicultural empathy that can help us become actively engaged for social justice. Since the venerable liberal arts tradition has been historically (and inseparably) tied to a realistic and normative concept of *eidos* and essence (as per Plato, Aristotle, Augustine, Thomas, Hegel, and Husserl), we should not be surprised to find some modification of classical realism (and *not the value relativism* the conservative culture warriors claim) in Marcuse's aesthetics and ontology. Indeed, chapter three of *One-Dimensional Man* highlights the importance of the aesthetic Form as the dimension where both reality and truth are disclosed. He also generally shares with Plato and Schiller the philosophical conviction that the most meaningful and beautiful works of art are also the soundest foundation for an education to social justice. ODM's chapter 8 argues the historical reality of universals: "The universal comprehends in one idea the possibilities which are realized, and at the same time arrested, in reality" (210).

82 Herbert Marcuse as Social Justice Educator

Herbert Marcuse's writings as a whole display caustic condemnations of U.S. military aggression, its need for an "enemy," the irrationality of U.S. economic waste, destruction, and wealth distortions, etc. They are all particularly timely and deserve invigorated attention across this nation's campuses as well as in other cultural and political circles today. His philosophical vision, political critique, and social activism continue to offer intelligent strategic perspective on such current concerns as repressive democracy, political and racial inequality, education as social control, and the radical meaning of socialism—especially where issues of alienation, war, oppression, critical inquiry, critical media literacy, and civic/revolutionary action are involved. He maintained that the most important duty of the intellectual was to investigate destructive social circumstances—and be engaged in activities of transformation (209) toward justice and peace (Marcuse 1987, 182). This is the activist legacy of *One-Dimensional Man*.

Notes

1 All page numbers in parenthesis refer to Marcuse, *One-Dimensional Man* (1964).
2 Marcuse, *Schriften 7, Der eindimensionale Mensch* (1989). See also this volume, Chapter 3, note 2.
3 See Outlaw, Jr., "Critical Social Theory: Then and Now" (2016, 232).
4 See Gordon, *Assimilation in American Life* (1964). Also Hofstadter, *Social Darwinism in American Thought* (1955).
5 See the inclusion of this essay in Boss, *Analyzing Moral Issues* (1999, 607–615). See also Bloom (1987) and Kors and Silverglate, *The Shadow University* (1998). In addition: Reitz, "Herbert Marcuse and the New Culture Wars" (2009a).
6 In England, Ernest Gellner (like Marcuse a Jewish intellectual and émigré from Nazi Germany) confronted the linguistic philosophy of Ludwig Wittgenstein and Gilbert Ryle at Cambridge University through his 1959 book, *Words and Things*. Gellner's book was supported by Bertrand Russell, and a huge row developed between Ryle and his defenders on the one side and Russell and Gellner on the other. It must also be noted that in the 1930s Marxism (and near-Marxism) found a variety of viable forms in the U.S.A., including the social reconstructionist perspective in politics and education by George Counts, Charles Beard, Merle Curti, and Theodore Brameld. See Reitz, "A Critical Outline of the Political Philosophy of Social Reconstructionism" (1976, 21–29). McCarthyism cleansed the Ivory Tower however (Schrecker 1986).
7 Echoes of this anti-intellectual scorn roundly resounded in the halls of Congress in December 2023 as MAGA Republicans like Elise Stefanik and Virginia Foxx and billionaires like Bill Ackman and Ross Stevens scolded the presidents of America's most prestigious universities. As was discussed in Chapter 1 above, these academic administrators were explaining the intricacies of their campus codes against hate speech and hate crimes such as antisemitism as well as the doctrine of pure tolerance.
8 Bloom, *The Closing of the American Mind* (1987, 152).
9 That is to say, a comparative and multidisciplinary approach drawing from heterodox perspectives political economy, sociology, philosophy, anthropology, and history.
10 Schwarz, *Keine Zeit für Eichendorff* (1992).
11 Kahane and Cavender, *Logic and Contemporary Rhetoric* (2006, 121).
12 Hegel, *Preface to the Phenomenology* (1986, 48, 20).
13 Daniel, "The Second Assassination of Dr. Martin Luther King, Jr" (2015, 237–238).
14 See Colombo, Cullen, and Lise, *Rereading America* (2004). Also see, Chrisoffel, Finkelhor, and Gilbarg, *Up Against the American Myth* (1970).

The Activist Legacy of One-Dimensional Man   83

15 "The root of the controversy is the pluralists' complaint that the association has failed to represent the full range of philosophical interests being pursued in American universities. Instead, they say, the association's leadership and programs presented at its annual meetings have been dominated by representatives of a single school of philosophical thought, which they term the 'analytic' tradition." Hook, "'Analytic' vs. 'Pluralist' Debate Splits Philosophical Association" (1981, 3), and Hook, "Association Officer Calls for 'Recovery of Philosophy'" (1982, 8); see also Bernstein, "Philosophical Rift" (1987).
16 *The Chronicle of Higher Education*, January 21, 1981, p. 3.
17 Dewey, "The Need for a Recovery of Philosophy" (1917, 3–69); Kasulis and Cummings Neville, *The Recovery of Philosophy* (1997).
18 Charles M. Sherover in Bernstein, "Philosophical Rift: A Tale of Two Approaches" (1987).
19 The wide-spread admiration for Marcuse's critical perspective on the political concerns of philosophy had also been reflected in the manifold essays in his honor (26 in all) published by Wolff and Moore, Jr., *The Critical Spirit* (1967).
20 Marcuse, "The Relevance of Reality" (1969).
21 See Farr, "An Essay on Repressive Education" (2015). Also Reitz, "Herbert Marcuse and the Humanities" (2009b).
22 Sernau, *Worlds Apart* (2001, 52–55). Also see Reitz and Spartan, "The Political Economy of Predation and Counterrevolution" (2015).
23 Reitz and Spartan (2015, 36). See also Reitz, "A Labor Theory of Ethics and Commonwealth" (2015).
24 Marcuse, "Lecture on Education, Brooklyn College, 1968" ([1968] 2009, 37).
25 Neumann, *Up Against the Wall Motherf**ker* (2008, 197).

References

Bernstein, Richard. 1987. "Philosophical Rift: A Tale of Two Approaches," *The New York Times*, December 29, A-1.

Bloom, Allan. 1987. *The Closing of the American Mind*. New York: Simon & Schuster.

Boss, Judith A. 1999. *Analyzing Moral Issues*. Mountain View, CA: Mayfield Publishing Company.

Chrisoffel, Tom, David Finkelhor, and Dan Gilbarg (Eds.). 1970. *Up Against the American Myth: A Radical Critique of Corporate Capitalism Based Upon the Controversial Harvard College Course, Social Relations 148–149*. New York: Holt, Rinehart, Winston.

Colombo, Gary, Robert Cullen, and Bonnie Lise (Eds.). 2004. *Rereading America: Cultural Contexts for Critical Thinking and Writing*. Boston, MA: Bedford/St. Martin's.

Daniel, Lloyd. 2015. "The Second Assassination of Dr. Martin Luther King, Jr," in Charles Reitz (Ed.), *Crisis and Commonwealth: Marcuse, Marx, McLaren*. Lanham, MD: Lexington Books.

Dewey, John. 1917. "The Need for a Recovery of Philosophy," in *Creative Intelligence: Essays in the Pragmatic Attitude*. New York: Holt.

Farr, Arnold. 2015. "An Essay on Repressive Education: Marcuse, Marx, Adorno and the Future of Emancipatory Learning," in Charles Reitz (Ed.), *Crisis and Commonwealth: Marcuse, Marx, McLaren*. Lanham, MD: Lexington Books.

Feenberg, Andrew. 2023. *The Ruthless Critique of Everything Existing: Nature and Revolution in Marcuse's Philosophy of Praxis*. London: Verso.

Feenberg, Andrew. 2014. *The Philosophy of Praxis: Marx, Lukács, and the Frankfurt School*. London: Verso.

84 Herbert Marcuse as Social Justice Educator

Feenberg, Andrew. 1991. *Critical Theory of Technology*. New York: Oxford University Press.

Feenberg, Andrew. 1981. *Lukács, Marx and the Sources of Critical Theory*. Towata, NJ: Rowman & Littlefield.

Gordon, Milton M. 1964. *Assimilation in American Life*. New York and Oxford: Oxford University Press.

Hegel, G.F.W. 1986. *Preface to the Phenomenology*. Translated by Walter Kaufmann. Notre Dame, IN: Notre Dame University Press.

Hofstadter, Richard. 1955. *Social Darwinism in American Thought*. Boston, MA: Beacon Press.

Hook, Janet. 1982. "Association Officer Calls for 'Recovery of Philosophy'," *Chronicle of Higher Education*, January 13.

Hook, Janet. 1981. "'Analytic' vs. 'Pluralist' Debate Splits Philosophical Association," *Chronicle of Higher Education*, January 12.

Kahane, Howard and Nancy Cavender. 2006. *Logic and Contemporary Rhetoric*. Belmont, CA: Thompson Wadsworth.

Kasulis, Thomas P. and Robert Cummings Neville (Eds.). 1997. *The Recovery of Philosophy: Essays in Honor of John Edwin Smith*. Albany, NY: SUNY Press.

Kors, Alan C. and Harvey Silverglate. 1998. *The Shadow University: The Betrayal of Liberty on American Campuses*. New York: Free Press.

Lamas, Andrew. 2016. "Accumulation of Crises, Abundance of Refusals," Guest Editor's Introduction to *Radical Philosophy Review*, Special Issue: *Refusing One-Dimensionality*, Volume 19, Number 1.

Maley, Terry (Ed.). 2017. *One-Dimensional Man 50 Years On: The Struggle Continues*. Halifax: Fernwood Publishing.

Marcuse, Herbert. [1968] 2009. "Lecture on Education, Brooklyn College, 1968," in Douglas Kellner, Tyson Lewis, Clayton Pierce, and K. Daniel Cho, *Marcuse's Challenge to Education*. Lanham, MD: Rowman & Littlefield.

Marcuse, Herbert. 1989. *Schriften 7, Der eindimensionale Mensch*. Frankfurt: Suhrkamp.

Marcuse, Herbert. 1987. *Schriften 9, Zeit-Messungen*. Frankfurt: Suhrkamp.

Marcuse, Herbert. 1969. "*The Relevance of Reality*," Proceedings of the American Philosophical Association. 1968–1969. See also in Douglas Kellner and Clayton Pierce (Eds.). 2011. *Philosophy, Psychoanalysis and Emancipation: Volume 5, The Collected Papers of Herbert Marcuse*. New York: Routledge.

Marcuse, Herbert. 1964. *One-Dimensional Man: Studies in the Ideology of Advanced Industrial Society*. Boston, MA: Beacon Press.

Neumann, Osha. 2008. *Up Against the Wall Motherf**ker: A Memoir of the '60s, with Notes for Next Time*. New York: Seven Stories Press.

Outlaw, Jr., Lucius T. 2016. "Critical Social Theory: Then and Now," *Radical Philosophy Review*, Volume 16, Number 1 (edited by Andrew Lamas, Douglas Kellner, Arnold Farr, and Charles Reitz).

Radical Philosophy Review. 2016. Special Issue: *Refusing One-Dimensionality*, Volume 19, Number 1 (edited by Andrew Lamas).

Reitz, Charles. 2015. "A Labor Theory of Ethics and Commonwealth: Recalling a 'New' Marcuse," in Charles Reitz (Ed.), *Crisis and Commonwealth: Marcuse, Marx, McLaren*. Lanham, MD: Lexington Books.

Reitz, Charles. 2009a. "Herbert Marcuse and the New Culture Wars," in Douglas Kellner, Tyson Lewis, Clayton Pierce, and K. Daniel Cho, *Marcuse's Challenge to Education*. Lanham, MD: Rowman & Littlefield.

The Activist Legacy of One-Dimensional Man   85

Reitz, Charles. 2009b. "Herbert Marcuse and the Humanities: Emancipatory Education vs. Predatory Capitalism," in Douglas Kellner, Tyson Lewis, Clayton Pierce, and K. Daniel Cho, *Marcuse's Challenge to Education*. Lanham, MD: Rowman & Littlefield.

Reitz, Charles. 1976. "A Critical Outline of the Political Philosophy of Social Reconstructionism," *Cutting-Edge: Journal of the Society for Educational Reconstruction*, Summer.

Reitz, Charles and Stephen Spartan. 2015. "The Political Economy of Predation and Counterrevolution: Recalling Marcuse on the Radical Goals of Socialism," in Charles Reitz (Ed.), *Crisis and Commonwealth: Marcuse, Marx, McLaren*. Lanham, MD: Lexington Books.

Schrecker, Ellen W. 1986. *No Ivory Tower: McCarthyism and the Universities*. New York: Oxford University Press.

Schwarz, Egon. 1992. *Keine Zeit für Eichendorff*. Frankfurt: Büchergilder Gutenberg.

Sernau, Scott. 2001. *Worlds Apart: Social Inequalities in a New Century*. Thousand Oaks, CA: Pine Forge Press.

Wolff, Kurt H. and Barrington Moore, Jr. 1967. *The Critical Spirit*. Boston, MA: Beacon Press.

5 What Makes Higher Education *Higher*?

The Philosophical Foundations for Critical Social Research

> Everyone knows that the shape of the world in which we are now living is not its final form. … . It is the hope of humanity to find peace, not through transcendence, but by changing the world—*believing in the possibility of earthly perfection.*
> —Karl Jaspers ([1931] 1999, 5–6)

Critical social theory discloses how capitalist priorities in social affairs distort both our learning and our larger cultural formation (Giroux 2022; Absher 2021; Loughead 2015). The U.S. empire has long encouraged a false patriotism revolving around white supremacy, violent masculinity, and endless militarism. Financial powers control production, politics, and the press. So-called freedoms in this nation have been poisoned by the historically unrepentant conquest of Native American land and violent expropriation of African-American labor. Hideous principles of accumulation and power have undergirded (and continue to define) the U.S. political-economic system and its foreign policy, with war crimes having killed thousands of civilians in Vietnam, Iraq, Afghanistan, and now Gaza. The policies and paramilitary tactics of "ICE" (Immigration and Customs Enforcement) directed at undocumented immigrants have mistreated thousands of immigrants (Jordan 2019). The White House of ex-president Trump emboldened a neofascist rhetoric of hate and fear, and mobilized militarized white supremacist kill squads, including those who encouraged Kyle Rittenhouse to use his military-grade automatic weapon to threaten and shoot down antiracist protestors in Kenosha, Wisconsin, in late August 2020. Can a scholar be oblivious to all of the above and still be a critical social theorist? According to Roy Bhaskar,

> When you think about it, most people who go into the social sciences do so because they think something is profoundly wrong with the social and human world. There are very few social scientists who don't have that initial impulse. "There's something wrong. That's why I want to be a sociologist. There's something wrong with the ways human beings treat each other, that's why I want to be a social psychologist." … So the critical impulse was there at the beginning of social science.
> (Bhaskar, Singh, and Hartwig [2001] 2020, 30–31)

DOI: 10.4324/9781003571582-5

What Makes Higher Education Higher? 87

The global economy's intensifying inequalities are leading to a reconsideration of who produces and who appropriates, who benefits, who is hurt. The Occupy Wall Street movement made a central critical contribution, with the "1 percent" representing the concentration of property ownership in the U.S.A. and the "99 percent" signifying a potential unity of the rest of us in the fullest, richest, most intercultural of terms. The sovereign "1 percent" will also commit ghastly future crimes. Chapters 1 and 2 began to emphasize these points, and let me repeat Marcuse's critical perspective on education:

> To create the subjective conditions for a free society [it is] no longer sufficient to educate individuals to perform more or less happily the functions they are supposed to perform *in this* society or extend "vocational" education to the "masses." Rather ... [we must] ... educate men and women who are incapable of tolerating what is going on, who have really learned what *is* going on, has always been going on, and why, and who are educated to resist and to fight for a new way of life. By its own inner dynamic, education thus *leads beyond the classroom*, beyond the university, *into the political* dimension, and into the *moral*, instinctual dimension.
>
> ([1975] 2009a, 35, emphasis in original)

Marcuse has further emphasized:

> In the United States, students are still in the forefront of radical protest: the killings at Jackson State, and Kent State testify to their historical role. Black militants pay with their lives: Malcolm X, Marin Luther King, Fred Hampton, George Jackson. The new composition of the Supreme Court institutionalizes the progress of reaction. And the murder of the Kennedys shows that even Liberals are not safe if they appear too liberal.
>
> (1972, 1)

Marcuse's perspicacious insight here was articulated almost fifty years before the unmistakably counterrevolutionary physical attack on January 6, 2021 or the Rufo-DeSantis political attack on Florida's New College in January 2023.

Critical educationists Henry Giroux (2012), Peter McLaren, and Michael W. Apple (2001) (as I shall elaborate in Chapter 8 below) have due respect for the research conclusion of educational sociologists Samuel Bowles and Herbert Gintis (1976) that the latent function of our schools and colleges has long been education for the perpetuation of inequalities of wealth, work, and social power. There have been, of course, intermittent free spaces in educational institutions where faculty and students engaged in real intellectual contestation that superseded the insistent single-dimensionality of society. A critical educationist too little honored for his profound work in arduous and conflicted circumstances in Buffalo, New York, Michael L. Simmons, Jr. protected one such space during the 1970s and '80s, in the (now dismantled) Department of Social, Philosophical, and Historical Foundations of Education in the Graduate School

88 Herbert Marcuse as Social Justice Educator

of Education at the State University of New York with a cadre of other progressive and radical educationists: Roger Woock, Gene Grabiner, Ronald Goodenow, Warren Button, Maxine Seller, Charles Fall, Gail Kelly, Lois Weis, Philip Altbach, and renowned philosopher of naturalism, education, and critical social theory Marvin Farber (on Farber, see Reitz 2023, 73–73). Simmons (1997) assimilated the naturalism, humanism, and social theory of Farber and John Dewey to the Frankfurt School theorists Horkheimer, Marcuse, and Habermas as well as the critical realism of Roy Bhaskar. He oversaw the development of my dissertation, published as *Art, Alienation and the Humanities: A Critical Engagement with Herbert Marcuse* (SUNY Press, 2000).

Simmons conducted discussions in terms of Socratic themes and questions. For instance, how can we create a social system that makes living according to the principles of goodness possible? Is it necessary to do so? Why? How and why must science itself be rethought? His work demonstrated that the serious critical social theorist must enter into the search for the as yet undisclosed nature of rigorous knowing in both social science and educational philosophy. He introduced students to Horkheimer and Marcuse's appreciation for the critical dimension of classical philosophy: "Ever since the trial of Socrates, it has been clear that [philosophers] have a strained relationship with reality as it is, and especially with the community in which they live" (Horkheimer quoted in Simmons 1974, 6). Simmons offered a capsule historical description of critical social theory as: "the experience of, and expression on the philosophical plane, of the theory of Marx, working class politics, the rise to power of Hitler, the history of the Soviet revolution and state, and the continued power of world capitalism" (Simmons 1974, 9). Simmons also argued that …

> … critical social theory has several functions. It presents a model for the general critical comprehension of society, provides stimulus for the shaping of specific research projects, and it offers a social orientation for philosophic analysis and criticism of concepts and practices generally accepted within the educational community.
>
> (Simmons 1982)

Simmons saw our contemporary problems as connected to the pivotal issue in Plato's *Meno*:

> Society in crisis, with philosophy attempting to instantiate virtue … . One comes to see and understand and define inadequacies in the abstract, as it were, and in light of social reality as it is and as it can become given the state of current science, technology, values, tradition, class relations, political formations etc., all rethought in order to be realized in restructured social relations.
>
> (Simmons n.d., 12)

In addition to the work of Horkheimer and Marcuse (and Plato and Dewey), Simmons recommended a consideration of Habermas on the role of human

What Makes Higher Education Higher? 89

interests in knowledge production: our *technical* interests, our interests in *shared understanding*, and our *emancipatory* interests. He also introduced graduate students to Paulo Freire's theory of cultural action for freedom and the pedagogy of the oppressed.

Simmons recommended study of the philosophical realism of Roy Bhaskar as one of the most innovative theorists of critical social theory of the last few decades (see also Barnett 2024, 2018 on Bhaskar's engagement with the ecological movement). Bhaskar's chief contribution was his conception that the natural (and social) world is a *layered* or *stratified* composite reality: the empirical layer, the actual event layer, and a generative layer; all three must be considered for a comprehensive understanding of the reality of nature and society. Our empirical observations, while factual, do not represent the real world wholly, but only partially. Reality is deeper and is composed of generative processes and structures that produce manifest phenomena. These processes and structures, while not visible, are knowable. They are open rather than closed systems, and they contain event possibilities that may be actualized or *not* actualized. Reality is composed of the empirical, the actual, and the underlying structural generative mechanisms (the dynamics of nature and society). The generative layer gives rise to the actual events and to the empirical phenomena; some real possibilities remain absent. Real systems are open, having multiple dimensions and depth. Consciousness "… is a complex or set of powers … historically emergent from and present only in association with (certain complex forms of) matter" (Bhaskar [1979] 2015, 98).

Likewise, critical realism understood human existence in a manner that challenged the methodological individualism of much contemporary social science, especially economics. Bhaskar saw the subject matter of sociology as the *relations* that obtain between people, not simply the agency of individuals, even masses of individuals. In this view, societies are irreducible to people, irreducible to data points along a supply curve or a demand curve, and irreducible to a "rational" utilitarian calculation of advantage. For Bhaskar, as with Aristotle, Marx, and Durkheim, *nothing* done by any individual is *not* social. As the *zoon politikon*, humanity is social in speech, labor, wisdom, and politics. Methodological individualism has hindered us from appreciating what is essential to our freely flourishing well-being, and thus it has contributed to our alienation. Bhaskar, like Horkheimer, Habermas, and Marcuse, seeks to emancipate social theory such that it might transform rather than reproduce contemporary social structures of domination.

Critical Realism and Critical Social Theory

Bhaskar's approach is in agreement with Marcuse on the historical truth of universals and is equally radical politically. Echoing Marcuse's critique of Auschwitz and Vietnam, he concurs that—

> Our world, the planet, which is the habitat of the human species, is in ecological crisis and chronic economic imbalance and is afflicted by

90 *Herbert Marcuse as Social Justice Educator*

alienation and anomie, and many other things that threaten its survival, including the ever-continuing possibility of a holocaust ... . No century before the twentieth has known more killing ... as a result of conscious intentional decisions at the level of military chiefs of staff and governments. No century has seen more killing of civilians by both armies and other people.

(Bhaskar, Singh, and Hartwig [2001] 2020, 83)

Bhaskar's emphasis is reminiscent of Marcuse's insight that science and technology are social and politically implicated in systems of oppression. Against commercial and military interests, Marcuse counterposes an emancipatory critique employing the concepts *logos* and *eros*. Andrew Feenberg stresses that Marcuse's critical theory of science and technology embodies a "logos of life" (Feenberg 2023, 76). As he sees it, for Marcuse, "reason has from the beginning been oriented to a specific value: the service and affirmation of life" (Feenberg 2023, 94). This is a central contention of Marcuse's *Eros and Civilization*.

Bhaskar proposes a naturalist view of humanity that sees every human being as having ontological "ground state" (Bhaskar, Singh, and Hartwig [2001] 2020, 65). We are conditioned by communal experience to perform spontaneously creative and loving (i.e. right) actions. Ethical understanding and partnership behavior is said to be intrinsic to our generic social nature as humans. In this view (and much in the manner of Marcuse's political Eros), when confronted with localized warfare and the possibility of even greater global conflagration, visceral revulsion drives the world to condemn and oppose the invasion of Ukraine as well as the genocide in Gaza.

Today's global capitalist crisis has brought about a huge *legitimation crisis* as well as a crucial opportunity for a new political beginning. Marcuse's call for a Great Refusal during the '60s meant that he saw a *universalization of resistance* underway. The Great Refusal envisaged "a new culture which fulfills the humanistic promises betrayed by the old culture" (1969, 10). As *a collective project*, it constituted a multidimensional expression of negation against systems of domination—and represented the new *general interests* of humanity. The multiplicity of possible refusals, each for the sake of our deepest love of life, could and should be consolidated. As emphasized above, key is the revolt of youth as a global phenomenon: today against guns, war, women's oppression, racial animosity, labor force precarity, LGBTQ stigmatization, and the devastation of the earth—and increasingly for solidarity with immigrants and for ecosocialism. Ecology is central because human beings uniquely appreciate the awesome power of the earth and its remarkable beauty.

The ecology movement reveals itself in the last analysis as a political and psychological movement of liberation. It is political because it confronts the concerted power of big capital, whose vital interests the movement threatens. It is psychological because (and this is a most important point) the pacification of external nature, the protection of the life-environment, will

What Makes Higher Education Higher? 91

also pacify nature within men and women. A successful environmentalism will, within individuals, subordinate destructive energy to erotic energy.

(Marcuse 2019, 17; [1979] 2011a, 212)

Marcuse's essay "Ecology and Revolution" (Marcuse 2019; [1972] 2005) noted the revival of the women's movement and student anti-war protest in 1972. The ecology movement joined these in protesting against the capitalist "violation of the Earth" (2019, 1; [1972] 2005, 174). As noted earlier—

The revolt of youth (students, workers, women), undertaken in the name of the values of freedom and happiness, is an attack on all the values which govern the capitalist system. And this revolt is oriented toward the pursuit of a radically different natural and technical environment; this perspective has become the basis for subversive experiments such as the attempts by American "communes" to establish non-alienated relations between the sexes, between generations, between man and nature—attempts to sustain the consciousness of refusal and of renovation.

(2019, 3–4; [1972] 2005, 174)

As we have seen, Marcuse would valorize those responding to the sensuous and emancipatory core of their political Eros in opposing the genocidal warfare and ecocide in Gaza today. He points to the need for a "reorienting of philosophical desire" (Absher 2021, 81). "The erotic element is captured … in the very name 'philosophy'—*love* of wisdom … . Knowledge, according to Marcuse is … bound to libidinal striving for self-actualization" in an age when global capitalism encourages incessant growth amounting to a "global warming induced suicide pact" (Absher 2021, 82–83). In Marcuse's view, global humanity is seeking a form of democratic self-governance such that we might acquit ourselves honorably and generously during this dark time, mindful of the love and gratitude we owe to planet earth.

Ecological Materialism and Critical Naturalism: The Reality and Dialectics of the Human Condition

Herbert Marcuse was in many regards the foremost critical social theorist of the 20th-century. He saw nature *as an ally* rather than a "resource" and insisted on our earthly intercultural interconnectedness as the foundation of an ethics and politics of empathy, mutual aid, and this-worldly human flourishing. Marcuse's revolutionary Marxist writings were the avant-garde of *what we need today*. We need to be reading and re-reading Marcuse and Bhaskar, not as a nostalgic pastime but *because our lives depend upon it*.

[T]he restoration of the earth as a human environment, is not just a romantic, aesthetic, poetic idea which is a matter of concern only to the privileged; today, it is a question of survival.

(Marcuse 2019, 4–5; [1972] 2005, 175)

92　Herbert Marcuse as Social Justice Educator

The evidence today of impending natural catastrophe is mounting; so too our awareness that the climate crisis is the outcome of economic and governmental business as usual. Without ecosocialism's most radical goals—I call them collectively the *EarthCommonWealth Counteroffensive* (Reitz 2023)—there is no sufficient negation, and there will be no sufficient transformation from oligarchy toward a new world system when conditions are ripe for revolution.

Philosophy, emergent over centuries, has endeavored to understand and comprehend the dynamic material conditions that have generated the history of nature, society, and thought. Historical materialism is a name relatively recently given to this endeavor within Marxism (Plekhanov [1897] 1940; Marcuse [1932] 1973). Historical materialism signals the intellectual emergence of the recognition (central to philosophical rationality) that the natural world as well as social life have undergone multiple transformations over time in terms of patterns of geological change, bio-ecological development, and socioeconomic transformations. Frederick Engels confides something to us about the ontology (the dialectics) of things in nature as well as those constructed through human ingenuity, like buildings, books, and governments:

> [T]he world is not to be comprehended as a complex of ready-made *things*, but as a complex of *processes*, in which the things apparently stable ... go through uninterrupted change of coming into being and passing away, in which in spite of all seeming accidentality and all temporary retrogression, a progressive element asserts itself in the end ...
>
> (Engels [1888] 1974, 44)

> The new conception of nature [is] complete in all its main features; all rigidity [is] dissolved, all fixity dissipated, all particularity that had been regarded as eternal became transient, the whole of nature shown as moving in eternal flux and cyclical course.
>
> (Engels [1872–1882] 1973, 13)

Engels is elaborating the dynamics and the dialectics of matter and nature, the unity of body and mind, with an emphasis on human creativity (and intelligence itself) as "the highest product of matter" (Engels [1888] 1974, 25). Modern science and philosophy have emphasized humankind as a part of nature and thought as a social product. In contemporary sociology, an *ecological-evolutionary* perspective stresses that human societies are embedded in the natural world and humans are part of the global ecosystem—influenced by such things as soil, water and mineral resources, climate, terrain, plants, animals, and other features of the territory in which they live (Nolen and Lenski 2011). An *ecological materialism* sees the world and human societies in terms of systems of interrelated parts, the whole often being greater than the sum.

It is worth repeating that the methodologies of ecology, critical philosophy, and sociology take interconnected *systems* to be the focus of analysis (in terms

What Makes Higher Education Higher? 93

of statics and dynamics, structures and processes), rather than isolated particular units, individuals, experiences, or inert machinery. Hegel and Marx studied the systemic interconnectivities in nature and the social world in terms of reciprocities and mutualities, as well as tensions, conflicts, and antagonisms, where opposition can lead to contradiction as well as qualitative transformation. These are the methodologies of dialectical materialism. For Michael L. Simmons, Jr.—

> Dialectic treats existence, whatever its domain, size, form, importance, as a totality (or a unity) comprising elements or factors that stand in opposition, in conflict, even contradiction, to each other. Movement of the object results primarily from the oppositions, etc. The particular relations of any oppositions, conflicts, or contradictions are the necessary condition of the existence and particular nature of the very totality which contains them; it is [sic] them.
>
> (Simmons, "Dialectic," n.d.)

Simmons explains that the materialist dialectic understands actual inadequacies and absences in light of real and better human possibilities in order that these "be realized in restructured social relations." Higher learning *is* dialectical understanding, incipient critical social science and radical political education. Where science looks for lawfulness, Simmons acknowledges the critical realism of Bhaskar (*The Possibility of Naturalism*, [1979] 2015), as well as the naturalism of Dewey (*Human Nature and Conduct*, 1922; *Experience and Nature*, 1925)—and Marvin Farber (*Naturalism and Subjectivism*, [1959] 1968) allows us to understand these "laws" as *tendencies* within the underlying structures internal to nature and social reality that generate empirical data. For Bhaskar, the tendencies can be understood dialectically as actualized and as not actualized depending on conditions, time, and place. From the perspective of the critical realists and naturalists mentioned above, science and philosophy inherently entail a dialectical logic supporting emancipatory cultural action for freedom and justice.

Marcuse was the critical theorist to develop a uniquely explicit ecosocialist critique of capitalism and develop a strategy of revolutionary ecological liberation. Marcuse's revolutionary ecological legacy points out something seldom taken note of in environmentalist thinking or in Marcuse studies for that matter. We have noted above that Marcuse propounds the idea that "*nature is an ally*" in the "Nature and Revolution" chapter of *Counterrevolution and Revolt* (1972)—

- Nature is a dynamic force, without telos or plan, but Beauty pertains to nature as well as Art.
- Nature can be hostile to humanity, a circumstance against which we must struggle, but the unfriendly aspects of nature subside.
- Human beings uniquely recognize the awe-inspiring, astounding, and humbling qualities (Schiller calls them the "serene or regal" *erhaben*

94 *Herbert Marcuse as Social Justice Educator*

features) of beauty in the natural world, and these prefigure the promise of human freedom, collective happiness and fulfilment.

- Human senses and impulses do shape our rationality and experience.
- Nature is an educator. It teaches us to think of the ecological system as the unit of analysis.

Nature as an *Ally,* Nature as *Educator*

It's extraordinary that Marcuse sees nature as an *ally* in the struggle for liberation! What revelations await? Can we even imagine it? It is not as if nature is a *subject* that can choose to act on our behalf (or not) by giving us "following seas" or a tail wind—one might just as often be randomly becalmed or swamped. Nature is in motion; it is dynamic, and it is because humanity and nature are *dialectically interdependent* that the "liberation of nature" can be a "vehicle for the liberation of man" (1972, 59). Marcuse rejects the theology implied if one holds that nature can be a "manifestation of subjectivity" (1972, 65).

Like Goethe and Schiller, American transcendentalist Ralph Waldo Emerson *did* classically propose certain advantages we owe to nature: refreshed sensations and awareness, our essential bond with both the living and the non-living features and creatures of the material world.

> To the body and mind which have been cramped by noxious work or company, nature is medicinal and restores their tone … . [T]he universe is the property of every individual in it. Every rational creature has all nature for his dowry and estate … he is entitled to the world by his constitution.
>
> (Emerson [1836] 2009a, 6–7)

To Emerson we are also *educated* through the study of the environment:

> To the young mind everything is individual, stands by itself. By and by, it finds how to join two things and see in them one nature … it goes on tying things together, diminishing anomalies, discovering roots running under ground, whereby contrary and remote things cohere, and flower out from one stem.
>
> (Emerson [1837] 2009b, 151)

One might say with Emerson that such education affords insights into an underlying *dialectics of nature*. Emerson's views resonate with Engels. We stand to benefit as Marcuseans when re-reading Emerson's work on nature: we need to better appreciate Emerson's pantheistic tendencies, as well as to critique and sublate them, thereby preserving and elevating his ecological strengths.

Marcuse's philosophy helps in this regard with his recognition of the humanizing propensities of nature. Appreciating the Romantic and naturalistic insights of Goethe and Emerson, Marcuse agrees that nature has been a "symbol of beauty, of tranquility, of a nonrepressive order" (2019, 2; [1972]

What Makes Higher Education Higher? 95

2005, 174). Yet his contention that "nature is an ally" entails not only that, but that "[t]hanks to these values, nature was the very negation of the market society, with its values of profit and utility" (2019, 2; [1972] 2005, 174). He emphasizes that human beings and the earth are enmeshed in an ecological web of mutuality and interdependence: nature will "help" liberate us—if we help liberate *it*. Nature itself requires liberation because we now encounter nature "as transformed by society, subjected to a specific rationality which became, to an ever-increasing extent, technical, instrumentalist rationality bent to the requirements of capitalism" (Marcuse 1972, 59–60). Nature needs us as an ally to prevent its destruction and we need nature as an ally given its power to ensure that we can endure.

> The liberation of nature cannot mean returning to a pre-technological stage, but advancing to the use of the achievements of technological civilization for freeing man and nature from the destructive abuse of science and technology in the service of exploitation. Then, certain lost qualities of artisan work may well reappear on the new technological base.
>
> (Marcuse 1972, 60)

Marcuse's *ecological materialism* sees the world and human societies in terms of systems of interrelated parts, the whole often being greater than the sum. In societies, the basic needs of the system are met through cooperation of one sort or another, often a customary solidarity and egalitarian partnership, sometimes compulsion or coercion. This cooperation is reproduced by the basic forms of social learning, an enculturation; the mode of cooperation can also be challenged and transformed, sometimes successfully. Fundamental conflicts are endemic to most modern human societies existing within a globalized political-economic system, a world system that has tended toward patterns of dominator power and inequality.

Marcuse's ecological materialism is also historical. Even a stone has a history (Lenin [1914] 1972, 111) as does every species of life. Geology and biology must explain this history as well as describe it. Nature is *not* a collection of inert hunks of matter or molecules but an interactive ecological totality of material forces and processes engaged in various interrelated sets and schemes of protracted and/or rapid change in living and nonliving systems. As Marx, Engels, and critical Marxist materialists like Herbert Marcuse were well aware, the interactive and dynamic qualities of the material world were evident in the ancient Greek writings of Heraclitus, Thales, Democritus and Leucippus. Likewise, the works of the elder Pliny and Lucretius in the Roman era. Renewed publications of these writers during the Renaissance marked the modern beginning of a unified theory of the material world. Science was attempting to eliminate the "meta" from metaphysics and stress the "uni" in universe. Mind and humankind were starting to be understood as integral parts of nature. Comprehension, itself, was thought to require broadly based scientific knowledge of the macrocosm, as well as humanistic expertise in such fields as art and

96 Herbert Marcuse as Social Justice Educator

anatomy. Indeed, the Renaissance recognition of the inherent interconnections linking different areas of theoretical endeavor and practical concern was the most remarkable event of all.

Historical materialism attempts to understand the philosophical problem central to human history and human liberation: theoretical explanation and its relation to reality. Alexander Humboldt's "everything is interconnected" approach (especially in *Kosmos*) recognized how humanity's inner capacities adapt to the world's ecosystems, and that our insight into these ecosystems builds our fuller, more comprehensive understanding of life as a whole—i.e. including aesthetics, ethics, and politics. Humboldt's writing on plant ecology, geography, geology, and much more of necessity also condemned sugar plantation slavery as a denatured and disfiguring economic form where he found it in Cuba. Humboldt maintained the unity of the human race against Agassiz, who promoted racial hierarchy. Humboldt's work was also a manifest or a latent background influence on Henry David Thoreau, John Muir, Friedrich Engels, and a generation later, Herbert Marcuse.

Marcuse's final monograph links his materialism to his critical Marxism. "History is also grounded in nature. Marxist theory has the least justification to ignore the metabolism between the human being and nature ..." (1978, 16).

The ecological materialism of Marcuse can be illumined by bringing it into juxtaposition with that of Aldo Leopold ([1942] 1991; [1949] 1966b). A forester, nature writer, and the nation's first professor of wildlife management at the University of Wisconsin in 1933, Leopold is renowned as one of the world's foremost philosophers of conservation and ecology. Leopold's philosophy was not a narrow instrumental rationality of resource management, but rather in dialectical sympathy with wildlife, plant life, ice, water, air, and the land (Brennan 2007, 519). He understood earth (i.e. land) scientifically as a biotic system. "Land ... is not merely soil, it is a fountain of energy flowing through a circuit of soils, plants, and animals" (Leopold [1953] 1966a, 231). It is a fundamental constituent of a "biotic pyramid."

> Plants absorb energy from the sun. This energy flows through a circuit called the biota ... A plant layer rests on the soil, an insect layer on the plants, a bird and rodent layer on the insects, and so on up through various animal groups to the apex layer, which consists of the larger carnivores ... .
> Each successive layer depends upon those below it for food and often for other services, and each in turn furnishes food and services to those above ... lines of dependency for food and other services are called food-chains. Thus soil-oak-deer-Indian is a chain that has largely been converted to soil-corn-cow-farmer.
>
> (Leopold [1953] 1966a, 230–231)

Above and beyond nature's beauty, Leopold saw that living on the face of our planet with dignity is possible. Our historical and material condition holds the promise of ethical, political, and aesthetic meaning for human communities. To

Leopold, nature was considered to be a community to which humanity belongs. "The culture of primitive peoples is often based on wildlife. Thus, the plains Indian not only ate buffalo, but buffalo largely determined his architecture, dress, language, arts, and religion" (Leopold [1949] 1966b, 195). Ultimately, Leopold came to replace the term "wildlife" with the term "land" because he saw the former as inextricably bound to the latter. Leopold explicitly developed what he called a "land ethic," which led him to a logic of protection, love, and respect for nature—both in recreation and in social production. "That the land is a community is a basic concept of ecology. But that the land is to be loved and protected is an extension of ethics" (Leopold [1953] 1966a, x). He replaced a view of humanity as conqueror of the land-community with a vision of the planet's inhabitants as a commonwealth of earth. "EarthCommonWealth" is my term, not his, but it encapsulates his conviction that ecological science can lead to ecological conscience: to conservation and cooperation. "Ecology is the science of communities, and the ecological conscience is therefore the ethics of community life" (Leopold [1942] 1991, 340). Ecological science discloses "the tendency of interdependent individuals or groups to evolve modes of cooperation ... All ethics so far evolved rest upon a single premise: that the individual is a member of a community of interdependent parts" (Leopold [1949] 1966b, 218–219). Leopold argues that "for the purposes of a liberal education ecology is superior to evolution as a window through which to view the world" (Leopold [1942] 1991, 305).

> Much of the damage inflicted on land is quite invisible to laymen. An ecologist ... must be the doctor who sees the marks of death in a community that believes itself well and does not want to be told otherwise.
>
> (Leopold [1953] 1993, 165)

Leopold's hitherto largely unheralded ecological vision embraced all living things as an earthly community capable of measured and dignified coexistence with our planet and its surroundings. Leopold, like Humboldt and Engels—and Marcuse—did not limit himself to the description of immediate abuses or the observation of ecological marvels. His analysis was grounded in an appreciation of the dynamism and mediated dialectical interdependencies of nature that could also make recovery and ecological/ethical advance possible. Leopold developed an ecological critique of private property rights in land ownership, since such rights undergirded social and environmental destruction:

> When god-like Odysseus returned from the wars in Troy, he hanged all on one rope a dozen slave-girls of his household whom he suspected of misbehavior during his absence ... The girls were property. The disposal of property was then, as now, a matter of expediency, not right and wrong ... The ethical structure of that day covered wives, but had not yet been extended to human chattels ... Land, like Odysseus' slave girls, is still property.
>
> (Leopold [1953] 1966a, 217–218)

98   Herbert Marcuse as Social Justice Educator

> [E]thics, so far studied only by philosophers, is actually a process in ecological evolution. Its sequences may be described in ecological as well as in philosophical terms. An ethic, ecologically, is a limitation on freedom of action in the struggle for existence. An ethic, philosophically, is a differentiation of social from anti-social conduct. These are two definitions of one thing. The thing has its origin in the tendency of interdependent individuals or groups to evolve modes of cooperation ... cooperative mechanisms with an ethical content.
>
> (Leopold [1953] 1966a, 217–218)

Leopold's Land Ethic contains a critique of private property ownership that leads him to valorize commonality and cooperation given our societal interdependence. He connects the aesthetic realm also to the land: "What is art? Only the drama of the land's workings" (Leopold [1942] 1991, 303). Aside from humans, does any other living being on the face of the planet appreciate its beauty, its ethical promise?

> The practice of conservation must spring from a conviction of what is ethically and aesthetically right, as well as what is economically expedient. A thing is right only when it tends to preserve the integrity, stability, and beauty of the community, and the community includes the soil, waters, fauna, and flora, as well as people ... Economic provocation is no longer a satisfactory excuse for unsocial land use ... for ecological atrocities ... I have no illusions about the speed or accuracy with which an ecological conscience can become functional.
>
> (Leopold, [1947] 1991, 345)

Aldo Leopold's ecology and ethics of commonwealth epitomize what he had in common also with Vine Deloria, Jr. ([1992] 1995), one of the most highly regarded literary and political figures of the Standing Rock Sioux. Humans, wildlife, plants, and land form a larger inclusive community relationship—one to be respected and held in the highest regard. Deloria writes with wry irony: "[I]t is the white man with his careless attitude toward life who is actually in danger of extinction" (Deloria [1992] 1995, 250).

> The native peoples of the American continents ... have managed to survive. Now, at a time when the virtues they represented, and continue to represent, are badly needed by the biosphere struggling to remain alive, they must be given the participatory role which they might have had in the world if the past five centuries had been different.
>
> (Deloria [1992] 1995, 252)

Daniel R. Wildcat, professor of sociology and academic administrator at Haskell Indian Nations University in Lawrence, Kansas, who has worked closely with Vine Deloria, Jr., offers us a set of exceptionally worthy resources allowing serious readers to discover America's indigenous ecological ingenuity.

What Makes Higher Education Higher? 99

> Those expecting to find reassuring romantic reveries about noble savages living close to nature should turn elsewhere for their reading pleasure ... New Age secrets and formulae, and exoticized platitudes of mythological tribal origin, are absent in these pages.
>
> (Wildcat 2009, 20, 74)

Wildcat's volume *Red Alert!: Saving the Planet with Indigenous Knowledge* (2009) cogently makes the case for an "Indigenous Realism."

> To know reality we need to respect the dynamic material relationships that constitute the complex web of life. This ... is *not* a call to anthropology and archeology as these disciplines have been practiced throughout much of their Western academic existence, but a challenge to replace a search for humankind's general development along a Western-inspired universal timeline with a rethinking of our diverse human cultural development as shaped by places.
>
> (Wildcat 2009, 11)

Daniel R. Wildcat's perspective on saving the planet with indigenous knowledge delves into the historic American sources on the "web of life" from which Leopold unfolded his own appreciation of indigenous ecophilosophy: humanity needs to adhere to a partnership-oriented land ethic and land aesthetic.

> In order to deal with the array of social and ecological issues we will face across nearly every dimension of the complex life system of Mother Earth, we must begin to understand our lives as essentially *not* only about us but about our human selves in what environmental scientists and ecologists, without the least hint of romanticism, call the web of life.
>
> (Wildcat 2009, 5)

> [W]e have no tradition of religious writings ... . [W]e have saved ourselves from religious wars ... . [W]e are, as my northern plains friends say *mitakua oysin,* "all related."
>
> (Wildcat 2009, 57–59)

Wildcat's writing also takes us behind Marcuse's 1972 insight that *nature is an ally,* reminding us that it is *Mother Earth herself* who has been admonishing us to act boldly to stop the climate catastrophe that he calls "global burning."

Marcuse argues for *a modern historical materialism* on the basis of Marx's *Philosophical Manuscripts* of 1844, Plato's dialectical idealism, Kant's transcendental humanism, Hegel's historization of conceptual concreteness—and critical consciousness under the impact of the women's movement. Extrapolating from all of this permits also a vital philosophical synthesis of the ideas of Leopold, Deloria, and Wildcat with Herbert Marcuse (Reitz 2023).

100 _Herbert Marcuse as Social Justice Educator_

Disrupting the Pre-established Harmony Between Scholarship and the Power of the 1 Percent

The critical Marxism of Marcuse's _One-Dimensional Man_ sought to break through the "pre-established harmony between scholarship and national purpose" (1964, 19). In a wide-ranging series of publications after _One-Dimensional Man_, he reiterated that we must use "all possible means of protest" to present the "indictment of what those who rule our lives are doing with this country …" ([1969] 2011b, 187). This was an ongoing expression of his critical social impulse, his own political Eros.

> [W]e live in a profoundly immoral and profoundly inhuman society behind the veil of a free democratic process and behind the veil of prosperity. Behind the veil of prosperity, waste, destruction, and war, the brutalization of entire populations, and poverty and misery are not only abroad but within our national frontiers—and all this in a historical period in which the resources for the liberation of all men would be available if they would be rationally used in the interests of man and not only certain vested interests. Now, against this society you see today the global rebellion of the youth, together with the liberation movements of the oppressed people in the Third World [i.e. Global South], and in the Black liberation movement.
> ([1969] 2011b, 185)

In the absence of an overarching commonwealth ethos, knowledge is merely technique, an uncritical methodology for expedient manipulation and control (as in capitalism's conduct of "warrior science" condemned by ecofeminists). This reduces its practice to positivism, empiricism, and pragmatism. It becomes single-dimensional in its promotion of the valorization of capital at the expense of nearly everything else. "When we discover a fantastic new fertilizer or new kind of gas, we change the material world, that is, the natural environment—which may of course be economically fantastic, but ecologically horrendous" (Bhaskar, Singh, and Hartwig [2001] 2020, 32).

Revolts arise from a striving to reduce destructive violence, often enough expressing a love of beautiful work and play, love of beautiful knowledge instead of psychopathic political disregard for the future. Struggles and revolts against racist practices, sexist practices, exploitative labor practices, and war have elevated our sense of the intersectionality of diverse forms of oppression and for a fuller, more concrete sense of the necessity of _system_ change. Participation in multiple righteous revolts can indicate a series of committed activist interventions and oppositions to injury and injustice, _but without a strategic view for real prospects of system transformation, revolts have limited revolutionary power._

Marcuse's theory of culture pivots on critical social learning linked to an _emancipatory political action_ component. As outlined in Chapter 2 above, in 1975 he gave a "Lecture on Higher Education and Politics" at Berkeley:

What Makes Higher Education Higher? 101

To attain our goal, we need *knowledge*. It is still true that *theory* is the guide of radical practice. *We need history* because we need to know how it came about that civilization is what it is today: where it went wrong. And we need the history not only of the victors, but also of the victims. *We need a sociology* which can show us where the real power is that shapes the social structure. *We need economics* which are not "sublimated" to mathematics. *We need science* in order to reduce toil, pain, disease, and to restore nature.

([1968] 2009b, 43, emphasis in original)

Marcuse's focus was on social transformation—toward a better future condition for humanity. "*The alternative* is not a free-wheeling emotionalism, intolerance, but another concept and another practice of objectivity, another interpretation of facts, namely in terms of the given possibilities to build a better society through radically changing the established one" ([1968] 2009b, 42). In our society today, technology tends to facilitate forces of domination, but Marcuse makes clear that it also has the capacity to overcome alienated labor and bring qualitative change to our lives with generous amounts of leisure and free time if propelled by eco-socialist politics as we build a new world system.

Capitalism's fetish with commodity production and profit is poisoning the earth. Profit comes before all else: gun manufacturers before victims in schools and churches. Drug manufacturers before diabetics and opioid addicts. On one of the most divisive issues in public health today was explored in the article "Gas Stoves Are Just Fine, Claims the Scientist Paid to Say So" (*The New York Times*, January 30, 2023 A1). This obsession with profit is a many-headed hydra: cut off one head and five more appear; e.g., control cigarettes then vaping generates renewed revenue for the tobacco industry. For Marcuse, Simmons, and Bhaskar, science and technology must be enlisted in the service of humanity, *not* capital accumulation. They understand commercialized exploitation of the earth as the source of social injustice and environmental violations of the planet that must be ended.

The general form of the internal contradictions of capitalism has never been more blatant, more cruel, more costly of human lives and happiness. And— this is the significance of the Sixties—this blatant irrationality has not only penetrated the consciousness of a large part of the population, it has also caused, mainly among the young people, a radical transformation of needs and values which may prove to be incompatible with the capitalist system, its hierarchy, priorities, morality, symbols (the counter-culture, ecology) ...

(Marcuse [1975] 2015, 114–115)

It is clear that we need science, philosophy and religious studies that function in a humane, critical, and creative manner, such that our works of higher learning are consecrated in service to the qualitative improvement of human life on earth. Change starts with the pleasure we find in meaningful work, mindful

102 *Herbert Marcuse as Social Justice Educator*

of our need for a livelihood that is more than "making a living;" we need to be making a life of love and justice, leisure, abundance, and peace.

Consistent with Marcuse's utopianism, we must hammer out what we really desire. What are the most intelligent/wisest uses of labor and wealth? Commodified human labor must be negated and sublated into *public* work, i.e. *common* work that aims at *common* wealth and the public good, rather than private accumulation.

Ecosocialism, Ecopedagogy, and the Future of Higher Education

How *do* we contend with the power of the 1% that distorts today's material human condition? The owners and managers of the world's largest income-producing properties, international banks and financial institutions, landowners and developers, the agribusiness oligopoly, timber interests, the corporate media, are not friends of a common humanity. The coercive power of the CIA, and the FBI, and the U.S. military, is real. Yet the money-is-speech U.S. Supreme Court incurred much damage to its reputation during the confirmation hearings of two notorious male justices, Clarence Thomas (in 1991) and Brett Kavanaugh (in 2018). Their toxic masculinity was excused as natural and expected; their sexual harassment and victim shaming was denied. Recently, a white masculinist assault was launched against a new nominee to the Supreme Court, Judge Ketanji Brown Jackson, a black woman, by the Republican party's most toxic Senators and future presidential candidates, Ted Cruz and Josh Hawley, accusing her of an allegiance to "woke" racialized education. "A snarling pack of white male Republicans ripping apart a poised, brainy Black woman …" as Maureen Dowd (2022) put it, comparing the treatment of Ketanji Brown Jackson to that of Anita Hill before a Senate Judiciary Committee. To Dowd, this abuse was galling, appalling, and repulsive; it is representative of the counterrevolutionary values and practices of the prevailing dominator power in the U.S.A.

The corporatization of the university displaces the university's traditionally critical function and threatens critical education in a number of particular ways. Higher education administrators, trustees, and regents are increasingly coming from the corporate world. Faculty increasingly find themselves with little choice but to accept unilateral administrative decision making if they are without sufficient tenure protections, and/or adequate protection through unionization for due process. For example, faculty senates at universities across Wisconsin in 2016 struggled to preserve their voice in campus governance, but their rights were withdrawn unilaterally through the electoral success of reactionary state politicians. Organized faculty (unionized or not) across the state voiced their discontent through campus votes of no-confidence in UW System President Ray Cross, who acquiesced to former Wisconsin governor Scott Walker's political success. Faculty thus have a real need to be involved in the shared governance process broadly conceived and be prepared politically to support organized labor. Faculty across the nation have witnessed significant reductions to the

What Makes Higher Education Higher?   103

instructional sides of their institutional budgets while the administrative side has grown, sometimes enormously. Some accreditation boards in social work and nursing, for example, stipulate proportions of full-time faculty to students that must be maintained. Tanya Loughead sees a dynamic here that could be extended if the latent power of accrediting agencies were liberated to require across the board "that a college or university be structured such that a minimum of 85 percent of courses in every department be taught by full-time, qualified professors with terminal degrees in their fields" (Loughead 2015, 9). She acknowledges, however, that this is not how accrediting boards now function, however. Instead, a grants culture sponsored by corporate, military, and federal governmental interests leads to universities becoming less and less critical or questioning of the society around them. Loughead, an educational philosopher, states: "universities as critical sites of inquiry can only exist when professors themselves model the critical life" (Loughead 2015, 15).

We must intervene in the generative systems that are the engines of inequality in the economy, politics, and culture. We need to apply an ecological materialist analysis to the internally conflicted economic and political systems wreaking havoc today, and (in terms of a unity of theory and practice) assess how we might best utilize the real but latent powers of labor to begin to establish realistic methods and goals for an *EarthCommonWealth Alternative* (Reitz 2023). The classic contributions to power structure research by C. Wright Mills ([1956] 2000), G. William Domhoff ([1967] 2022), and Michael Parenti ([2002] 2011) have much to offer in terms of explanation. The task now, however, is how to *dismantle* and replace these structures. This is necessary to attain goals of global disarmament and demilitarization with the elimination of nuclear arms. The latent power of labor is central to emancipatory theory and praxis. In this regard, we need to extend the dialectical philosophical perspective on the material human condition of both Marcuse and Charles Woolfson's *Labor Theory of Culture* (1982). This stresses the cultural context of cooperation and caring in the earliest human societies, which fostered interdependence and an awareness of the customary power of partnership. Partnership customs and behaviors had the capacity to ensure survival. Subsistence needs were met with relatively little time spent in the collaborative acquisition of necessities, i.e. three to four hours a day (Sahlins [1968] 2017); thus, the foundation was established for the fuller species' life to flourish within the human community. This included the development of language as a derivative of the communal human condition (Leakey 1994, 124).

The radically socialist logic of commonwealth production, ownership, and stewardship can facilitate a movement for social transformation that can, within the realm of necessity, construct an architecture of intercultural equality, dis-alienation, ecological balance, abundance, and freedom. Marx and Marcuse emphasized that collective effort is what makes us prosperous: labor occurs in social relationships and is a communal project of social beings to meet human needs and promote human flourishing. Furthermore, social productivity is the political-philosophical foundation of the call for socialized ownership. Yet

104   *Herbert Marcuse as Social Justice Educator*

capitalism's fetish for commodity production and for growth in exchange values (enhancing surplus value) has become the be-all and end-all of the business system (no limits to profit accumulation). At the same time, the workforce is a resource with programmatic power. It is the creative force in the economy. Wealth derives from this collective production process (as was notably described by Adam Smith on the power of the division of labor). Included in the outputs of this collective process are also our common human heritage of science, technology, math, etc., even language, each of which develops primarily within the context of social labor. When these multiple efforts at labor combine judiciously with our common earthly comrades—the land, wildlife, flora, sea, air, etc.—humanity's CommonWealth emerges. Conditioned upon proper respect for the earth's rights and resources, laboring humanity, as society's foundational collective, has a legitimate right to the control, disposition, and ownership of this socially produced wealth. This is a *supply-side* economic theory. In contrast to the conservative capitalist fable that economic growth is driven through corporate tax breaks and business deregulation; supply-side here draws attention to the economic significance of the expanded production of real output increasing the society's supply of use-values, *not* the paper wealth of asset price inflation as pursued in financialized capitalism. Commonwealth productivity indicates what social living labor accomplishes in terms of real tangible value creation. Our very humanity is grounded in the legacy we have inherited from our earliest forms of production in partnership societies with their ecologies of caregiving and commonwealth. There will be no restoration of nature and no re-humanization of our coarsened and divided culture, our damaged and precarious world, without the radical regulation of globally financialized monopoly capitalism—or its *elimination*. Socialism's minimum standards require the provision of adequate social needs-oriented programs and services such as housing, health care, childcare, and education, to everyone, as well as government policy, law enforcement, and public media that ensure the optimization of the human material condition.

Today's global capitalist crisis has brought about a huge *legitimation crisis* as well as a crucial opportunity for a new political beginning. The goal of building a universal human community on the foundation of universal human well-being must acknowledge the fundamental role of the labor process in the sustenance of human social life. Human labor has the irreplaceable power to build the commonwealth, past and future. Our current conditions of insecurity and risk make it imperative that we undertake a deeper understanding of the necessity of a humanist commonwealth alternative: radical ecosocialism as an egalitarian, abundant, and green political-economy, through which humanity may govern itself honorably, in terms of our fullest potentials, mindful of the care and gratitude we owe to planet earth.

References

Absher, Brandon. 2021. *The Rise of Neoliberal Philosophy: Human Capital, Profitable Knowledge, and the Love of Wisdom*. Lanham, MD: Lexington Books.

Apple, Michael W. 2001. *Educating the 'Right' Way: Markets, Standards, God and Inequality*. New York and London: RoutledgeFalmer.

Barnett, Ronald. 2024. *Realizing the Ecological University: Eight Ecosystems, Their Antagonisms, and a Manifesto*. New York: Bloomsbury Publishing.

Barnett, Ronald. 2018. *The Ecological University: A Feasible Utopia*. New York: Routledge.

Bhaskar, Roy, Savita Singh, and Mervyn Hartwig. [2001] 2020. *Reality and Its Depths: A Conversation Between Savita Singh and Roy Bhaskar*. Singapore: Springer.

Bhaskar, Roy. [1979] 2015. *The Possibility of Naturalism: A Philosophical Critique of the Contemporary Human Sciences*. London and New York: Routledge.

Bowles, Samuel and Herbert Gintis. 1976. *Schooling in Capitalist America*. New York: Basic Books.

Brennan, Jason. 2007. "Dominating Nature," *Environmental Values*, Volume 16, Number 4.

Deloria, Jr. Vine. [1992] 1995. "Afterword" to *America in 1492* edited by Alvin Josephy in *Voices of Diversity*, edited by Pat Andrews. Guilford, CT: The Dushkin Publishing Group.

Dewey, John. 1925. *Experience and Nature*. Chicago, IL: Open Court.

Dewey, John. 1922. *Human Nature and Conduct*. New York: Henry Holt.

Domhoff, G. William. [1967] 2022. "Who Rules America?" in *The Corporate Rich, White Nationalist Republicans, Inclusionary Democrats in the 2020s*. New York: Routledge.

Dowd, Maureen. 2022. "Real Justice: Justice Jackson," *The New York Times*, March 27, SR9.

Emerson, Ralph Waldo. [1836] 2009a. "Nature," in *Nature and Other Essays*. Mineola, NY: Dover Publications.

Emerson, Ralph Waldo. [1837] 2009b. "The American Scholar," in *Nature and Other Essays*. Mineola, NY: Dover Publications.

Engels, Frederick. [1888] 1974. *Ludwig Feuerbach and the Outcome of Classical German Philosophy*. New York: International Publishers.

Engels, Frederick. [1872–1882] 1973. *Dialectics of Nature*. New York: International Publishers.

Farber, Marvin. [1959] 1968. *Naturalism and Subjectivism*. Albany, NY: SUNY Press.

Feenberg, Andrew. 2023. *The Ruthless Critique of Everything Existing: Nature and Revolution in Marcuse's Philosophy of Praxis*. London and Brooklyn: Verso.

Giroux, Henry A. 2022. *Pedagogy of Resistance: Against Manufactured Ignorance*. London: Bloomsbury Academic.

Giroux, Henry A. 2012. *On Critical Pedagogy*. New York: Bloomsbury.

Jaspers, Karl. [1931] 1999. *Die geistige Situation der Zeit*. Berlin: Walter de Gruyter.

Jordan, Miriam. 2019. "ICE Arrests Hundreds in Mississippi Raids Targeting Immigrant Workers," *The New York Times*, August 7.

Leakey, Richard. 1994. *The Origin of Humankind*. New York: Basic Books.

Lenin, V.I. [1914] 1972. *Philosophical Notebooks*. Moscow: Progress.

Leopold, Aldo. [1953] 1993. *Round River*. New York: Oxford University Press.

106 *Herbert Marcuse as Social Justice Educator*

Leopold, Aldo. [1942] 1991. "The Role of Wildlife in Liberal Education," in Susan L. Flader and J. Baird Callicott (Eds.), *The River of the Mother of God and Other Essays by Aldo Leopold*. Madison, WI: University of Wisconsin Press.

Leopold, Aldo. [1953] 1966a. "The Land Ethic," in *A Sand County Almanac*. New York: Oxford University Press.

Leopold, Aldo. [1949] 1966b. *A Sand County Almanac*. New York: Oxford University Press.

Loughead, Tanya. 2015. *Critical University: Moving Higher Education Forward*. Lanham, MD: Lexington Books.

Marcuse, Herbert. 2019. *Ecology and the Critique of Society Today: Five Selected Papers for the Current Context*. Philadelphia, PA: International Herbert Marcuse Society.

Marcuse, Herbert. [1975] 2015. "Why Talk on Socialism?" in Charles Reitz (Ed.), *Crisis and Commonwealth: Marcuse, Marx, McLaren*. Lanham, MD: Lexington Books.

Marcuse, Herbert. [1979] 2011a. "Ecology and the Critique of Modern Society," in Douglas Kellner and Clayton Pierce (Eds.), *Herbert Marcuse, Philosophy, Psychoanalysis and Emancipation: Volume 5, Collected Papers of Herbert Marcuse*. New York and London: Routledge.

Marcuse, Herbert. [1969] 2011b. "The Role of Religion in a Changing Society," in Douglas Kellner and Clayton Pierce (Eds.), *Herbert Marcuse, Philosophy, Psychoanalysis and Emancipation: Volume 5, Collected Papers of Herbert Marcuse*. London and New York: Routledge.

Marcuse, Herbert. [1975] 2009a. "Lecture on Higher Education and Politics, Berkeley, 1975," in Douglas Kellner, Tyson Lewis, Clayton Pierce, and K. Daniel Cho, *Marcuse's Challenge to Education*. Lanham, MD: Rowman & Littlefield.

Marcuse, Herbert. [1968] 2009b. "Lecture on Education, Brooklyn College, 1968," in Douglas Kellner, Tyson Lewis, Clayton Pierce, and K. Daniel Cho, *Marcuse's Challenge to Education*. Lanham, MD: Rowman & Littlefield.

Marcuse, Herbert. [1972] 2005. "Ecology and Revolution," in Douglas Kellner (Ed.), *Herbert Marcuse, The New Left and the 1960s: Volume 3, Collected Papers of Herbert Marcuse*. New York and London: Routledge.

Marcuse, Herbert. 1978. *The Aesthetic Dimension*. Boston, MA: Beacon Press.

Marcuse, Herbert. [1932] 1973. "The Foundation of Historical Materialism," in *Studies in Critical Philosophy*. Boston, MA: Beacon Press.

Marcuse, Herbert. 1972. *Counterrevolution and Revolt*. Boston, MA: Beacon Press.

Marcuse, Herbert. 1969. *An Essay on Liberation*. Boston, MA: Beacon Press.

Marcuse, Herbert. 1964. *One-Dimensional Man: Studies in the Ideology of Advanced Industrial Society*. Boston, MA: Beacon Press.

Mills, C. Wright. [1956] 2000. *The Power Elite*. New York: Oxford University Press.

Nolan, Patrick and Gerhard Lenski. 2011. *Human Societies*. Boulder, CO: Paradigm Publishers.

Parenti, Michael. [2002] 2011. *Democracy for the Few*. Boston, MA: Wadsworth.

Plekhanov, Georgi. [1897] 1940. *Essays in Historical Materialism*. New York: International Publishers.

Reitz, Charles. 2023. *The Revolutionary Ecological Legacy of Herbert Marcuse: The Ecosocialist EarthCommonWealth Project*. Cantley, Quebec, CA: Daraja Press.

Sahlins, Marshall. [1968] 2017. "The Original Affluent Society," in *Stone Age Economics*. New York and London: Routledge.

Simmons, Michael L. Jr. 1997. "Certainty, Harmony and the Centering of Dewey's Aesthetics," in *Philosophy of Education 1997*. Urbana, IL: Philosophy of Education Society.

What Makes Higher Education Higher? 107

Simmons, Michael L. Jr. n.d. [but after 1982]. "Dialectic: Philosophy of Education's Missing Essence." Personal copy.

Simmons, Michael L. Jr. 1982. "The Present Position of Marvin Farber's Materialism," personal copy of unpublished paper presented at the International Conference on Philosophy and Science in Phenomenological Perspective, SUNY Buffalo, March 11–13.

Simmons, Michael L. Jr. 1974. "Critical Social Theory and the Social Foundations of Education: Philosophical, Historical, Political and Pessimistic Reflections," personal copy of paper delivered at the American Educational Studies Association.

Wildcat, Daniel R. 2009. *Red Alert! Saving the Planet with Indigenous Knowledge.* Golden, CO: Fulcrum Publishers.

Woolfson, Charles. 1982. *The Labor Theory of Culture: A Re-examination of Engels's Theory of Human Origins.* London: Routledge and Kegan Paul.

6 Critical Teaching and Learning
On the *Origins* of Social Inequality

> We submit to the peaceful production of the means of destruction, to the perfection of waste, to being educated for a defense which deforms the defenders and that which they defend.
>
> —Herbert Marcuse (1964, ix)

An in-depth examination of political economy, especially the social dynamics of economic inequality, is a vital part of critical pedagogy. Marcuse's critical pedagogy understands economic inequality as critical pedagogy's material core. The basic fact of the economy, its unequal distribution of wealth and life chances, is generally overlooked (and actively suppressed) by mainstream analysts, policy makers, commentators, and educationists. How well equipped are teachers to direct dialogue regarding the complex underlying structures of economic functioning?

This chapter, completed with insights provided in conversation with my economics colleague Stephen Spartan, will attempt a critical philosophical analysis of work, the origins of wealth, and contemporary propensities toward military spending and war. Our purpose is to provide key materials and insights that can function critically in a variety of lesson plans to help teachers and students better *understand, question, and challenge* the deeply rooted origins of U.S. inequality by comprehending the unequal patterns in the distribution of wealth and in forms of economic compensation. The objective of this piece is, thus, a fundamental empowerment: to develop, through fact-based observations drawn from the national income accounts and critical social analysis—a fuller awareness of underlying generative structures—and also to evoke a "new sensibility" with regard to the prospects for radical social change.

We have noted above that economics for Aristotle was the study and practice of improving the human material condition, enabling human families and communities to flourish. The capitalist system is obviously *dis*-economic in its extreme inequalities of immiseration and wealth, limitations on quality of life, and undemocratic monopolization of power. In economics and ethics, Aristotle believed the chief vice was the boundless pursuit of private property accumulation; the chief virtue, the pursuit of the well-being of the family and community (*Politics*, chapter IX).

DOI: 10.4324/9781003571582-6

In the U.S.A. today, excessive military spending illustrates this vice most vividly. Aside from the fuller costs of U.S. wars in terms of lives lost, government lies and illegalities, and torture, as these are repeatedly emphasized by Marcuse (1969, 1972, 2019), the U.S. military budget is far greater than needed, and in fact could be reduced if the sole goal were national defense. In reality, the military budget does more than provide for defense; it is a major mechanism to subsidize owners of the military-industrial complex and thus keep the nearly unbounded profits flowing. Military spending is one of the most wasteful projects in the U.S.A. and elsewhere around the globe. It could be substantially reduced and public welfare would not be impaired. All of this doesn't even begin to get at the fact that U.S. media are generally uncritical about the U.S. military being the largest polluter in the world. According to FAIR (Fairness and Accuracy in Reporting), "Major Media Bury Groundbreaking Studies of Pentagon's Massive Carbon Bootprint" (2019), with the U.S. military as the largest single source of greenhouse gasses on the planet.

Marcuse's Critique of Militarism and the Global Political Economy

In *One-Dimensional Man* (1964), Herbert Marcuse had stressed the nearly total absorption of the populations of advanced industrial societies within a completely administered political universe of a liberal welfare/warfare state. Ten years later—after having emphasized in stark contrast notable outbreaks of activist political radicalism in *An Essay on Liberation* (1969) and in *Counterrevolution and Revolt* (1972)—he argued the growing political opposition to U. S. militarism and global capitalism quite compellingly. He did so in a series of seven rather recently discovered and newly published lectures delivered at Vincennes University, Paris, in 1974 (2015).

As was noted above in Chapter 2, Marcuse's *Paris Lectures* (2015) foresaw the possible end of capitalism precisely at a time of its greatest productive capacities and its greatest wealth accumulations. He believed he could discern U.S. societal disintegration from what was actually happening in the process of production itself. First, there was the increasing unproductivity of those who control the destructive and wasteful productive forces today (Marcuse 2015, 32–33). When he wrote in 1974, he pointed out that the Pentagon was the nation's biggest single industrial enterprise with 14.2 million workers directly or indirectly dependent on military spending.

> [I]f you throw together—which as an orthodox Marxist you might well do— unemployment and employment for the military services, you arrive at the following figures: a total of over 25% of the labor force, i.e. 22.3 million, were either unemployed or dependent on military spending directly or indirectly.
>
> (Marcuse 2015, 42)

Marcuse saw a capitalism that had become more and more militarist and predatory; super profits were generated by wasteful war production. Likewise,

110 *Herbert Marcuse as Social Justice Educator*

any limited prosperity among war production workers eluded masses of people whose conditions of life had become increasingly precarious.

Accounting for Inequality

Educators at every level face the necessity of building the theory and practice for a free world order today. To do so one must talk about established institutions, not individuals; systems as the unit of analysis, not just individuals.

The following presentation and discussion of patterns of wealth and income distribution and other specific exhibits will endeavor to furnish theoretically and politically powerful aids for teachers in several interrelated disciplines—sociology, economics, history, and ethics, as well as logic and critical thinking. Our thesis is that inequality is not simply a matter of *distance* between rich and poor but of the *structural relationships* in the economic arena of propertied and non-propertied segments of populations. Like Marcuse, our aim here is to aid an emancipatory form of critical education theory and practice—to mobilize students and faculty to challenge the conditions, educational and otherwise, that serve to perpetuate increasingly alienating, unequal, and undemocratic realities in the global economy and in the political and cultural life of the U.S.A.

The analytical innovations presented here can be regarded as a contribution to critical social theory insofar as they "project potentiality in the objective conditions" (Marcuse 2015, 18) and embody a newer form of concrete critical social science inquiry that examines *the structures and dynamics of capital formation and the problematic patterns of workforce compensation* in the U.S.A. while also projecting the possibilities derived from this analysis for radical social change in the conditions of labor.

The observations made here on the origins and outcomes of income inequality in the nation's manufacturing sector offer several persistent principles that can be applied more generally to the production and sale of products in other sectors of the U.S.A. and global economies, such as the financial system and information-based services. This approach draws out implications latent in standard economic data and arrives at certain significant findings and conclusions that have been avoided in standard economics and business textbooks. It also fills in some of the key and notable economic deficits of contemporary forms of cultural critique stemming from postmodern literary and aesthetic theory.

Students—and faculty—typically have little awareness of the nature of wealth or the pattern of its distribution in society. They also lack insight into the connection of income flows to relations of property ownership. According to *The Washington Post*'s piece by Christopher Ingraham, "The richest 1 percent now owns more of the country's wealth than at any time in the past 50 years" (2017). Ingraham draws on data from Edward N. Wolff's *A Century of Wealth in America* (2017), still in 2024 one of the most reliable sources of information on the unequal distribution of wealth in the U.S.A. The disparities in the shares of *total wealth held in all U.S. households* are described by Ingraham as follows:[1]

Critical Teaching and Learning   111

90% is held by the richest quintile (one fifth of U.S. households)
8% by the second wealthiest quintile
2% by the middle quintile
0% by the second lowest quintile
-1% by the poorest quintile

A starkly unequal pattern of the concentration of wealth has persisted during every decade in the U.S.A. since the end of World War II. *Sociology* and *Social Problems* textbooks by authors like Ian Robertson, D. Stanley Eitzen, and John J. Macionis ([2012] 2018) have tracked this concentration through the years. In the 1980s, the uppermost quintile held 78% of the wealth. After 2000, this had risen to 84% (Reitz 2004; Reitz and Spartan (2015).

This intensifying pattern of unequal wealth distribution has enormous implications for the distribution of income. Those *households with the greatest wealth also receive the greatest incomes, inasmuch as their incomes derive from their vast property holdings.* Most of the wealth in high-wealth families is inherited and most of the income is unearned.

If the facts of increasing economic inequality are largely undisputed, the same may not be said of their social significance. The prevailing views among economists and business idealists/apologists represented in the writings of George Gilder, for example, hold that these inequalities are natural and normal, a positive social good.

Despite all the publicity given to the analysis of inequality presented by Thomas Piketty (2014) with regard to capital and inequality in the 21st century, way beyond what Wolff has received, his study (and most commentary upon it) offers no radical challenge to corporate liberalism (Andrews 2016; Reitz 2016). Yet, the profoundly negative impacts of this vastly unequal wealth distribution on *life chances* must be addressed. "Life chances" is the sociological term used to indicate the relative access a household has to the society's economic resources: decent housing, health care, education, employment, etc. The greater the wealth in one's household, the greater one's life chances. The less the wealth in one's household, the fewer the life chances.

The question of where wealth comes from was classically posed by the early modern social philosophers John Locke and Adam Smith, though this is seldom discussed with students. Precursors to Marx, they in large measure settled the question by maintaining that a person's labor is the real source of all property that one might have the right to call one's own.

Marx and Marcuse encompassed the theories of Locke and Smith within a larger philosophy of labor. Where Locke and Smith saw individual labor as the source of private property, in an atomistic (Robinsonian) manner, Marx recognized that all humans are born into a social context. Humanity's earliest customs, i.e. communal production, shared ownership, and solidarity assured that the needs of all were met, by right not by charity—i.e. including those not directly involved in production, like children, the disabled, and the elderly. This right to a commonwealth economy, humanity's earliest ethic of holding

112 Herbert Marcuse as Social Justice Educator

property in common, derives only secondarily from any individual's factual individual contributions to production; it is rooted primarily in our essentially cooperative and empathic species nature as humans. Marx and Marcuse stressed that labor is a *social* process; that the value created through labor is most genuinely measured by socially necessary labor time; and its product rightfully *belongs* to the labor force as a *body*, not to individuals as such—i.e. grounding a theory of common ownership and social justice; the rights of *CommonWealth* (Reitz 2015). In advocating that labor has the right to retain the full value of the wealth it creates, Marx was simply carrying the abstract philosophies of Locke and Smith through to their concrete social conclusions.

The labor theory of value, even in Locke and Smith, is rejected by most conventional economists, who contend that labor is merely a cost of doing business, and that profit accrues from entrepreneurial skill, technological innovation, and risk-taking. These factors may increase profit in the short run in a sub-division of any given industry, where fractions of capital compete, yet in the long run the innovative production processes and reduced costs and payrolls become the new social average. What has meaning for an individual entrepreneur does not explain the aggregate picture. *National income accounts*, on the other hand, reveal the structural fundamentals of the value production process. Very importantly, these national income accounts—unlike the prevailing business idealist models—do *not* include the "cost" of labor among the input costs in the conception of the production process they utilize. Instead, they treat workforce compensation as do Locke, Smith, and Marx above—as an income flow stemming from the value production process itself. These accounts are therefore insightful and useful in Marxist terms in that they presuppose that labor in each firm (and by extension each branch of production) is paid for through *payroll outlays* from the total value that is added *through the firm's value production process*.

To explain the mechanism generating inequality, a model is required that can depict and clarify *income flows* in terms of differential returns *to labor and capital* as the two basic factors in the production process itself. Figure 6.1 offers such a model. Usually concealed, the structure and dynamics of the value production process will be made visible here in their material form.

Modeling Income Flows and the Capital/Labor Split: The Capital/Labor Antagonism

The model we have developed illustrates the dynamics of wealth acquisition and accumulation and the generative mechanisms that are the dynamic structural origins of inequality (Figure 6.1). This illustrates our thesis that inequality is not simply a matter of the gap between rich and poor but of the structural relationships in the economic arena between propertied and non-propertied segments of populations (the capital/labor split). Our goal is to present in theoretical form the inner necessity of exploitative class relations within capitalism. This model may serve as a small but necessary contribution to the

Critical Teaching and Learning 113

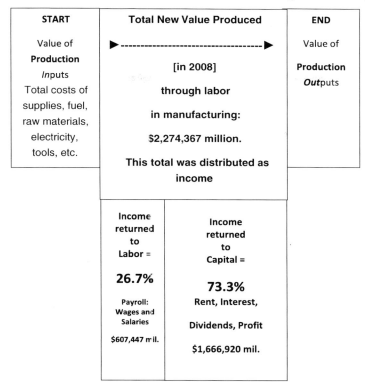

Figure 6.1 Income Flows under Capitalism: The Capital/Labor Split

advancement of a more economically informed critical theory of society and indicate how and why *property relations* must be addressed in order to root out recurring crises.

Figure 6.1 outlines the structure and the dynamics of the value *production* process—in manufacturing—and depicts the essential working of the *substantive* economy. The *value-added* approach emphasizes the importance of production as the key factor in the generation of substantive growth in national wealth and in the assessment of national income in terms of substantive, value-added outputs. Central to the model is an understanding of the process of adding value to economic inputs by working them up by the end of the process into finished products. The amount of *new wealth created* through production is calculated by subtracting the dollar costs of the *inputs* (supplies, raw materials, tools, fuel, electricity, etc.) from the dollar value of the *outputs*. The difference equals the *value added*, and the value added is distributed as income to the two major factors in production, labor and capital. Every dollar of the value added is distributed into one of the two basic income categories: 1) returns to the workforce (in terms of the *payroll*—wages and salaries), or 2)

114   *Herbert Marcuse as Social Justice Educator*

returns to owners and investors (in terms of profit, rent, dividends, interest). Subtracting the *payroll* from the *value added* discloses the income flow returning to capital, which accumulates as new wealth. Thus, this model actually represents the three inextricably interconnected activities of production, distribution, and capital accumulation. The model discloses the fundamental *distributive* structures of the contemporary business economy: capital acquisition/ accumulation and workforce compensation. If labor *fundamentally* creates all wealth, as John Locke and Adam Smith maintained, then labor creates all the value that is distributed as income to the labor force (wages and salaries) *and to capital* (rent, interest, dividends, and profit). We emphasize that incomes returned to capital and labor are *structurally determined*, i.e. conditioned primarily by societal, rather than individual, factors. A major portion of the value employees add to the economy is legally appropriated by employers as a return to capital. This is the meaning of exploitation and wasted abundance.

Figure 6.2 presents data from the Statistical Abstract of the United States 2011, which measures the wealth created in every manufacturing sector of the economy in 2008. This substantive, real-world data can be plugged into the model outlined above to gain a concrete understanding of how the economy functions, especially the dynamics of capital accumulation, which results from the differential incomes distributed to labor and to capital. Every dollar of the value added in U.S. manufacturing—for example in 2008, $2,274,367 million (the most recent available figure as this study was initially undertaken)—was distributed into one of the two basic reproduction categories: 1) as income to the workforce—as *payroll* (wages and salaries)—$607,447 million; and 2) as income to owners and investors—as *profit, rent, dividends, and interest*—$1,666,920 million. In other words, unequal property relations structure this disproportionate division of the added value proportionately as follows: capital 73.3 percent/labor 26.7 percent. Such are the dynamics of compensation in U.S. manufacturing.

A critical philosophical perspective consistent with the critical realism of Bhaskar and Marcuse demonstrates that labor has *a reality and a capacity beyond its theoretical and practical confinement within its commodified form* (i. e. a wage or salary). The fuller potential and power of labor, as recognized also by Locke and Smith, challenges the presumption that capital produces value, the view that profit *unilaterally* accrues as a reward for the contribution of the investor/employer. Labor provides the total value added in the production process. Profit is a *subtraction* from the value produced. The workforce is a resource with *programmatic power*. It is the creative force in the economy. Everything depends on labor. Labor occurs in social relationships; it is a communal project of social beings to meet human needs and promote human flourishing (see Woolfson's *Labor Theory of Culture*, 1982). Because social labor is the source of social wealth, only the labor force, as a group, has a legitimate right to the ownership of this wealth.

Private ownership of capital is clearly not socially necessary for *value (i.e. wealth) production*. The necessary component is *labor*. A *critical* appreciation

Table 1006. Manufactures—Summary by Selected Industry: 2008

[12,781.2 represents 12,781,200. Based on the Annual Survey of Manufactures; see Appendix III]

Industry based on shipments	2002 NAICS code[1]	All employees			Production workers[2] (1,000)	Value added by manufactures[3] (mil. dol.)	Value of shipments[4] (mil. dol.)
		Number[2] (1,000)	Payroll Total (mil. dol.)	Per employee (dol.)			
Manufacturing, total	31–33	12,781.2	607,447	47,527	8,872.9	2,274,367	5,486,266
Food[5]	311	1,437.8	51,818	36,039	1,113.7	246,222	649,056
Grain and oil seed milling	3112	53.2	2,817	52,953	39.5	28,988	94,000
Sugar and confectionery poducts	3113	61.9	2,625	42,431	47.3	13,184	26,648
Fruit and vegetable preserving and specialty food	3114	167.7	6,232	37,161	138.5	28,045	63,187
Dairy products	3115	132.3	5,899	44,592	95.6	27,072	98,118
Animal slaughtering and processing	3116	505.7	15,217	30,094	438.9	50,823	169,925
Bakeries and tortilla	3118	271.6	9,442	34,760	172.8	34,108	58,701
Beverage and tobacco products	312	152.8	7,322	47,905	87.0	76,292	125,520
Beverage	3121	134.7	6,223	46,196	73.5	44,833	88,085
Textile mills	313	135.6	4,661	34,383	113.1	12,471	31,845
Textile product mills	314	136.3	4,151	30,455	104.9	11,540	26,630
Apparel	315	148.9	3,887	26,112	116.2	9,237	19,596
Cut and sew apparel	3152	118.5	3,075	25,951	92.2	7,385	15,608
Leather and allied products	316	31.7	994	31,361	23.9	2,619	5,411
Wood products[5]	321	461.6	15,619	33,834	365.5	34,577	88,004
Sawmills and wood preservation	3211	91.7	3,394	37,024	76.9	7,278	24,272
Paper	322	403.2	20,546	50,957	311.6	79,175	178,749
Pulp, paper, and paperboard mills	3221	117.8	7,794	66,142	93.6	40,476	82,923
Converted paper products	3222	285.4	12,752	44,687	218.0	38,700	95,826
Printing and related support activities	323	605.9	25,138	41,491	422.4	60,003	99,167
Petroleum and coal products	324	105.9	8,415	79,444	68.2	91,559	769,886
Chemical[5]	325	780.1	50,766	65,074	448.8	355,481	751,030
Basic Chemical	3251	151.8	10,880	71,656	92.2	83,629	244,174
Pharmaceutical and medicine	3254	249.1	18,771	75,347	117.8	142,773	194,478
Soap, cleaning compound, and toilet preparation	3256	104.4	5,667	54,259	62.7	46,661	97,431
Plastics and rubber products	326	796.5	31,580	39,651	613.2	91,431	204,679
Plastics products	3261	651.8	25,299	38,815	499.7	76,503	167,423
Rubber products	3262	144.7	6,281	43,415	113.5	14,929	37,256
Nonmetallic mineral products	327	443.4	19,372	43,694	338.0	61,994	115,920
Glass and glass product	3272	93.9	4,227	45,042	74.0	12,562	23,197
Cement and concrete products	3273	213.6	9,106	42,637	161.8	29,774	57,779
Primary metal[5]	331	418.3	22,693	54,245	328.7	93,564	282,141
Iron and steel mills and ferroalloy	331	109.3	7,668	70,150	87.4	43,036	126,332
Foundries	3315	144.0	6,435	44,689	116.3	15,492	31,842
Fabricated metal products[5]	332	1,572.7	69,231	44,021	1,153.4	188,072	358,363
Forging and stamping	3321	123.5	5,763	46,663	92.0	15,834	34,899
Architectural and structural metals	3323	408.5	17,253	42,239	293.1	44,878	94,980
Machine shops, turnd product and screw, nut, and bolt	3327	398.5	17,748	44,537	298.5	39,941	64,064
Coating, engraving, heat treating, and allied activities	3328	136.0	5,360	39,403	104.0	16,432	27,740
Machinery[5]	333	1,127.4	57,212	50,749	726.1	168,453	356,954
Agriculture, construction, and mining machinery	3331	209.2	10,279	49,147	143.0	39,037	94,334
Industrial machinery	3332	127.6	7,648	59,919	67.6	18,703	35,612
Ventialtion, heating, air conditioning, and commercial refrigeration equipment	3334	145.8	6,019	41,297	104.7	19,092	40,702
Metalworking machinery	3335	161.3	8,305	51,502	112.1	17,325	29,764
Computer and electronic products[5]	334	1,034.1	66,345	64,156	492.8	234,390	391,082
Computer and peripheral equipment	3341	92.6	5,908	63,792	34.7	38,727	68,110
Communications equipment	3342	132.8	8,961	67,481	53.9	30,504	53,865
Semiconductor and other electronic component	3344	371.6	20,486	55,123	227.9	71,258	116,809
Navigational, measuring, medical, and control instruments	3345	395.4	29,038	73,475	151.3	88,473	139,775
Electrical equipment, appliance, and component	335	411.9	19,038	46,226	285.3	61,975	131,759
Electrical equipment	3353	144.4	6,890	47,705	96.1	21,840	44,301
Transportation equipment[5]	336	1,474.4	82,532	55,976	1,018.6	252,187	666,807
Motor vehicle	3361	163.0	11,318	69,424	139.5	52,337	210,978
Motor vehicle body and trailer	3362	123.5	4,789	38,790	95.0	10,208	29,764
Motor vehicle parts	3363	523.7	24,771	47,297	391.6	62,812	174,646
Aerospace product and parts	3364	439.8	30,898	70,240	235.2	93,036	178,709
Ship and boat building	3366	149.0	6,857	46,016	103.1	16,665	30,430
Furniture and related products[5]	337	459.8	16,344	35,544	243.3	43,965	80,466
Miscellaneous[5]	339	642.9	29,782	46,322	397.1	99,460	153,200
Medical equipment and supplies	3391	313.7	16,151	51,491	188.3	60,424	84,029

[1] North America Industrial Classification System, 2002; see text, Section 15. [2] Includes employment and payroll at administrative offices and auxiliary units. All employees represents the average of production workers plus all other employees for the payroll period ended nearest the 12th of March. Production workers represent the average of the employment for the payroll periods ended nearest the 12th of March, May, August, and November. [3] Adjusted valur added; takes into account (a) value added by merchandising operation (that is difference between the sales valu,e and cost of merchandise sold without further manufature, procssing, or assembly), plus (b) net change in finished goods and work-in-process inventories between beginning and end of year. [4] Includes extensive and unmeasurable duplication from shipments between establishments in the same industry classification. [5] Includes industries not shown separately.

Source: U.S. Census Bureau, Annual Survey of Manufactures, "Statistics for Industry Groups and Industries: 2008," June 2010, <http://www.census.gov/manufacturing/asm/index.html>.

Figure 6.2 Income Returned to Capital: Value Added by Manufactures Minus Total Payroll

116 *Herbert Marcuse as Social Justice Educator*

of work turns right side round the empiricist assertion that "job creators" are paying their employees and demonstrates that employ*ees* are paying their employ*ers*. This exposes the Jobs Shell Game. The theory that businesses can reduce inequality by "creating jobs" is politically deceptive and pathetic for labor, given that each quantity q of income flowing through the aggregate manufacturing payroll (i.e. including CEOs and all managers) in the form of wages, salaries, and benefits is outdone by an accompanying compensation of $3q$ to capital (i.e. to a relative handful of households) in the private manufacturing sector—as *profit, rent, dividends, and interest.*

In any society, the labor force must produce a surplus of value/wealth to maintain infrastructure and provide for social goods such as health care, education, etc., over and above incomes to individuals. Marx's point is that *only the labor force as a social body* has a legitimate right to manage this surplus. When it does, the first condition for a *humanist commonwealth* has been met.

Teaching the Necessity of a New World System Today

Peter McLaren (2015) has something for us all to consider in his "Revolutionary Critical Pedagogy for a Socialist Society, A Manifesto"—

> We are faced with two choices about how to live our humanity—the liberal model of pleading with corporations to temper their cruelty and greed, and the reactionary model that has declared war on social and economic equality. And on the evidence that each of these models is fiercely and hopelessly entangled in each other's conflictual embrace, we can accept neither.
>
> (McLaren 2015, 260)

> As advocates of revolutionary critical pedagogy ... we participate in an analysis of the objective social totality ... *we simultaneously struggle for a social universe outside the commodity form of labor. If we are to educate at all, we must educate for this*!
>
> (McLaren 2015, 260, emphasis added)

> It is precisely the socialist partisanship of critical pedagogy—not to the point of dogmatism or inflexibility—that reveals its power of critique. We need to reclaim the power of critique as the sword arm of social justice and not relinquish it. For in doing so we reclaim our humanity and the world.
>
> (McLaren 2015, 261)

Marcuse in 1972 made a similar, striking statement linking socialism in its most radical form to the authentically aesthetic form of a free society. Today the *radical* socialist opposition has "a strange unorthodox character ... . [T]his opposition is directed against the totality of a well-functioning, prosperous society—a protest against its Form—the commodity form of men and things" (1972, 49, 51).

No non-socialist theory of society or education has any profound quarrel with wage labor or the general system of commodity dependency. Marx admonishes workers: "... instead of the *conservative* motto '*A fair day's wage for a fair day's work!*' they should inscribe on their banner the *revolutionary* watchword, '*Abolition of the wages-system!*'" (Marx [1865] 1965, emphasis in original). Marx clarified capitalist society's obsession with production for profit rather than human need. This is its structurally generated fetish/addiction to production for commodity exchange rather than for use-values. Production for *use* rather than *exchange* would optimize living conditions within the social formation as a whole. Capitalist productive relations are driving global labor to its knees. Only the abolition of wage labor and commodity fetishism in the economy can restore satisfaction and dignity to an uncommodified labor process.

Commodified existence is not natural; it is contrived. Significant portions of commodified social life need to be rethought and reconstructed. Realigning the social order to conform with the highest potentials of our economy, technology, and human nature requires the decommodification of certain economic minimums: health care, childcare, education, food, transportation, housing— and work, through a guaranteed income. These are pre-revolutionary, *transitional* goals. *Revolutionary* goals envisage a more encompassing view of human flourishing: the passage from wages and salaries to voluntary public work in the public interest—*voluntary public work within a commonwealth of freedom.*

There must also be the decommodification of the electoral process and political leadership! Note Marcuse's statement in the *Paris Lectures* that "If it is impossible to become a candidate in the elections without disposing of a fortune of around a million dollars, this is in any case a strange form of democracy" (2015, 5).

> [W]e have to become aware of the real possibility of a revolution in the most advanced industrial countries taking place not on a basis of poverty and misery, but rather on the basis of wasted abundance. And if this paradoxical concept is correct, it would mean that we have to become aware of new motives for revolution—new motives for revolution and new goals of revolution that no longer focus on the possibility or necessity of revolution born of misery and material privation, but a revolution on the basis of increasing social wealth for increasing strata of the population.
>
> (2015, 49)

Without a world economic system based on equality and democracy, there will be no peace and no survival. McLaren (1995; 1997; 2000; 2015) has long called for a pedagogy of revolution and revolutionary multiculturalism—that is, teaching the truth about ending class exploitation, racism, gender inequality, empire, and war.

118   *Herbert Marcuse as Social Justice Educator*

The abolition of the wages-system is necessary, but not sufficient, to secure the conditions for human beings to become all that they are capable of being. The alienation and exploitation of labor is the enabling material core that permits, if not to say requires, society to legitimate a variety of other forms of social oppression. The movements against racism and sexism have educated the nation that class relations do not wholly demarcate structures of dominator power. Racism, patriarchy, antisemitism, homophobia, and other forms of discrimination, disrespect, and inequality sorely inhibit our powers of actualization. To theorize scientifically the cultural transformation of each of these negations and to be engaged politically and culturally with the labor force to end them must be the essential logic and manifesto of all future critical teaching. We saw above that at the conclusion of Marcuse's *Paris Lectures* he calls for:

> a new form of socialism, namely socialism as in any and every respect qualitatively different and a break with capitalism … and it seems to me that only a decisive redirection of production itself would in this sense be a revolutionary development. A total redirection of production, first of all, of course, towards the abolition of poverty and scarcity wherever it exists in the world today. Secondly, a total reconstruction of the environment and the creation of space and time for creative work; space and time for creative work instead of alienated labor as a full-time occupation.
>
> (2015, 69)

Marcuse's emphasis on creative work leads him from the fundamental goals of socialism to the radical aesthetic ethos of authentically free human society residing in dignity with the living and non-living entities on planet earth.

Note

1   Thanks to Christopher Ingraham (2017) for this clarity because Wolff's data are daunting; see Table 2.2 and Figure 2.5 (Wolff 2017, 55–58). Wolff documents "the sharp increase in wealth inequality in the United States over the last four decades … . Almost the entire growth in household wealth accrued to the richest 20 percent … . There is clear evidence of a growing bifurcation in the United States between the 'favored fifth' and almost all the rest" (Wolff 2017, xiii). These data were collected in 2013, and the tendencies toward wealth inequality no doubt have continued over the ensuing decade. Wolff acknowledges that family wealth is an indicator of well-being and that "wealth-generated income does not require the same trade-offs with leisure as earned income … the distribution of power is often related to the distribution of wealth" (2017, 44–45).

References

Andrews, Charles. 2016. "Book review of Thomas Piketty's Capital in the Twenty-first Century," *Review of Radical Political Economics*, Volume 48, Number 2, Summer.

FAIR (Fairness and Accuracy in Reporting). 2019. "Major Media Bury Groundbreaking Studies of Pentagon's Massive Carbon Bootprint," October 10. Retrieved November 17, 2019.

Ingraham, Christopher. 2017. "The richest 1 Percent Now Owns More of the Country's Wealth Than at Any Time in the Past 50 Years," *Washington Post*, December 6. https://www.washingtonpost.com/news/wonk/wp/2017/12/06/the-richest-1-percent-now-owns-more-of-the-countrys-wealth-than-at-any-time-in-the-past-50-years/.

Macionis, John J. [2012] 2018. *Social Problems*. Boston, MA: Prentice-Hall.

Marcuse, Herbert. 2019. *Ecology and the Critique of Society Today*. Sarah Surak, Peter-Erwin Jansen, Charles Reitz (Eds.). Philadelphia, PA: The International Herbert Marcuse Society.

Marcuse, Herbert. 2015. *Paris Lectures at Vincennes University 1974*. Peter-Erwin Jansen and Charles Reitz (Eds.). Philadelphia, PA: The International Herbert Marcuse Society.

Marcuse, Herbert. 1972. *Counterrevolution and Revolt*. Boston, MA: Beacon Press.

Marcuse, Herbert. 1969. *An Essay on Liberation*. Boston, MA: Beacon Press.

Marx, Karl. [1865] 1965. *Wages, Price, and Profit*. [Beijing] Peking: Foreign Languages Press.

Marcuse, Herbert. 1964. *One-Dimensional Man*. Boston, MA: Beacon Press.

McLaren, Peter. 2015. "Revolutionary Critical Pedagogy for a Socialist Society, A Manifesto," in Charles Reitz (Ed.), *Crisis and Commonwealth: Marcuse, Marx, McLaren*. Lanham, MD: Lexington Books.

McLaren, Peter. 2000. *Che Guevara, Paulo Freire, and the Pedagogy of Revolution*. New York and Oxford: Rowman & Littlefield.

McLaren, Peter. 1997. *Revolutionary Multiculturalism: Pedagogies of Dissent for the New Millennium*. Boulder, CO: Westview Press, HarperCollins.

McLaren, Peter. 1995. *Critical Pedagogy and Predatory Culture*. London and New York: Routledge.

Piketty, Thomas. 2014. *Capital in the Twenty-first Century*. Cambridge, MA: Harvard University Press.

Reitz, Charles. 2016. "Accounting for Inequality," *Review of Radical Political Economics*, Volume 48, Number 2, Summer.

Reitz, Charles. 2015. *Crisis and Commonwealth: Marcuse, Marx, McLaren*. Lanham, MD: Lexington Books.

Reitz, Charles. 2004. "Teaching About Oppression and Exploitation: Critical Theory and the Origins of Inequality," *Cultural Logic*, Volume 7. https://ojs.library.ubc.ca/index.php/clogic/article/view/191893/188856.

Reitz, Charles and Stephen Spartan. 2015. "The Political Economy of Predation and Counterrevolution," in Charles Reitz (Ed.), *Crisis and Commonwealth: Marcuse, Marx, McLaren*. Lanham, MD: Lexington Books.

Wolff, Edward N. 2017. *A Century of Wealth in America*. Cambridge, MA: Belknap/Harvard University Press.

Woolfson, Charles. 1982. *The Labor Theory of Culture*. London: Routledge and Kegan Paul.

7 Ecosocialism and the Revolutionary Goals of Reason

We need a philosophically grounded alternative to capitalism.
—Peter McLaren (2016, xiii)

Herbert Marcuse was a philosophical advocate of revolutionary social change in pursuit of the *freedom* he believed to be the innermost dynamic of human existence and a core feature of authentic social life.

He stood in solidarity with the movements against the Vietnam War and ecological destruction and for women's rights and civil rights for oppressed social groups. A similar spirit of revolt is resurgent especially among young people now in the 2020s—as diverse, global phenomena of protest have appeared against the ecological crisis, gun availability, militarism, gender oppression, police violence, and labor force precarity—Black Lives Matter, Me Too, Occupy!

Marcuse saw the French Revolution as *tapping reason* to "assert the reality" of this freedom (*Reason and Revolution: Hegel and the Rise of Social Theory* [1941] 1960, 4), yet at this stage it was the bourgeoisie and their business organizations, rather than the labor force, that enjoyed freedom's newest historical prerogatives. Nineteenth-century labor would remain alienated in a new form of unfreedom and environmental devastation in the new business/industrial society. Marcuse's study of the "and" in *Reason and Revolution* turned to Marx's *Economic and Philosophical Manuscripts of 1844* (the latter newly published in 1932 by the Frankfurt Institute for Social Research in conjunction with the Marx-Engels Institute of Moscow) for help in understanding the modern predicament of labor and the prospect of attaining the full political potential of free human beings within a new communist order. He notes that, for Marx and for communism, *radical* means *going to the root*, and this means "the real appropriation of the essence of man by man and for man, therefore it is man's *complete conscious ... return to himself as a social, that is, human being*" (Marx, in Marcuse [1941] 1960, 286, emphasis added).

Marcuse's emphasis on the *radically reasonable and humanist* goals of political economic change builds a through-line linking the critical theoretical work of his eight monographs and over eighty journal publications. Realigning the social order to conform rationally with the highest potentials of our economy, technology, and human nature requires radical politics—the de-commodification of

DOI: 10.4324/9781003571582-7

Ecosocialism and the Revolutionary Goals of Reason   121

certain economic minimums: health care, childcare, education, food, transportation, housing—and work. These are transitional proto-revolutionary goals. The radical and revolutionary goals of reason envisage a more encompassing view of liberation and human flourishing: the passage from wages and salaries to public work in the public interest—socialist work in and for a commonwealth of freedom, with work transformed into life's prime want. Radical change aims at the elevated pleasure we can only find in meaningful creative effort, mindful of our need to be of service to humanity. We need the deepest gratification that comes from a life filled with labors of love, abundance, leisure, peace, and justice.

> [W]hat is at stake in the socialist revolution is not merely the extension of satisfaction within the existing universe of needs, nor the shift of satisfaction from one (lower) level to a higher one, but the rupture with this universe, the *qualitative leap*. The revolution involves a radical transformation of the needs and aspirations themselves, cultural as well as material; of consciousness and sensibility; of the work process as well as leisure. The transformation appears in the fight against the fragmentation of work, the necessity and productivity of stupid performances and stupid merchandise, against the acquisitive bourgeois individual, against the servitude in the guise of technology, deprivation in the guise of the good life, against pollution as a way of life. Moral and aesthetic needs become basic, vital needs and drive toward new relationships between the sexes, between the generations, between men and women and nature. Freedom is understood as rooted in these needs, which are sensuous, ethical, and rational in one.
>
> (1972, 16–17)

Marcuse proposes a vision of *intercultural solidarity against* the resurgent politics of white supremacy, oligarchic wealth idolization, and profitable waste, as well as the toxic masculinity characteristic of the authoritarian populism. Here a struggle for *the radical transformation of the labor process itself—* labor's liberation from commodification and alienation—*stands centermost*. As a species we have endured because of our sensuous appreciation of our emergent powers: the power to subsist cooperatively, to create, communicate, and care communally. The very foundation of ethics and reasoned discourse is to be found in commonwealth labor (Reitz 2019, 93–118). Humanity's earliest customs—i.e. communal production, shared ownership, and solidarity—give rise to a social logic that assures that the needs of all for sustenance and life satisfaction are met, including those not directly involved in the labor process, such as children, the disabled, and the elderly.

Sensuous Living Labor: *Logos* and *Ethos* of Humanism

The right of the commonwealth to govern itself and humanity's earliest ethic of holding property in common derive only secondarily from factual individual contributions to production; they are rooted primarily in our essentially shared

122 Herbert Marcuse as Social Justice Educator

species life and our being as humans, *as sensuous living labor*. Humanity's rights to a commonwealth economy, politics, and culture reside in our commonwork. Our earliest proverbs, fables, and riddles from the oldest African cultures teach the sustaining power of partnership and cooperation and the categorical ethical advantages of empathy, reciprocity, hospitality, and respect for the good in common. Satisfactions and dissatisfactions are differentiated according to standards bioecologically emergent within our economic and cultural lives, gravitating toward the humanism of a communally laboring commonwealth. Humanism in ancient times (Plato and Aristotle) was *not* a philosophy of the natural and unmediated goodness of human beings, as in the Romanticism of a latter-day Rousseau. It was a philosophy of the *humanizing influence of education*—parents and teachers, customs, culture, and laws—within a sustaining societal context.

As a species, we have endured because of our sensuous appreciation of our emergent powers: the power to subsist cooperatively; to create, to communicate, and to care communally within that form of society that we may rightly call a commonwealth. Sensuous living labor is the substrate of our being as humans. It is the foundation of our affective and intellectual capacities (and vulnerabilities), bioecologically developed within history. Marcuse's insights into the power of sensuous living labor to liberate itself from commodification and exploitation in order to make commonwealth a universal human condition are underappreciated.

Marcuse saw the liberation of labor from commodification as the ground of authentic dis-alienation and freedom, not in terms of greater more efficient production but in terms of an ethics of partnership, racial and gender equality, and gratification through work, earth admiration, and ecological responsibility. The convergence of the environmentalist and labor movements is essential in terms of a unified emancipatory praxis if the human species is not only to endure but to flourish. A philosophical and political recognition of the meaning of commonwealth labor serves as the fundamental legitimation of ecosocialist philosophy and its promise of abundance and leisure for all within a context of respect for the earth.

The Teachers of Virtue

Humanity's first teachings on ethics are to be found in ancient Africana philosophy. A commonwealth sense is present in traditional African proverbs that has continued as a moral guide to social behavior up to the present. I argue that a *commonwealth ethos* is the intercultural core of humanity's historical wisdom traditions and needs to be at *the heart of critical theory and a future ecosocialist society*.

Today we are aware of the African and Asian roots of Plato's view of the world (Bernal 1991): how the *Republic* and the *Meno*, especially, share with Egyptian, Indian, and Buddhist philosophies cultural notions of communal harmonization, transmigration of souls and reincarnation in a caste system,

Ecosocialism and the Revolutionary Goals of Reason 123

enlightenment and equanimity. Plato's *Republic* did not include the general public as participants at any level of government unless they first met educational qualifications, and this reflected existing aristocratic practice. Thus, many have seen his particular political and educational recommendations as authoritarian and conservative. His guardians seem legitimated as elite human beings. Still, in the *Meno*, Socrates demonstrated his own ability as a teacher to help an unlettered slave boy fully comprehend the highest forms of mathematical reasoning; thus, if virtue and justice are knowledge, they might likewise be taught. The *Meno* holds that no teachers of virtue are to be found, however. Persons who exemplify virtue seem to get this through divine dispensation. Plato's more mature work, *The Republic*, on the other hand, does acknowledge that virtue and the ideal of the Good can be imparted: dialectical pedagogy can make this and a vision of the just society possible. Herbert Marcuse stresses the practical and subversive nature of Plato's philosophy: "[T]he authentic, basic demand of idealism is that this material world be transformed and improved by knowledge of the Ideas. Plato's answer to this demand is his program for a reorganization of society" ([1937] 1968, 91–92).

According to Edmund Akwasi Agyeman, African philosophy's renowned Zulu principle of *ubuntu* underscores the *sociality of personhood*: "I am because we are, and since we are, therefore I am" (Agyeman 2021, 63, 154). This stands in sharp contrast to Descartes' theory of human personhood that begins with an asocial and ahistorical "I think therefore I am." "African philosophers, sociologists and social anthropologists have for decades asserted that African social organization is communal" (Agyeman 2021, 61). Agyeman points out that the conviction that each of us needs the other for sustenance is key to Africana philosophy and undergirds its communal ethic. Micere Githae Mūgo, emerita professor of African American Studies at Syracuse University, extends the concept of *ubuntu*, linking it to the Kiswahili term *utu*—"the capacity to exhibit behavior that is humane" (Mūgo 2021, 6). She stresses "an *utu/ubuntu* imperative" in African indigenous knowledge that also applies to scholarly research and writing. She emphasizes the obligation of the Africana professoriate to create "liberated academic zones" in which scholarship is to be animated through "the heart of the mind" (Mūgo 2021, 10, 20). I shall argue, utilizing also insights from the philosophical work of Ato Sekyi-Otu (2019), that *ubuntu* and *utu* offer universalizable moral principles of general education and also an impeccable idea of what it takes to make higher education *higher*. This significantly augments the arguments presented on that theme in the previous chapter.

I have reflected on the proverbs of Africa, focusing especially on those which address collective approaches to *work* in society. These also vividly illustrate the philosophical materiality of traditional African thought. Such proverbs remind us that "effort is expected on the part of community members for their welfare and for the welfare of the community at large" (Agyeman 2021, 71), and even if some individuals have become rich or powerful, they "need to be constantly mindful that their fortune and authority result not so much from the individual effort but from the labor and sacrifice of others and see themselves

124   *Herbert Marcuse as Social Justice Educator*

more as custodians and servants than as owners and masters" (Nyamnjoh et al. 2021, 33). Renowned and primordial proverbs about collective effort undergird the critical theory of labor I have been developing as this impacts our being and becoming human:

- "The cotton thread says that it is only as a team that you can carry a stone."
- "Many hands make light work."
- "It takes a whole village to raise a child."

These aphorisms constitute *universalizable* humanist, i.e. not narrowly tribal, teachings for the guidance of practical life. According to Ghanaian-born Ato Sekyi-Otu, we must understand "that indigenous ethical judgments are already universalizing in their justificatory grounds, inescapably humanist in their critical vocabulary" (Sekyi-Otu 2019, 18). Further, they are in no way to be confused with purely religious teachings. Not gods, but communally laboring humanity can be seen as the source of ethics here. Like Marx, Sekyi-Otu holds that religion is not relevant in terms of its truth value, but rather in terms of the human needs it may disclose as a haven in a heartless world. He sees moral universals as embodied in the Africana sense of a "vernacular Kantianism" (Sekyi-Otu 2019, 18) and as being native to every culture. Among humanity's earliest proverbs, fables, and riddles are those that teach the sustaining power of partnership and cooperation, drawn toward the humanist happiness of a communally laboring commonwealth. We work for the good in common because it is through our community that we each flourish (Jolley 2011). "It takes a village" to make humanity humane.

Roy Bhaskar's writing, in its later stages, similarly came to theorize, in Vedic fashion, that human beings have a "ground state" (Bhaskar, Singh, and Hartwig [2001] 2020, 65) in which we spontaneously perform right actions that are creative and loving. Ethical understanding and partnership behavior is said to be ingrained over time into our generic nature and corporeal substance as humans. Furthermore,

> … saving yourself and ourselves from this social crisis that we are all in won't wait until you develop the theory [of human emancipation]. Rather, you need to work on, pare yourself down and do what you feel is correct, operating from your ground state in as pure and clear a way as you can.
>
> (Bhaskar, Singh, and Hartwig [2001] 2020, 192)

Much like Bhaskar, anthropologists Riane Eisler (1987) and Richard Leakey (1994), and primatologist Frans de Waal (*The Bonobo and the Atheist: In Search of Humanism among the Primates* 2013; 2006, 2009), have emphasized the cooperation and caring featured in the earliest human societies. This fostered communal interdependence and an awareness of the customary power of partnership. Communal customs and behaviors had the capacity to ensure our endurance.

Ecosocialism and the Revolutionary Goals of Reason   125

We have seen in Chapter 2 that Bhaskar called for an advanced level of our understanding of science and nature outside of what is traditionally taught in graduate school or utilized in business: a new *critical naturalism* that includes a restructuring of science and social science: such that we can *love* them (Bhaskar, Singh, and Hartwig [2001] 2020, 35). In Bhaskar's estimation, the dynamic realities of nature and society operate independently of any human mind, but *without love*, philosophical accounts of nature, science, and society do not present a cogent explanation of the full secular and material reality. In his view, teaching and research must return to principles of compassion, mercy, and love, in order to care adequately and effectively for our societal and planetary futures.

Likewise, Chapter 2 discussed the ecofeminists Silvia Federici (2020), Vandana Shiva, Maria Mies, and Ariel Salleh ([1993] 2021), who criticize the "warrior science" of the sort practiced at Los Alamos (where the Manhattan Project's research was tethered to atomic bomb making), or at Monsanto (where research aimed at altering and patenting genetic life into GMO seed for profit maximization in spite of ecological destruction). Ecofeminism urges instead a science of degrowth, common wealth, and *buen vivir*.

For Marcuse, "reason has from the beginning been oriented to a specific value: the service and affirmation of life" (Feenberg 2023, 94). This is a central contention of Marcuse's *Eros and Civilization*. "There is an unbroken ascent in erotic fulfillment from the corporeal love of one to that of others, to the love of beautiful work and play, and ultimately to the love of beautiful knowledge" (Marcuse [1955] 1966, 211). Eros ultimately seeks a serene, stately, noble logic of gratification for humanity, where "the right and true order of the Polis is just as much an Erotic one as the right and true order of love" ([1955] 1966, 211). Likewise, Horkheimer's critical theory emphasized: "Plato held that Eros enables the sage to know the ideas" (Horkheimer and Adorno [1944] 1972, 267). Critical social theory understands Eros as an essential element of an emancipatory philosophical naturalism and ecological materialism. As Thomas Alexander (1987; 2013) argues: our deepest need is "to create a civilization that fulfills the Human Eros ... realizing as much as possible every individual's capacities to live a fully human life" (Alexander, in Simmons 1997).

Marcuse's writings contain essential philosophical resources for critical social theory and revolutionary ecological liberation. His work models the path by which we, an international political force of "the 99 percent," can be politically prepared and strengthened. With his insights, we can reconceptualize our understanding of our world and our work in order collectively to retake and repossess our commonworld and commonwealth.

The global system of advanced capitalism is poisoning and depleting the resources of our material environment; a politics of neofascism is increasingly contorting our political lives. Refugees migrate from the Middle East to Europe and from the Global South to the U.S.A. only to be denied their rights to asylum. Establishment politicians in and out of office promote racist animosity and anti-immigrant scapegoating as they orchestrate social control polices in service to this system. There can be no escape from these crises without a

126   *Herbert Marcuse as Social Justice Educator*

global ethic comprehending the embeddedness of individual well-being within communal well-being. This is true also for ecological devastation and the generalized economics of despair world-wide.

This interpenetration of our common economic, environmental, and ethical injuries was comprehended in the intersectional philosophy of emancipation developed over fifty years ago by Marcuse. His political-philosophical vision continues to offer intelligent strategic perspectives on current concerns—especially issues of neofascist white supremacy, hate speech, toxic masculinity, misogyny, hate crimes, police brutality, environmental destruction, and education as monocultural, nationalistic, and patriotic manipulation. These troubles are profound, and they can be countered overall through a Marcusean strategy of revolutionary ecosocialism and ecofeminist liberation.

In his posthumously published *Paris Lectures at Vincennes University, 1974,* Marcuse underscored his belief that the women's movement was one of the most important political forces for system change. He saw this movement as key in the transformation of civilization's traditionally patriarchal values, and this as *central* to what he saw as the "context of the enlarged depth and scope of the revolution, of the new goals and possibilities of the revolution" (Marcuse [1974] 2015a) such that the movement for the liberation of women finds momentous significance in his overall perspective. In the same year in which he delivered these Paris lectures, Marcuse's essay "Marxism and Feminism" also appeared ([1974] 2005a; more on this below).

Marcuse's ecological writings emphasize how both the earth and human life are distressed under the conditions of global financial capital. His little known, yet crucial, ecological essays (2019; [1979] 2011; [1972] 2005b) are eminently cognizant of the interconnectedness of the biosphere and the negative impacts of the capitalist political economy. As we have seen, these proposed a program of global action against capitalism's wasted abundance and climate crisis, revolving around what Marcuse considered to be the radical rather than minimum goals of socialism. We have also seen that Marcuse was the only figure of the first-generation Frankfurt School who developed writings directly concerned with ecological and feminist problems and the counterstrategies to confront and overcome them.

> [T]he restoration of the earth as a human environment is not just a romantic, aesthetic, poetic idea which is a matter of concern only to the privileged; today, it is a question of survival. People must learn for themselves that it is essential to change the model of production and consumption, to abandon the industry of war, waste, and gadgets, replacing it with the production of those goods and services which are necessary to a life of reduced labor, of creative labor, of enjoyment.
>
> (2019, 4–5; [1972] 2005b, 174)

Capitalism's fetish with commodity production and profit was and is poisoning the earth. Marcuse found that environmentalist criticisms of extractive and polluting economic policies tended implicitly or explicitly to involve

Ecosocialism and the Revolutionary Goals of Reason   127

system-negations and epitomize a visceral repugnance at the totality of the efficiently functioning social order of advanced industrial society.

"Commercialized Nature, Polluted Nature, Militarized Nature ..." May Day! May Day!

In 1972 Marcuse understood that nature was under attack: "Commercialized nature, polluted nature, militarized nature cut down the life environment of man, not only in an ecological, but also in a very existential sense" (1972, 60). He regarded the environmental movement of his time as the embodiment of a life-affirming energy directed toward the protection of earth and toward bringing peace and harmony to human existence overall. He recognized the importance of ecology to the revolutionary movement and the importance of the revolutionary movement for ecology. Both are linked through Eros into a campaign for revolutionary ecological liberation. To him this reflected the vernal spirit of "May Day" (colorful ribbons and flowers, Mother Earth etc.), while embodying also the combative spirit of the revolutionary international labor force. May Day, as a revolutionary holiday, means protesting wrongs— fighting reform struggles within capitalism as part of the struggle for system change. May Day is thus a fight at a higher level of engagement, protesting a political-economic wrong in general having fateful implications for our future on the face of the planet—capitalism. He advocated not only the Great Refusal but what he called "revolutionary ecological liberation." Wasted abundance and environmental degradation required a radical systems-critique and political opposition that Marcuse believed needed to become a revolutionary force.

Nature's power to soothe and quiet our souls and bring peace to the human heart was famously praised in 19th-century German Romanticism via poems like Goethe's classic "*Über allen Gipfeln* [Wanderer's Night Song]" and his "Song of May"—"O *wie herrlich leuchtet mir die Natur* [Oh how Nature's splendor radiates within me!]." For critical theorists Max Horkheimer and Theodor Adorno—in 1944 after Auschwitz—all of the grand-sounding nature veneration rang hollow and left a bitter distaste for the myriad poetic praises sung to nature in German high culture. They wrote in *Dialectic of Enlightenment*:

> Only when seen for what it is, does nature become existence's craving for peace, that consciousness which from the very beginning has inspired an unshakable resistance to Führer and collective alike. Dominant practice and its inescapable alternatives are not threatened by nature, but by the fact that nature is remembered.
>
> (Horkheimer and Adorno [1944] 1972, 254–255)

For Horkheimer and Adorno, *not* nature but its remembrance was key. Material nature required the reflective powers of the human mind to itself be understood and liberated. Herbert Marcuse, on the other hand, held *nature itself* in higher esteem. In 1972 his *Counterrevolution and Revolt* contained a

128 *Herbert Marcuse as Social Justice Educator*

notable chapter on "Nature and Revolution." He theorized in a more optimistic vein:

> What is happening is the discovery (or rather, rediscovery) of *nature as an ally* in the struggle against the exploitative societies in which the violation of nature aggravates the violation of man. The discovery of the liberating forces of nature and their vital role in the construction of a free society becomes a new force in social change.
>
> (1972, 59, emphasis added)

Science and technology must be enlisted in the service of humanity, not capital accumulation. The violations of the earth entailed in its commercialized exploitation must be halted and remedied. Marcuse *does* say that in a sense we must recognize "nature as a subject in its own right—a subject with which to live in a common universe" (1972, 60). From this perspective, nature must be made whole where it has been damaged. The Preamble to the Constitution of Ecuador (Political Database of the Americas 2008) includes a recognition of nature's rights in an explicit provision: "We hereby decide to build a new form of public coexistence, in diversity and harmony with nature, to achieve the good way of living [*buen vivir, sumac kawsay*]." Marcuse's ecosocialism is likeminded: "The Marxian conception understands nature as a universe which becomes the congenial medium for human gratification to the degree to which nature's *own* gratifying qualities and forces are recovered and released" (1972, 67).

A Labor Theory of Partnership and Governance

We live in a (massively) built environment: this built environment constitutes an ecology of commonwealth labor, a human community's social effort exteriorized in curbs, pavement—every square inch around us, including gardens, parks, etc.—worked by human hands, yet we are largely oblivious of this circumstance. This is the process of human making (Marx: human objectification) by which new tangible value is produced—new tangible value is added to our socially created fund of communal wealth. Wealth derives from this collective production process. Collective effort makes us prosperous, not primarily the contributions of investors or entrepreneurs, which become more and more marginal over time. Included in this collective process is collective product: our common human heritage of language, science, technology, math, etc., which develop primarily within the context of commonwealth labor. When this combines with our common earthly heritage of land, sea, air, etc., there emerges humanity's CommonWealth. At the same time, the high productivity of modern technology allows tremendous output with a small amount of labor time. Production of a sufficient quantity of goods need not therefore be solely a function of the quantity of labor employed. Automated technology provides the potential for an abundant leisure without the need for excessive drudgery. Yet, the tremendous productivity of modern technology does not allow the citizenry of the

Ecosocialism and the Revolutionary Goals of Reason

U.S.A., or the globe for that matter, to reduce their toil and enjoy abundant leisure. Recognition of the commonwealth nature of labor—as possessing the promise of abundance and leisure—validates a global movement for labor's liberation and the transformation of the economy's wasted abundance.

This society is fully capable of abundance as Marcuse recognized in *One Dimensional Man*, yet the material foundation for the persistence of economic waste and want and political unfreedom is *commodity dependency*. Work, as the most crucial of all human activities by which humanity has developed to its present stage of civilization, can be and should be a source of human satisfaction. Under capitalism it is reduced to a mere means for the receipt of wages. Sensuous living laborers are reduced to being mere containers for the only commodity they can bring to the system of commodity exchange—their ability to work. This represents the commodification of the most essential aspect of human life under global capitalism. Necessities of life are available to the public nearly exclusively as commodities through market mechanisms based upon ability to pay.

The 1 percent's enormous accumulation of private property has not led to the self-actualization of the human species or its individual constituents, as the neoliberal business utopians assert, but to the continuation of war and poverty, in Iraq, Afghanistan, Gaza, and to the delusions of grandeur and self-destruction on the part of cryptocurrency moguls and our current masters of the universe on Wall Street. Marx and Marcuse held that the labor force, through its own agency and revolutionary humanism, had within it the power to transform the social wealth production process into the production of our *common wealth*.

Despite our grief at the multiform ways in which labor and the realm of necessity have been dehumanized and degraded, Marcuse acknowledges the fundamental role of the labor process in the liberation and realization of this new form of human community.

System Negation as New General Interest

Marcuse noted that the development of the women's movement and intensifying student anti-war protests were resonant with the ecology movement, and that they could be united in protesting against the capitalist "violation of the earth" (2019, 1; [1972] 2005b, 174; Sukhov 2020, 372–373). I have noted that Marcuse's pronounced feminist commitment was explicitly expressed in his 1974 essay "Marxism and Feminism" ([1974] 2005a):

> I believe the women's liberation movement today is perhaps the most important and potentially the most radical political movement that we have … . [T]he very goals of this movement require changes of such enormity in the material as well as intellectual culture that they can be attained only by a change in the entire social system.
>
> ([1974] 2005a, 165–166)

130   *Herbert Marcuse as Social Justice Educator*

They required also a modification of the essential goals of socialism which were at times oblivious to the discrimination against women. Beyond that, for Marcuse, feminism had emphasized

> ... making life an end in itself, for the development of the senses and the intellect for pacification of aggressiveness, the enjoyment of being, for the emancipation of the senses and the intellect from the rationality of domination: creative receptivity versus repressive productivity.
>
> ([1974] 2005a, 170)

The extraordinary value of Marcuse's feminist-informed and ecologically-conscious strategy—*against* the sociopathic disregard for our future and *for* our common humanity—is that *system negation* can have the appeal of a *new general interest*—offering a constellation of radical goals and forces moving toward racial equality, women's equality, the liberation of labor, the restoration of nature, leisure, abundance, and peace. These goals, and the means to them, can bring together a global alliance of transformative forces. Such a strategy forms the key to the *emancipatory universalization of resistance*—the revolt of youth as a global phenomenon. Marcuse knew we needed a "New Global Left for The Revolution of 20XX" (Chase-Dunn and Nagy 2018, 262–263).

The EarthCommonWealth Alternative

EarthCommonWealth is a term I have coined for the Marcusean vision of an *ecosocialist system-alternative*. Its environmental vision sees all living things and their non-living earthly surroundings as a global community capable of a dignified, deliberate coexistence. The ecological work of Aldo Leopold ([1942] 1991; [1949] 1966; [1953] 1993), as I have described it above, also comes into play here. Understanding the earth in global ecological terms, Leopold saw it as a fountain of energy flowing through a circuit of land, minerals, air, water, plants, and animals, including the human species. He proposed a dialectical and materialist "land ethic" as a call to conservation and cooperation, in which the individual's rights to private property in land are contrasted unfavorably with historical patterns of communal ownership (Leopold [1949] 1966). The EarthCommonWealth Alternative seeks to restore nature's bounty and beauty by opposing the profitable misuse of limited natural resources, in large measure by negating planned obsolescence and its attendant wasted abundance. Having such an alternative perspective on what socialism is *for* is a prerequisite for overcoming the climate crisis and launching the restoration of our much-too-much abused natural world as well as the reclamation of our human nature from its alienated condition.

Marcuse is thus proposing that revolutionary socialism operate on a new Reality Principle—what, in social action, we are to be engaged *for*—in keeping

Ecosocialism and the Revolutionary Goals of Reason   131

with the transvaluation of values represented in his *Eros and Civilization* (Kellner 1984, 338).

The "Green New Deal" of Bernie Sanders and Alexandria Ocasio-Cortez, and others, is about climate change and much more too; higher education for all; affordable housing; high quality health care; clean manufacturing with creation of union jobs; supports for family farming, repair of damages to native lands. This is a necessary part of a radical electoral strategy. It tries to tame a bestial and destructive capitalist oligarchy. Zero CO_2 emissions in ten years, "all power clean power," no fossil fuels; no nuclear power, clean up earth, restore nature. Moving Dems to the left is part of a transformational/transitional program away from oligarchic capitalism toward democratic socialism. The Green New Deal proposes that the public receive ownership stakes when they invest in renewable power generation, for example. All of this is good—as far as it goes.

Revolutionary ecological liberation in Marcuse's sense requires more: EarthCommonWealth is a vision transcending capitalist oligarchy, as such, not simply its most bestial and destructive components. Revolutionary ecological liberation decouples income from individual labor activity/property ownership altogether, with an ecosocialist form of Universal Guaranteed Income. We must expose capitalism's "Capital/Labor Split" and "Jobs Shell Game," as I discussed in Chapter 6 above. I have shown (Reitz 2016) that in the U.S. manufacturing sector "job creating" investors tend to create *no* jobs *unless* on average these jobs in total return three times as much income to the holders of capital as is returned to the labor force in terms of its total wages and salaries (including even the salaries of the topmost echelons of managerial labor). Therefore, policies must do more than "tax the rich"—we must "expropriate the expropriators;" forgive the debts of the current labor force; redistribute property/land; eliminate universal commodity dependency through the decommodification/socialization of the economy, one sector after the other. System transformation is the goal: implementing new forms of communal democracy to govern economic production, consumption, exchange, and distribution as an EarthCommonWealth.

A commonwealth worthy of the name requires new institutional relationships of ownership, production, distribution—a new way of holding property in which resources would be held and controlled and conserved publicly; rent-seeking and the for-profit financial industry eliminated as modes of privilege; incomes distributed without reference to individual productivity according to need and as equally as feasible; hours of labor substantially reduced, and the well-rounded scientific and philosophical development of the young made possible through a public system of multicultural general education. Without an adamant ideology of EarthCommonWealth, there is no sufficient negation, and there will be no sufficient program away from the capitalist political oligarchy. EarthCommonWealth liberates labor's aesthetic and ethical form, society as a

132　*Herbert Marcuse as Social Justice Educator*

work of art. The strategic relevance of Marcuse's view of radical socialism is its usefulness as a clear alternative to global capitalism's intensifying destruction of the natural and social world. An egalitarian and ecological prosperity is not an "unattainable" utopia—it is possible now. To be *radical*, socialism must ensure the ecological well-being of humanity, the biosphere, and the earth. A humanist ecosocialism must be free of the familiar discriminatory patterns of the past and eliminate the infamous (if unacknowledged) caste status of racial minorities as well as gender-based abuse and violence. It must deconstruct all customary obstacles to human actualization and lead to a better future condition for humanity as such. Our task is to contribute as best we can to help future generations make EarthCommonWealth, universally, the material human condition.

The Call to Revolutionary Ecological Liberation

Chapters 1 and 2 have emphasized that Marcuse addresses "the destruction of nature in the context of the general destructiveness which characterizes our society."

> Under the conditions of advanced industrial society, satisfaction is always tied to destruction. The domination of nature is tied to the violation of nature. The search for new sources of energy is tied to the poisoning of the life environment.
>
> (2019, 12; [1979] 2011, 209)

Marcuse's essay additionally frames a discussion of destructive and authoritarian personality structures within "the concerted power of big capital" (2019, 17; [1979] 2011, 212). For him there is no separation between individual psychology and social psychology: "[T]he potential forces of social change are there. Those forces present the potential for emergence of a character structure in which emancipatory drives gain ascendency over compensatory ones" (2019, 17; [1979] 2011, 210). Chapter 1 has highlighted his theory of our political Eros:

> Can we now speculate, against Freud, that the striving for a state of freedom from pain pertains to Eros, to the life instincts, rather than to the death instinct? If so, this wish for fulfillment would attain its goal not in the beginning of life, but in the flowering and maturity of life. It would serve, not as a wish to return, but as a wish to progress. It would serve to protect and enhance life itself. The drive for painlessness, for the pacification of existence, would then seek fulfillment in protective care for living things. It would find fulfillment in the recapture and restoration of our life environment, and in the restoration of nature, both external and within human beings. This is just the way in which I view today's environmental movement, today's ecology movement. The ecology movement reveals itself

Ecosocialism and the Revolutionary Goals of Reason   133

in the last analysis as a political and psychological movement of liberation. It is political because it confronts the concerted power of big capital, whose vital interests the movement threatens. It is psychological because (and this is a most important point) the pacification of external nature, the protection of the life-environment, will also pacify nature within men and women. A successful environmentalism will, within individuals, subordinate destructive energy to erotic energy.

(2019, 17; [1979] 2011, 212)

At the present stage of development, the absolute contradiction between social wealth and its destructive use is beginning to penetrate people's consciousnesses, even in the manipulated and indoctrinated conscious and unconscious levels of their minds. There is a feeling, a recognition, that it is no longer necessary to exist as an instrument of alienated work and leisure.

(2019, 3; [1972] 2005, 174)

So, for Marcuse, "the issue is not the purification of the existing society but its replacement" (2019, 5; [1972] 2005, 175). In a 1975 essay on issues of socialism, he maintains:

Capitalism destroys itself as it progresses! Therefore, no reforms make sense. The notion that the society, as a whole is sick, destructive, hopelessly outdated, has found popular expression: "loss of faith" in the system; decline in the work ethic, refusal to work, etc. ... . The general form of the internal contradictions of capitalism has never been more blatant, more cruel, more costly of human lives and happiness. And—this is the significance of the Sixties—this blatant irrationality has not only penetrated the consciousness of a large part of the population, it has also caused, mainly among the young people, a radical transformation of needs and values which may prove to be incompatible with the capitalist system, its hierarchy, priorities, morality, symbols (the counter-culture, ecology).

([1975] 2015b, 304–307)

I encountered the above Marcuse statement in a 1975 typescript "Why Talk on Socialism?" in the Frankfurt Archive and published it for the first time in 2013 (Marcuse, in Reitz [2013] 2015). Marcuse's philosophy, practically from the beginning, addressed the deep roots of the capitalist system's functioning and its crisis: the commodification of labor, burgeoning inequality, wasted abundance (especially in war), lives without meaningful purpose. The inadequacy of one-dimensional American liberalism was its obliviousness to the problematic nature of prevailing social and economic relations and its suffocation and repression of life's internal inconsistencies and contradictions. Yet pockets of protest emerged within it and created what he called a "New Sensibility" (1969, 23) comprising an oppositional philosophy and politics:

134 *Herbert Marcuse as Social Justice Educator*

[Changed] needs are present, here and now. They permeate the lives of individuals ... . First the need for drastically reducing socially necessary alienated labor and replacing it with creative work. Second, the need for autonomous free time instead of directed leisure. Third, the need for an end of role playing. Fourth, the need for receptivity, tranquility and abounding joy, instead of the constant noise of production ... . The specter which haunts advanced industrial society today is the obsolescence of full-time alienation.

(2019, 15; [1979] 2011, 211)

Marcuse's critical social theory sharpens environmentalist activism into radical ecology—seeing the damage as being done by capitalism's fetish with production for profitable commodity exchange and the attendant dehumanization of social life. Marcuse regarded the environmental movement as the embodiment of a life-affirming energy directed toward the protection of earth. It opposes the so-called free market economy, which means nothing but universal commodity dependency—that is, universal *un*freedom, a system of covert and overt control. Capitalism is not concerned with freeing mankind from the need to toil; it is concerned only with developing means to maintain a sufficient rate of profit. It represents the irrational perfection of waste; simultaneously also earth degradation—profitable plastic litter, air pollution, trash (planned obsolescence), toxic dumping, pollution of air and water, resource depletion, etc. If economics is (as Aristotle held) the study and practice of improving the human material condition—i.e. enabling the human community to flourish—the capitalist system is obviously wasteful in its excessive immiseration, limitations on quality of life, and undemocratic monopolization of power—not to mention excessive military spending. Production according to profit and exchange value, rather than use value, has given us the twisted dis-economics of advertising, planned obsolescence, and wasteful military spending.

Marcuse's political-economic critique is an ecological critique of "growth." Ostensibly durable goods like automobiles, washing machines, etc. are engineered with the premature break-down built in. Advertising adds to the waste by further boosting sales and the exchange value of a "new" product despite its diminished quality and use value. We get disposable consumer goods and a society in which lives become disposable too (as described decades ago by Vance Packard in *The Waste Makers*, 1960). Today, such corporate practices underlie the full spectrum of sales, from single-use plastics clogging landfills, rivers and oceans—to such contemporary innovations as Monsanto's seeds that produce crops artificially made sterile, such that the seeds are under monopoly control and must always be purchased anew. The military budget is far greater than needed already, and in fact could be reduced if the sole goal were national defense. In the present U.S. economy, however, the military budget does more than provide for defense; it is a major mechanism to subsidize owners of the military-industrial complex and thus keep the profits flowing.

The strategic relevance of Marcuse's view of *radical socialism* is its usefulness as a clear alternative to global capitalism's intensifying destruction of the natural and social world. His radical socialism offers a constellation of feasible (i.e. not utopian) goals that can hold together a global alliance of transformative forces. Advanced industrial society, functioning at the highest levels of technology and productivity, blocks any institutionalization of Marcuse's utopian vision, yet its very accomplishments show that a new intercultural architecture of commonwealth production, ownership, and stewardship could bring to fruition, within the realm of necessity, Marcuse's revolutionary goals of rehumanization (dis-alienation), economic and political equality, labor freedom, ecological balance, leisure, abundance, and peace.

I have noted above that the keys to an emancipatory universalization of resistance include the revolt of youth as a global phenomenon, today against guns, war, and weaponry; the resistance of women against their sexual and economic oppression; the multicultural movement against racial animosity and anti-immigrant hostility; the militance of organized labor and protest groups of working families seeking justice against food and housing precarity and exploitation; LGBTQ activists and allies against stigmatization; and the protective forces arrayed against the devastation of the earth—all increasingly in solidarity and for socialism. A convergence of these forces forms the core of a proposal for a counteroffensive to unleash the latent powers of the Left.

Principles of reciprocity and solidarity in communal life, teamwork, modesty, and mutuality show our humanity toward others. Ecosocialism means creating the most encompassing conditions of human flourishing—EarthCommonWealth—as the promise inherent in living labor. In accordance with the logic of critical political economy and revolutionary socialism utilized by Marcuse and Marx to spell out a utopian vision of a new world order, I stress our need for a new communal mode of common work as well as a communal mode of holding property. Commonwealth labor is not only a social and productive force but also a primordial source of ethical conviction and conduct.

Commonwealth Labor: Aesthetic Form of Free Society

Marcuse believed that among the most radical goals of socialism are the aesthetic ones and that social life needs to embody them. Not just the kind of aesthetic features that we could say distinguish the architecture of Haussmann's Paris or the Venetian Piazza San Marco from everyday life at home. These architectural jewels are wonderful emblems of freedom and dignity, but they nonetheless serve primarily as ornaments in high culture that also conceal the fundamental disfigurement of their societies through brutal economic, political, and libidinous oppression (even if the rulers were allowed transgressive excesses in their lives as less limited individuals). Paris and Venice do not represent (except as prefigurative impressions) the deeper aesthetic satisfactions that Marcuse proposed were needed for a truly liberated social formation. This would require all human lives to be associated

136   *Herbert Marcuse as Social Justice Educator*

in egalitarian partnership such that each could access (as the norm in political life) non-repressive gratification and freedom.

Marcuse (1969, 126) talks about the aesthetic ethos becoming a *gesellschaftliche Produktivkraft*. Social labor in this sense needs to become like the social artistry of an orchestral performance or sports team: persons who have met the challenges of being trained and skilled at an occupation they are attracted to performing difficult tasks with similarly accomplished peers—and with pleasure. The task to be performed having its own combination of physical, intellectual, and aesthetic demands and concomitant sensual, emotional, and cultural satisfactions. Much as Goethe recommended theater as a *Bildungsanstalt* (Marcuse [1922] 1987), social labor in commonwealth form has the power to confront the ongoing challenges and conflicts basic to the material human condition (rather than evading or suppressing them in single-dimensional fashion). In this manner, commonwealth labor may mold the character, conscience, and cultural-political fulfillment of each individual (recall Marcuse on Fourier's conception of an enjoyment of work, [1955] 1966, 216–217). Each of us thus *gebildet* in a commonwealth mode—i.e. formed and educated through freedom work, the directed discussion of the aims and ecological consequences of production, as well as an understanding of our great books legacy in the arts and sciences—would be prepared for a life of greater leisure, learning, and engagement for social justice, becoming all that we can be.

In his chapter on "The Aesthetic Dimension," in *Eros and Civilization*, Marcuse combines the aesthetic theories of Kant and Schiller with Freud. From Kant's treatment of imagination as a source of free creativity, he turns to Schiller's *Letters on Aesthetic Education*, in which Schiller, like Kant, describes human sensuality as the basis of aesthetics and as an impulse for a "new kind of civilization." Marcuse seeks a new civilization, challenging Freud's pessimism, in which *sexuality as beauty* promises dignity and fulfillment in life, actualizing the non-alienated self. And what he means here as "self" is our species-self or species-essence in which humanity's nature and an individual's freedom meet. Schiller's *Letters* are also the source of Marx's statement in his *Paris Manuscripts* (of 1844) that future production in a perfected communist society could occur beyond the commodity form and "according to the laws of beauty."

Ecosocialism delivers on art's *promesse de bonheur commun* and nature's promise that we can attain our happiness-in-common by learning to live with dignity and freedom on planet earth. "A successful environmentalism will, within individuals, subordinate destructive energy to erotic energy" (Marcuse 2019, 17; [1979] 2011, 212). Marcuse saw this energy as a political Eros in a twofold sense. First, it is the true labor of love—a Platonic, higher level, selfless regard for other humans as humans. Secondly, as the true love of learning, a Platonic desire that culminates in a conscious political struggle against institutional forces of destruction.

Marx's *Paris Manuscripts* of 1844 saw communism as represented in two ways: first, new possibilities of production and life occur in a kind of "raw communism"—people *liberated from* the formerly alienating conditions caused by private property and the private accumulation of the social product. This essential communism is intended to safeguard and increase the income of all workers as a minimum standard of society. The fuller development of communism is more radical and more rational: labor is freed from its commodity form (as wages or salaries) *to embody an aesthetic ethos, commonwork for the commonwealth.*

The Ecosocialist EarthCommonWealth Project

The latent emancipatory power of labor is axial to the ecosocialist Earth-CommonWealth project. The "New Social Movements" around the globe at the start of the 21st century learned to ally not only with nature but also crucially with labor. The militant anti-globalization action in Seattle 1999 against corporate capitalism and the World Trade Organization united progressive unions and environmentalists—"teamsters and turtles." Activist elements of organized labor in the U.S.A. and elsewhere in the world joined with environmental organizations, in a massive confrontation with the representatives of global capital as they consolidated their payroll-slashing and earth-bashing investment strategies through imperialist-style outsourcing and the "race to the bottom."

In 2001, a similar confrontation occurred in Genoa, Italy. This was one of the most enormous demonstrations against global finance capital Europe had seen in years. The 2011 and 2012 anti-austerity uprisings in Athens, Rome, Madrid, and elsewhere were equally spectacular and militant. So too the massive student protests against tuition increases in Montreal, Quebec, during March, May, and August 2012. These struggles echo the worker-student protests in Paris 1968 and the new forms of radical political-economic thinking emergent from the now regular meetings of the World Social Forum in Porto Alegre, Brazil and elsewhere. Then there were also the left populist movements of SYRIZA in Greece, Podemos in Spain, and the 2016 Bernie Sanders campaign in the United States, in which he nearly took the lead of the Democratic party. Today, Generation Z-ers are demonstrating for racial equality, women's equality, LGBTQ protections, the restoration of the natural environment, meaningful work and leisure, economic security, gun control, and world peace, as Volpe (2022) has indicated in *Fight*. "It's not American Zoomers driving this change, or Swedish, or French, or Nigerian Zoomers—It's just Zoomers. From 2011 to 2019, the number of general strikes, anti-government demonstrations and riots around the world increased by more than 200 percent" (Volpe 2022, 134). In France, 2020 was another year for protests and civil disobedience. The year began with tens of thousands of union members, public sector employees, "yellow vest" demonstrators, lawyers, rail workers, and students protesting government plans for pension reform (Volpe 2022, 147). Student protests against genocide and ecocide in Gaza are the most recent upsurge in the political Eros of young and militant humanitarian protesters.

It is hoped that the ecosocialist EarthCommonWealth project sketched here in its most general and aspirational features will appeal to the energies of those

138 *Herbert Marcuse as Social Justice Educator*

engaged in a wide range of contemporary social justice struggles, including those mentioned above: antiracism, the women's movement, LGBTQ rights, and antiwar forces. As the *dialectical counterpart* of the Great Refusal, the EarthCommonWealth Project is keyed to the *promesse du bonheur commun*—outlining what humanity's common struggle is *for*, as well as what it is struggling against.

This project argues that a new system of ecological production, egalitarian distribution, shared ownership, and democratized governance is within reach, having its foundation in the ethics of partnership productivity with an ecosocialist and humanist commitment to living our lives on the planet consistent with the most honorable and aesthetic forms of human social and political fulfillment. Based on the political logic of public purposes of work, ownership, and education, and in solidarity with the democratic rights of the global workforce, an equitable, sustainable, and peaceful global future is calling each of us to be its educational and political advocate. Critical pedagogy is animated by a real sense of hope and possibility. It is *necessary* to replace today's savage inequalities in schools and society; with the ongoing engagement of our most committed colleagues and the radical activism of youth, *it is possible*! As Marcuse encourages us with upper case enthusiasm: "*IT CAN STILL BE DONE!*" ([1975] 2009, 43).

Marcuse's advocacy of revolutionary ecological liberation contests the sovereignty of billionaire oligarchs and investors, the military-industrial complex, and Wall Street with the promise of socio-cultural equality and sustainable political-economic abundance. Human labor has the imperishable power to build the commonwealth; it has done so in the past and will in the future. Greatness in human governance is not to be measured through a militarized nation state, nor by a dictatorship of the proletariat, nor state capital ownership, but through *a commonwealth alternative*. Engels (Letter to Bebel, March 18–24, 1875) put this non-hierarchical vision of governance into words: "We would therefore suggest that *Gemeinwesen* [commonwealth] be universally substituted for state; it is a good old German word that can very well do service for the French 'Commune.'" A "commonwealth" worthy of the name requires institutions yet to be invented—new communal relationships of service and support, new forms of partnership ownership, production, distribution in which resources would be kept and controlled and conserved in a *res publica*, an association of free persons, understanding themselves as sensuous living labor *having the birthright to be unburdened by alienation*.

References

Agyeman, Edmund Akwasi. 2021. "The Community, Belonging and Agency in Akan Proverbs," in Francis B. Nyamnjoh, Patrick U. Nwosu, and Hassan M. Yosimbom (Eds.), *Being and Becoming African as a Permanent Work in Progress: Inspiration from Chinua Achebe's Proverbs*. Bamenda, Cameroon: Langaa Research & Publishing Common Initiative Group.

Ecosocialism and the Revolutionary Goals of Reason 139

Alexander, Thomas M. 2013. *The Human Eros: Eco-ontology and the Aesthetics of Existence*. Boston, MA: Fordham University Press.

Alexander, Thomas M. 1987. *John Dewey's Theory of Art, Experience and Nature: The Horizons of Feeling*. Albany, NY: SUNY Press.

Bernal, Martin. 1991. *Black Athena: The Afroasiatic Roots of Classical Civilization: The Fabrication of Ancient Greece 1785–1985*. New York: Random House.

Bhaskar, Roy, Savita Singh, and Mervyn Hartwig. [2001] 2020. *Reality and Its Depths: A Conversation Between Savita Singh and Roy Bhaskar*. Singapore: Springer.

Chase-Dunn, Christopher and Sandor Nagy. 2018. "The Piketty Challenge: Global Inequality and World Revolution," in Lauren Langman and David A. Smith (Eds.), *Twenty-First Century Inequality & Capitalism*. Chicago, IL: Haymarket Books.

de Waal, Frans. 2013. *The Bonobo and the Atheist: In Search of Humanism among the Primates*. New York: W.W. Norton.

de Waal, Frans. 2009. *The Age of Empathy*. New York: Random House.

de Waal, Frans. 2006. *Primates and Philosophers*. Princeton, NJ: Princeton University Press.

Eisler, Riane. 1987. *The Chalice and the Blade*. New York: HarperCollins.

Feenberg, Andrew. 2023. *The Ruthless Critique of Everything Existing: Nature and Revolution in Marcuse's Philosophy of Praxis*. London and Brooklyn: Verso.

Federici, Silvia. 2020. *Revolution at Point Zero: Housework, Reproduction, and Feminist Struggle*. Oakland, CA: PM Press.

Horkheimer, Max and Theodor W. Adorno. [1944] 1972. *Dialectic of Enlightenment*. New York: Herder & Herder.

Jolley, Dorothy R. 2011. *Ubuntu: A Person is a Person Through Other Persons*. Masters thesis. Southern Utah University.

Kellner, Douglas. 1984. *Herbert Marcuse and the Crisis of Marxism*. Berkeley, CA: University of California Press.

Leakey, Richard. 1994. *The Origin of Humankind*. New York: Basic Books.

Leopold, Aldo. [1953] 1993. *Round River*. New York: Oxford University Press.

Leopold, Aldo. [1942] 1991. "The Role of Wildlife in Liberal Education," in Susan L. Flader and J. Baird Callicott (Eds.), *The River of the Mother of God and Other Essays*. Madison, WI: University of Wisconsin Press.

Leopold, Aldo. [1949] 1966. *A Sand County Almanac*. New York: Oxford University Press.

Marcuse, Herbert. 2019. *Ecology and the Critique of Society Today: Five Selected Papers for the Current Context*. Philadelphia, PA: International Herbert Marcuse Society.

Marcuse, Herbert. [1974] 2015a. *Paris Lectures at Vincennes University, 1974*. Philadelphia, PA: International Herbert Marcuse Society.

Marcuse, Herbert. [1975] 2015b. "Why Talk on Socialism?" in Charles Reitz (Ed.), *Crisis and Commonwealth: Marcuse, Marx, McLaren*. Lanham, MD: Lexington Books.

Marcuse, Herbert. [1979] 2011. "Ecology and the Critique of Modern Society," in Douglas Kellner and Clayton Pierce (Eds.), *Herbert Marcuse, Philosophy, Psychoanalysis and Emancipation: Volume 5, Collected Papers of Herbert Marcuse*. New York and London: Routledge.

Marcuse, Herbert. [1975] 2009. "Lecture on Higher Education and Politics, Berkeley, 1975," in Douglas Kellner, Tyson Lewis, Clayton Pierce and K. Daniel Cho (Eds.), *Marcuse's Challenge to Education*. Lanham, MD: Rowman & Littlefield.

Marcuse, Herbert. [1974] 2005a. "Marxism and Feminism," in Douglas Kellner (Ed.), *Herbert Marcuse, The New Left and the 1960s: Volume 3, Collected Papers of Herbert Marcuse*. New York and London: Routledge.

140   *Herbert Marcuse as Social Justice Educator*

Marcuse, Herbert. [1972] 2005b. "Ecology and Revolution," in Douglas Kellner (Ed.), *Herbert Marcuse, The New Left and the 1960s: Volume 3, Collected Papers of Herbert Marcuse*. New York and London: Routledge.

Marcuse, Herbert. [1922] 1987. "Der deutsche Künstlerroman," in *Schriften 1*. Frankfurt: Suhrkamp.

Marcuse, Herbert. 1972. *Counterrevolution and Revolt*. Boston, MA: Beacon Press.

Marcuse, Herbert. 1969. *An Essay on Liberation*. Boston, MA: Beacon Press.

Marcuse, Herbert. [1937] 1968. "The Affirmative Character of Culture," in *Negations: Essays in Critical Theory*. Boston, MA: Beacon Press.

Marcuse, Herbert. [1955] 1966. *Eros and Civilization*. Boston, MA: Beacon Press.

Marcuse, Herbert. [1941] 1960. *Reason and Revolution*. Boston, MA: Beacon Press.

McLaren, Peter. 2016. "Foreword: Philosophy and a Pedagogy of Insurrection," in Charles Reitz, *Philosophy and Critical Pedagogy*. New York: Peter Lang.

Mies, Maria and Vandana Shiva. [1993] 2021. *Ecofeminism, With a Foreword by Ariel Salleh*. New York and London: Bloomsbury.

Mũgo, Micere Githae. 2021. *The Imperative of Utu/Ubuntu in Africana Scholarship*. Ottawa, CA: Daraja Press.

Nyamnjoh, Francis B., Patrick U. Nwosu, and Hassan M. Yosimbom (Eds.). 2021. *Being and Becoming African as a Permanent Work in Progress: Inspiration from Chinua Achebe's Proverbs*. Bamenda, Cameroon: Langaa Research & Publishing Common Initiative Group.

Packard, Vance. 1960. *The Waste Makers*. New York: David McKay.

Political Database of the Americas. 2008. "Preamble to the Constitution." Georgetown University, Center for Latin American Studies. https://pdba.georgetown.edu/Constitutions/Ecuador/english08.html.

Reitz, Charles. 2019. *Ecology & Revolution: Herbert Marcuse and the Challenge of a New World System*. New York and London: Routledge.

Reitz, Charles. 2016. "Herbert Marcuse and the New Culture Wars: Campus Codes, Hate Speech and the Critique of Pure Tolerance," in Charles Reitz, *Philosophy & Critical Pedagogy: Insurrection & Commonwealth*. New York: Peter Lang.

Reitz, Charles. [2013] 2015. *Crisis and Commonwealth: Marcuse, Marx, McLaren*. Lanham, MD: Lexington Books.

Sekyi-Otu, Ato. 2019. *Left Universalism: Africacentric Essays*. New York: Routledge.

Simmons, Michael L. Jr. 1997. "Certainty, Harmony and the Centering of Dewey's Aesthetics," in *Philosophy of Education 1997*. Urbana, IL: Philosophy of Education Society.

Sukhov, Michael J. 2020. "Herbert Marcuse on Radical Subjectivity and the 'New Activism': Today's Climate and Black Lives Matter Movements," *Radical Philosophy Review*, Volume 23, Number 2.

Volpe, John Della. 2022. *Fight: How Gen Z is Channeling Their Fear and Passion to Save America*. New York: St. Martin's Press.

8 Educating the Educator

Marx's third thesis on Feuerbach tells us: because human beings themselves must be actively engaged in changing social circumstances, "it is essential to *educate the educator*." Herbert Marcuse deserves to be recognized as a practitioner/theorist of *critical pedagogy as social justice education*. He became the *educator's educator* (alongside Paulo Freire), paving the way decades ago for some of today's most eloquent educational theorists: Henry Giroux, Angela Davis (2016), Douglas Kellner, and others, including especially Peter McLaren. These writers bring to bear critical pedagogy's most radical elements in a variety of ways. Douglas Kellner sees the United States today as a rogue nation that has thrown its historically flawed form of democracy into crisis. Decades before Trump, Kellner wrote: "Never before has a more vicious bunch occupied the highest levels of government" (Kellner 2005, x). Henry Giroux referred to these events as constituting a new dark age, with a "New Authoritarianism" putting "America at the Edge" (Giroux 2004, 2005, 2006). Even before the events of 9/11, Michael Apple likewise aptly described the system as "capitalism with the gloves off" (Apple 2001, 18). David Korten writes similarly of predatory finance:

> The global economy is not, however, a healthy economy. In all too many instances it rewards *extractive* investors who do not create wealth, but simply extract and concentrate existing wealth. The extractive investor's gain is at the expense of other individuals or the society at large.
>
> (Korten 1995, 195)

Critical pedagogy, according to Joe L. Kincheloe's classic description (2008), challenges the "Great Denial" of the political dimension of education. Like critical philosophy, critical pedagogy is centrally concerned with building a context for understanding, the alleviation of human suffering, resistance to dominant power, and agency for emancipatory social change (see also Giroux 2022; 2012; hooks 2000; McLaren 1995, 2005, 2015b). In their pathbreaking scholarship published as *Schooling in Capitalist America*, Samuel Bowles and Herbert Gintis (1976) established one of the most fundamental features of critical education theory—that the latent social function of schooling in the U.S.A.

DOI: 10.4324/9781003571582-8

142 *Herbert Marcuse as Social Justice Educator*

has long been the legitimation and replication of the unequal social division of labor. Peter McLaren's life's work advances this understanding substantively (2015b, 2010, 2005, 2000), as I shall soon elaborate. Others developing a nascent critical pedagogy (Giroux 1983; Apple 1982) had reservations regarding Bowles' and Gintis's emphasis on schooling as a social control mechanism, highlighting the critical subjectivity of students. To them it seemed the thesis defended by Bowles and Gintis presented a significant challenge to teachers working within the nation's system of education at every level, who believed in the progressive nature of teaching and who stood in solidarity with students, endeavoring toward mutual empowerment and social transformation. Speaking of their own methodology and conclusions, Bowles and Gintis were clear: "The ensuing study of historical change in the U.S. school system reveals not a smooth adjustment of educational structure to economic life, but rather a jarring and conflict-ridden course of struggle and accommodation" (Bowles and Gintis 1976, 161). Giroux's many subsequent volumes on the politics of class, race, and gender inequality in schooling came to employ critical political economics with activist verve and punch: "Americans live at a time in which the destruction and violence waged by neoliberal capitalism is unapologetic and without pause" (Giroux 2018, 291).

Likewise, Michael Apple gave one of his most critical subsequent works the ironic title, *Educating the 'Right' Way: Markets, Standards, God and Inequality* (2001). McLaren urges educators to "take the struggle over the social division of labor as seriously as we do the struggle over meaning and representation" (McLaren 1997, 13). Michael Apple concurs:

"There are gritty realities out there, realities whose power is often grounded in structural relations that are not simply social constructions created by the meanings given by an observer" (Apple 2001, 56). Apple also comments scathingly that "for a rapidly growing segment of the conservative population God's message to all of us is to turn both to capitalism and tradition" (Apple 2001, 22). In the eyes of such people, "Capitalism is 'God's economy'" (Apple 2001, 25).

Likewise, Douglas Kellner has written extensively on critical theory and the future of critical pedagogy (Kellner 2022). He argues that it is time that a new class analysis and a new class politics revitalize critical social theory (Best and Kellner 2001; Kellner 1989, 228–229; Kellner 2003b). This interest is central to his ongoing innovative work on the impacts on education of globalization, the restructuring of capital, media spectacle, and new technologies. Kellner emphasizes that when a critical pedagogy is tied to new critical theory it can have a real emancipatory impact:

> Critical social theories conceptualize the structures of domination and resistance. They point to forms of oppression and domination contrasted to forces of resistance that can serve as instruments of change. ... Thus, critical social theories are weapons of critique and instruments of practice as well as cognitive maps. ... If a theory illuminates a phenomenon ... and produces altered reception of it (or perhaps rejection), or inspires the

Educating the Educator   143

production of oppositional ... practices, then the theory turns out to be valuable both in its theoretical and practical effects.

(Kellner 1995, 25–27)

Human intelligence, for Kellner, is emergent from the need to overcome material, historical, and cultural oppression, hence his criticisms of the nation's post-9/11 warmongering, patriotism, and media propaganda (2003a, 67–70; 2005).

Each of these authors is focusing today on capitalism's incompatibility with democracy. They combine a critique of the logic of capital accumulation and global predation with a critique of education for social control and the replication of the unequal social division of labor. Giroux very correctly reproaches the reactionary culture warriors who claim multicultural reform in education has already gone "too far," with his studied assessment that it "hasn't gone nearly far enough" (Giroux 2004, 16). Today this attack continues on DEI, "diversity, equality, inclusion" and CRT "critical race theory." McLaren (1997, 2000) calls for the pedagogy of revolution and revolutionary multiculturalism—that is, teaching about more than diversity: about the structured social dynamics of class exploitation, racism, gender inequality, empire, and war. McLaren names the backlash to multicultural educational reform "white terror" (1995, 117). He urges radical education reform as a means of "unthinking" whiteness and "rethinking" democracy. As he sees it, we are compelled by the force of economic necessity as well as the ethics of equality to alter these reproductive processes and to pursue "the common goal of transforming the exploitative social relations of global capitalism" (McLaren 1995, 69; McLaren and Farahmandpur 2005).

McLaren (2000, 196–197) writes:

As it stands, the major purpose of education is to make the world safe for global capitalism ... . Revolutionary educators *refuse* the role that global capitalism has assigned to them: to become the supplicants of corporate America and to work at the behest of the corporate bottom line.

McLaren's stress on the *refusals* required of the revolutionary critical educator derives from Marcuse's concept of the "Great Refusal."

McLaren explains the origins of critical pedagogy:

The work that we do has been adapted from the pathfinding contributions of the late Brazilian educator, Paulo Freire, whose development of pedagogies of the oppressed helped to lay the foundations for additional radical approaches (feminism, Marxism) to teaching and learning that utilize the life experience of students in and outside of traditional classrooms to build spaces of dialogue and dialectical thinking.

(McLaren 2015a, 259)

This involves the teacher's serious commitment to developing the theoretical and practical talents of students and to facilitating student success in spite of

144 *Herbert Marcuse as Social Justice Educator*

institutionalized obstacles. It contrasts sharply with the lament of certain otherwise ostensibly competent faculty members who long simply "for better students." Coursework should develop in an intellectually participatory way, with the teacher posing *thematic questions* introducing students to a transformed approach both toward the educational institution and the subject matter, the latter involving a set of problems needing attention and ingenuity on the part of the student and teacher. Student-generated discussion topics must be elicited which require ongoing investigation. As has been mentioned in a discussion of Freire's work earlier in this volume, Freire (1993) suggests that this process should focus on three areas of inquiry, asking students to identify: (1) the most serious and disturbing *limit situations* (obstacles, contradictions, negations in their lives) that they (and by extension, all of us) need to know more about as challenges to their (and our) fulfillment and humanization; (2) student actions (negations) in response to these limit situations, both actual and possible; and (3) structures of society and institutional realities that require transformation (sublimation, *Aufhebung*) in order to obviate these limit situations in the future. This is a clear application of the Hegelian/Marxian dialectical method to research and learning, cultural action for freedom.

In this manner, critical pedagogy is intended to evoke *critical appreciation* of the emancipatory power of "directed dialogue" as a pedagogical method for collaborative political learning and political practice for social justice (Reitz 2002; Slater et al. 2002; Steiner 2000). During the discussions within student teams or small groups, the teacher should feel comfortable enough actually to walk away from the classroom. On the other hand, the teacher's presence during general group discussion with the entire class is indispensable in bringing the theoretical analysis of problems and prospects deftly to bear and to guide dialogue appropriately in a manner consistent with Freire's insights. The teacher's own analysis must be critically informed by the philosophy of social science and critical materialist sociological insights from research analysts like D. Stanley Eitzen, Maxine Baca Zinn, Joe R. Feagin, G. William Domhoff, Michael Parenti, Jonathan Kozol, Samuel Bowles, Herbert Gintis, Noam Chomsky, Holly Sklar, Barbara Ehrenreich, Howard Kahane, and Neil Postman, etc. A mastery of scholarship and knowledge furnishes the foundation for the power of critical analysis.

McLaren (2015a, 260) presented a *manifesto* for *socialist* teaching in *Crisis and Commonwealth* (Reitz 2015). He makes the most fundamental of radical proposals: "as we participate in an analysis of the objective social totality that we simultaneously struggle for a social universe *outside the commodity form of labor. If we are to educate at all, we must educate for this!*" McLaren is calling upon the teacher corps to challenge, creatively and militantly, the prevailing forms of educational administration and pedagogical practice in the U.S.A., which ultimately *replicate* the acceptance of wage labor and capital's fetishism of commodities. These must no longer be taken as natural and normal.

Peter McLaren's most recent book, *Pedagogy of Insurrection* (2015b), highlights a political economic focus. Its leading section, "Solving the Problem of

Educating the Educator 145

Inequality: The Market Is Not a Sustainable or Livable Community," begins with the foundational recognition that "Schools in the main reflect the inequality found in the structure of capitalist society" (2015b, 19). He makes clear:

> the market is not a community. It is only possible to realize your humanity if you are educated in an authentic community ... . Critical educators assume the position that equality is both a precondition and outcome for establishing community, and a community is a precondition for deep democracy.
>
> (2015b, 21, 23)

> Revolutionary critical educators question capitalist concepts—such as wage labor and value production—alongside their students in order to consider alternative ways of subsisting and learning in the world so as to continually transform it along the arc of social and economic justice ... . As such, critical pedagogy calls for a movement that is anti-capitalist, anti-imperialist, anti-racist, anti-sexist, anti-heterosexist and pro-democratic.
>
> (2015b, 35)

Today critical educators are faced with a heightened sense of political urgency:

> The fact is, surely, that we are faced with two [loaded] choices about how to live our humanity—the liberal model of pleading with corporations to temper their cruelty and greed, and the reactionary model that has declared war on social and economic equality. And on the evidence that each of these models is fiercely and hopelessly entangled in each other's conflictual embrace, we can accept neither.
>
> (McLaren 2015a, 260)

McLaren has renamed critical pedagogy *revolutionary critical pedagogy*. He and Nathalia Jaramillo have co-written *Pedagogy and Praxis in the Age of Empire: Toward a New Humanism* (2007). They denounce "the rising tide of belligerence" and "the emblematic war on the poor" (2007, 3–21) and call for a world economic system based on socialist equality and democracy, without which there can be no peace and no survival. Furthermore, McLaren (2000, 1997) develops a *pedagogy of revolution* and *revolutionary multiculturalism*—that is, a manner of teaching that refuses to be oblivious to class exploitation, racism, gender inequality, empire, and war.

For his part, Henry Giroux makes a powerful case for critical pedagogy as a force against inequality and for social transformation in a dazzling series of book-length publications (dozens of them from 1976 to the present). Here I shall report on one shorter essay possessing Giroux's critical perspective in highly concentrated prose, "Can Democratic Education Survive in a Neo-liberal Society?" (Giroux 2015, to which the following parenthetical page numbers refer).

146 Herbert Marcuse as Social Justice Educator

In this conservative right-wing reform culture, the role of public education, if we are to believe the Heritage Foundation and the likes of Bill Gates-type billionaires, is to produce students who laud conformity, believe job training is more important than education, and view public values as irrelevant. Students in this view are no longer educated for democratic citizenship. On the contrary, they are now being trained to fulfill the need for human capital.

(138)

Giroux states sharply that:

privatization, commodification, militarization and deregulation are the new guiding categories through which schools, teachers, pedagogy and students are defined. The current assault on public education is not new but it is more vile and more powerful than in the past.

(140)

Teachers need to spearhead a new social movement as a powerful force for critical consciousness and societal reconstruction. As he sees it:

Pedagogy is a mode of critical intervention, one that believes teachers have a responsibility to prepare students not merely for jobs, but for being in the world in ways that allow them to influence the larger political, ideological and economic forces that bear down on their lives. Schooling is an eminently political and moral practice, because it is both directive and actively legitimates what counts as knowledge, sanctions particular values and constructs particular forms of agency.

(140)

Because teachers are being put on the defensive by neoliberal reformers in education like Michelle Rhee and Christopher Rufo, Giroux stresses that the teacher corps needs to go on the offensive:

... *educators need to start with a project, not a method.* They need to view themselves through the lens of civic responsibility and address what it means to educate students in the best of those traditions and knowledge forms we have inherited from the past, and also in terms of what it means to prepare them to be in the world as critically engaged agents.

(141, emphasis added)

This means that:

Educators will have to focus their work on important social issues that connect what is learned in the classroom to the larger society and the lives of their students. Such issues might include the ongoing destruction of the ecological biosphere, the current war against youth, the hegemony of neo-liberal globalization, the widespread attack by corporate culture on public schools, the dangerous growth of the prison-industrial complex, the ongoing attack on the welfare system, the increasing rates of incarceration of people of color, the increasing gap between the rich and the poor, the rise of a generation of students who are laboring under the burden of debt and the increasing spread of war globally.

(142)

Educators need to do more than create the conditions for critical learning for their students; they also need to responsibly assume the role of civic educators willing to share their ideas with other educators and the wider public by writing for a variety of public audiences in a number of new media sites.

(142)

Giroux is thoughtful about the teacher's necessary political engagement and suggests:

One useful approach to embracing the classroom as a political site, but at the same time eschewing any form of indoctrination, is for educators to think through the distinction between a politicizing pedagogy, which insists wrongly that students think as we do, and a political pedagogy, which teaches students by example and through dialogue about the importance of power, social responsibility and the importance of taking a stand (without standing still) while rigorously engaging the full range of ideas about an issue.

(144)

Further,

political education foregrounds education not within the imperatives of specialization and professionalization, but within a project designed to expand the possibilities of democracy by linking education to modes of political agency that promote critical citizenship and address the ethical imperative to alleviate human suffering.

(145)

In sum:

[I]n opposition to the privatization, commodification, commercialization and militarization of everything public, educators need to define public education as a resource vital to the democratic and civic life of the nation.

(146)

148   *Herbert Marcuse as Social Justice Educator*

Philosophizing about higher education in a Marcusean fashion, contemporary critical theorist Tanya Loughead (2015) champions the ideal of the university as a critical site of humanist activism and creative labor. She discusses an array of radical philosophical and sociological perspectives that are absent from the generally prevailing, business-oriented views of U.S. higher education today. Extending the views of Herbert Marcuse, Henry Giroux, and Paulo Freire, her work is a source of new critical theoretical and practical insight. It offers a timely assessment and a powerful, engaging strategy for a change of direction moving to restore higher education's classic purpose, which Marcuse propounds in the tradition of Kant as an education *not* for the present but for the better future condition of the human race.

Loughead argues that the university needs to be a site where educators model the critical life through radical research, teaching, and service, writing that: "To fight for the scholarly meaning of the university nowadays is to be a radical" (Loughead 2015, 2). Like Marcuse, Loughead questions the overt and latent functions of U.S. higher education. We are invited to challenge the tendency of K-12 and post-secondary education to reproduce the unequal social division of labor and the one-dimensional corporate ideology that we live in and live through. Her philosophy of education is distinguished by its emphasis that radical teaching (2015, 37–47) means fostering in others aspirations for maturity and self-determination. Here we are back to Goethe as well as Kant on autonomy and the critical mind, but with a tip of the hat also to Marx and Marcuse because radical teaching means doing "freedom-work" (2015, 49–55). Radical teaching is a form of the work that must be done for a future of freedom!

Brandon Absher's (2021) book *The Rise of Neoliberal Philosophy* explicitly updates Marcuse's perspective, arguing that critical philosophy must challenge "the neoliberal reordering of higher education in the United States," which is characterized by "(1) defunding higher education and reframing it as a private consumer good, (2) reconceiving the purpose of higher education as training rather than education, (3) the instrumentalization and commodification of knowledge, and (4) the centralization and bureaucratization of administration" (Absher 2021, 23). Like Marcuse and Plato, Absher is bringing a multi-dimensional political philosophy and a normative ethics to bear on higher education in a manner that celebrates the classical vision of the humanities—mindfulness and a true love of knowledge.

Peter McLaren and Henry Giroux were the most prominent voices during the most intense and successful reform movements in education (especially higher education) during the last decades. The current volume acknowledges their immense contributions extrapolated from their understanding of Marx, Freire, and Marcuse. They have shown how critical educators may put critical pedagogy into practice in ways that can actually make teaching and learning a productive, emancipatory, and transformative experience. They have shown what it is exactly that may make our pedagogy critical.

References

Absher, Brandon. 2021. *The Rise of Neoliberal Philosophy: Human Capital, Profitable Knowledge, and the Love of Wisdom*. Lanham, MD: Lexington Books.

Apple, Michael W. 2001. *Educating the 'Right' Way: Markets, Standards, God and Inequality*. New York and London: RoutledgeFalmer.

Apple, Michael. 1982. *Cultural and Economic Reproduction in Education*. Boston, MA: Routledge and Kegan Paul.

Best, Steven and Douglas Kellner. 2001. *The Postmodern Adventure*. New York: Guilford.

Bowles, Samuel and Herbert Gintis. 1976. *Schooling in Capitalist America*. New York: Basic Books.

Davis, Angela. 2016. *Freedom is a Constant Struggle: Ferguson, Palestine, and the Foundations of a Movement*. Chicago: Haymarket Books.

Freire, Paulo. 1993. *Pedagogy of the Oppressed*. New York: Continuum.

Giroux, Henry A. 2022. *Pedagogy of Resistance: Against Manufactured Ignorance*. London: Bloomsbury Academic.

Giroux, Henry A. 2018. *The Public in Peril: Trump and the Menace of American Authoritarianism*. New York: Routledge.

Giroux, Henry A. 2015. "Can Democratic Education Survive in a Neoliberal Society?" in Charles Reitz (Ed.), *Crisis and Commonwealth*. Lanham, MD: Lexington Books.

Giroux, Henry A. 2012. *On Critical Pedagogy*. New York: Bloomsbury.

Giroux, Henry A. 2006. *America at the Edge*. New York: Palgrave Macmillan.

Giroux, Henry A. 2005. *Against the New Authoritarianism: Politics after Abu Ghraib*. Winnipeg, Manitoba, CA: Arbeiter Ring Publishers.

Giroux, Henry A. 2004. *Take Back Higher Education: Race, Youth, and the Crisis of Democracy in the Post Civil Rights Era*. New York: Palgrave Macmillan.

Giroux, Henry A. 1983. *Theory and Resistance in Education*. South Hadley, MA: Bergin and Garvey.

hooks, bell. 2000. *Where We Stand: Class Matters*. New York: Routledge.

Kellner, Douglas. 2022. *Critical Theory and Pedagogy*. New York: Peter Lang.

Kellner, Douglas. 2005. *Media Spectacle and the Crisis of Democracy: Terrorism, War, and Election Battles*. Boulder, CO: Paradigm.

Kellner, Douglas. 2003a. *From 9/11 to Terror War: The Dangers of the Bush Legacy*. New York and Oxford: Rowman & Littlefield.

Kellner, Douglas. 2003b. *Media Spectacle*. New York: Routledge.

Kellner, Douglas. 1995. *Media Culture: Cultural Studies, Identity and Politics Between the Modern and the Postmodern*. London and New York: Routledge.

Kellner, Douglas. 1989. *Critical Theory, Marxism, and Modernity*. Cambridge and Baltimore: Polity Press and Johns Hopkins University Press.

Kincheloe, Joe L. 2008. *Critical Pedagogy*. New York: Peter Lang.

Korten, David C. 1995. *When Corporations Rule the World*. West Hartford, CT: Kumarian Press.

Loughead, Tanya. 2015. *Critical University: Moving Higher Education Forward*. Lanham, MD: Lexington Books.

McLaren, Peter. 2015a. "Revolutionary Critical Pedagogy for a Socialist Society," in Charles Reitz (Ed.), *Crisis and Commonwealth: Marcuse, Marx, McLaren*. Lanham, MD: Lexington Books.

McLaren, Peter. 2015b. *Pedagogy of Insurrection*. New York and Bern: Peter Lang.

150   *Herbert Marcuse as Social Justice Educator*

McLaren, Peter. 2005. *Capitalists & Conquerors: A Critical Pedagogy Against Empire*. Lanham, MA: Rowman & Littlefield.

McLaren, Peter. 2000. *Che Guevara, Paulo Freire, and the Pedagogy of Revolution*. New York and Oxford: Rowman & Littlefield.

McLaren, Peter. 1997. *Revolutionary Multiculturalism: Pedagogies of Dissent for the New Millennium*. Boulder, CO: Westview Press.

McLaren, Peter. 1995. *Critical Pedagogy and Predatory Culture*. London and New York: Routledge.

McLaren, Peter, S. Macrine, and D. Hill (Eds.). 2010. *Revolutionizing Pedagogy: Educating for Social Justice Within and Beyond Global Neoliberalism*. London: Palgrave Macmillan.

McLaren, Peter and Ramin Farahmandpur. 2005. *Teaching Against Global Capitalism and the New Imperialism*. Lanham, MA: Rowman & Littlefield.

McLaren, Peter and Nathalia Jaramillo. 2007. *Pedagogy and Praxis in the Age of Empire: Toward a New Humanism*. Leiden: Brill.

Reitz, Charles (Ed.). 2015. *Crisis and Commonwealth: Marcuse, Marx, McLaren*. Lanham, MD: Lexington Books.

Reitz, Charles. 2002. "Elements of Edu*Action*: Critical Pedagogy and the Community College," in *The Freirean Legacy: Educating for Social Justice*. New York, Bern, and Frankfurt: Peter Lang.

Slater, Judith *et al*. (Eds.) 2002. *The Freirean Legacy: Educating for Social Justice*. New York, Bern, and Frankfurt: Peter Lang.

Steiner, Stanley F. 2000. *Freirean Pedagogy, Praxis, and Possibilities*. New York: Falmer Press.

9 Marcuse's Critical Pedagogy as Social Justice Education

Herbert Marcuse's philosophizing with respect to education has seldom been taken up as a research project. I have attempted in this volume to recapture the emancipatory power of one of this nation's most visionary social commentators of the '60s and '70s, in particular his views on matters of the theory and politics in teaching and learning. From his political perspective, what the world needed then and needs now is a strategy grounded in the most radical goals of reason to oppose resurgent racism, bigoted patriotism, and the warlike nationalism inherent in the "ripening and rotting" of global capitalism (Marcuse [1974] 2015, 13). Marcuse's work encouraged the U.S. anti-war movement, the student anti-racist movement, and the women's liberation movement. Yet he asked us to take both critical social theory and the constituents of education, especially higher education, as seriously as our social justice activism. Higher learning is qualitatively higher only where the liberal arts and sciences fulfill their potential to work against alienation. They must furnish a critique of (witting and unwitting) social complicity in psychological repression and/or economic exploitation—and become a means to emancipatory political engagement.

Marcuse's critical social theory dialectically transformed (through negation, preservation, and sublimation) a central assumption of classical German *Erziehungsphilosophie*: the challenge to become all that we can be through *Bildung* and *Kultur* (Marcuse [1937] 1968). He defends a philosophy of the emancipatory power of *education against alienation* and *for the cosmopolitan re-humanization of culture* (Marcuse [1955] 1966). Marcuse addresses questions such as these: How do you philosophize about teaching and learning under conditions of alienation? What are the intellectual, moral, and political qualities of life and thought that can make theory *critical*, society *democratic*, and education *liberating*? How is education to help us accomplish our own humanization and actualize our most humane powers? How shall we best protect human rights in an era of backlash to multiculturalism and amid rival redefinitions of freedom? How do we develop the character, conscience, and culture of students and the community such that we can reclaim our common humanity? These questions continue as central philosophical issues for critical educators in our own time.

Herbert Marcuse's work helps us understand the impact of the international economic, political and military contradictions underlying the contemporary

DOI: 10.4324/9781003571582-9

152 Herbert Marcuse as Social Justice Educator

human condition. His classic writings, as well as those less well known and brought to the fore in this volume, are a substantive lever to the transformation that the world today requires. Radically democratic organizations were emerging then, as now, and a wide variety of people were/are working to challenge the institutional inequalities of race, gender, and class—working to end the fundamental injustices of the global political economy and the dehumanization inherent in it.

Marcuse argued that the spirit of student rebellion in the U.S.A. and around the world in the 1960s expressed a *political form* of Eros, a visceral repugnance not only at U.S. militarism and war but also at the totality of the efficiently functioning social order of advanced industrial society. He described this opposition as a Great Refusal, which constituted a multidimensional expression of system negation. Capitalism's violation of the earth was of particular concern to Marcuse. Its political *dis*-economics of planned obsolescence, toxic dumping, air and water pollution, resource depletion, global warming, etc. was disfiguring and dishonoring humanity's relationship to nature. Today's intensifying levels of global economic inequality, climate change, and global warming necessitate intellectual and political advancement within this nation.

Herbert Marcuse as Social Justice Educator has been a philosophical excursion into the nature of emancipatory education in today's world. In some ways, it presents a "new" Marcuse for a new generation. It wants to serve as a countervailing force to the conventional wisdom in intellectual and political matters while also preserving the rational core of traditional educational theory. It has presented a detailed exposition of the emancipatory kind of *knowledge* and *praxis* Marcuse's dialectical philosophy makes possible. Dialectics has emerged as the method of working to improve relationships, particularly those that are changing and contradictory, as found in the realms of nature, society, and thought.

This volume has extended Herbert Marcuse's critical Marxism with an emphasis on today's predatory stage of capitalism and the *educative* power of struggle concerning issues of social justice. This emphasis on social reform-oriented practice also echoes the early 20th-century perspective of John Dewey, who broke radically (for his time) with the then usual rote emphasis on the 3Rs. He moved toward active learning methods including "learning through doing" and social reconstructionism as an educational philosophy. Dewey argued that:

> Philosophy is thinking what the known demands of us ... It is an idea of what is possible, not a record of accomplished fact ... it is hypothetical, like all thinking. It presents us an assignment of something to be done—something to be tried.
>
> (Dewey [1916] 1966, 326)

"Philosophy is a power to learn ... and to embody what is learned in an ability to go on learning" (325). Dewey further stressed that "European philosophy *originated* ... under the direct pressure of educational questions" (329, emphasis

Marcuse's Critical Pedagogy as Social Justice Education   153

added). We'll see below how it is humanity's *need* for education that spurred Plato's fuller philosophizing in the *Republic*.

Education and philosophy, for Dewey, as for Marcuse, were responses to alienation and social exigency, "needs, which are sensuous, ethical, and rational in one" (1972, 16–17). Any society requires intelligent public discussion and action if it is to attain justice. As we have seen, Marcuse's critical theory of democracy, education, and discourse is partisan not "content neutral" as some right-wing, "free-speech for racists" commentators (David Horowitz 2010) might like. The right wing has vociferously opposed campus speech codes restricting racist hate speech. Marcuse's "Repressive Tolerance" essay looked at the concrete consequences of hate speech and advocated the restriction of fascist speech. Yet, in the estimation of his right-wing critics Kors and Silverglate (1998), Marcuse's prescriptions are "the model for assaults on free speech in today's academic world" (1998, 71).

Alan Charles Kors and Harvey Silverglate have explicitly attacked Marcuse with regard to university policies in the U.S.A. They organized the Foundation for Individual Rights in Education, or FIRE, to help what they saw as a significant number of right-wing "victims of illiberal policies" subjected to violations of their free speech rights to engage in racist speech on college campuses. They present Marcuse as stark antipode to John Stuart Mill and as "betraying [the] liberty of America's campuses." Of course, they view Mill as *the* classic intellectual spokesperson for freedom of thought and action. They deflect attention away, however, from Mill's (as well as Marcuse's) progressive political emphasis on the rationality, social utility, and emancipatory function of dissent.

Kors and Silverglate read Mill according to their own libertarian emphasis and distort Mill's position as if he were advocating an abstract and indiscriminate defense of the (almost sacred) right of any person to express any opinion in any way, regardless of its content or meaning or repressive societal impact. Marcuse's authentically conservative *defense of Mill's standards of rationality in discourse* contrasts sharply with Kors and Silverglate. Marcuse's essay on repressive tolerance contends precisely that Mill would not have consented to any assertion (of the sort Kors and Silverglate propose) that his philosophy protects the abstract right of freedom of expression regardless of all content considerations. Mill writes, consistent with his defense of dissent:

> Undoubtedly, the manner of asserting an opinion, even though it be a true one, may be very objectionable and may justly incur severe censure … . Whatever unfair advantage can be derived by any opinion from this mode of asserting it accrues almost exclusively to received opinions … unmeasured vituperation employed on the side of the prevailing opinion really does deter people from professing contrary opinions and from listening to those who profess them. For the interest, therefore, of truth and justice it is far more important to restrain this employment of vituperative language than the other; and, for example if it were necessary to choose, there would be much more need to discourage offensive attacks on infidelity than on religion.
>
> (Mill [1859] 1963, 116–18)

154 *Herbert Marcuse as Social Justice Educator*

Mill, like Marcuse, agrees there is a "need to discourage offensive attacks" (i.e. hate speech) upon *the dissenting discourse of minoritized populations. This* is the speech to be protected from suppression by forceful voices speaking on behalf of the conventional wisdom asserting the traditional norms of Anglo-conformity. Champions of a First Amendment absolutism, like Kors and Silverglate, none-theless acquiesce when confronted with evidence of the discriminatory effects of abusive speech. They do not seem to think that an absolute right to abusive speech is profoundly problematic in a culture like that of the U.S.A., where there is no shortage of verbal vilification and acts of race and gender persecution.

Mill (as Marcuse stresses) advocates a more progressive stance than the pre-mise of the free speech absolutists about content neutrality: "... in Mill, every rational human being participates in discussion and decision—but only as a rational being" (Marcuse 1965, 106). It is in this sense that Marcuse builds explicitly upon Mill, maintaining that cogency and intellectual legitimacy are "... not a matter of value-preference but of rational criteria" (Marcuse 1965, 101). Mill stresses our obligation to know the grounds of our convictions, so that even true opinion might *not* abide "... as a dead dogma, ... as a prejudice, a belief independent of, and proof against, argument ..." (Mill [1859] 1963, 97). Both Marcuse and Mill conceive of authentic democracy as possessing a poli-tical culture that honors the collision of opposing arguments as a precondition for the pursuit of truth. In their common estimation, authentic democracy pre-supposes an educational and cultural context that facilitates autonomous and rational discourse. But it is exactly this authentically democratic educational and cultural context that is still lacking even today in the United States. Mar-cuse's point in 1965 remains as valid as ever: a genuinely democratic framework is a task yet to be accomplished. We must craft such a social foundation to attain the emancipatory goals of philosophy as well as politics.

Human life around the globe today is being threatened with destruction by brute force and subtle despoilation. Looking back in horror at genocide/ecocide, mass shootings, environmental disasters, and the violent suppression of ecological acti-vists, there is Auschwitz, Guernica, Wounded Knee, My Lai, Birmingham, Kent State, Attica ... Love Canal, Deepwater Horizon, Standing Rock, Flint ... more recently Kyiv, Mariupol, Buffalo, and Uvalde. By what powers on earth may we reclaim our common humanity and *act* such that "these dead shall not have died in vain." Like Hamlet, we must harken to the ghosts of those murdered with impu-nity by sovereign powers (Amadou Diallo, Laquan McDonald, Michael Brown, Eric Garner, Sandra Bland, Tamir Rice, Breonna Taylor, George Floyd, and Sonya Massey—and unnamed thousands in Iraq, Afghanistan, Syria, now Gaza). We are consigned *to consider* and *to act* against the disgrace and dishonor of passivity or complicity with a rotten (vile and grotesque) system supporting racialized police murder. There are more things on heaven and earth than are dreamt of in our philosophy, and we are to respond not with simple retribution but with elevated *Aufhebung* (sublation), restoration at a higher level. Like Prometheus, we are entrusted to care for the prophetic fire of engagement in cultural action for freedom.

Marcuse has offered us insight into the potentials and latent powers of critical pedagogy in the conscious formation of the Great Refusal, a united front of activist groups representing labor, anti-racism, feminism, gay rights, ecological conservation and restoration, and peace. Regressive political forces must be countered today, and this may be accomplished through radical collaboration around an agenda recognizing the basic economic and political needs of diverse subaltern communities. System negation must become a new general interest. Reality holds the promise of an egalitarian political economy through which human beings may govern in terms of our fullest potential and with integrity toward the planet through ecosocialist and humanist alternatives.

Marcuse's critical Marxism has responded creatively against alienation—asserting the power of our political Eros, the power of humanity's need for the *bonheur commun*, the power of EarthCommonWealth. Human labor (especially as the labor force within global capitalism) is a strategic resource with material momentum and political clout. The labor force may withhold its labor at a crucial juncture of social conflict and may ultimately liberate itself from the constraints of exploitation. It can shape the world anew. Today the 1% is armed with its own theory; the 99% needs a fundamentally different outlook. In the approach I extrapolate from Marcuse here, the main avenue of advance is to develop an incisive vision for humanity as sensuous living labor, including a *labor theory of ethics*.

Radical collective action, consistent with an ethical realism grounded on the mutual respect, cooperation, and reciprocity of *commonwealth labor* and the ecosocialist logic of commonwealth production, ownership, and stewardship, can bring to fruition, within the realm of necessity, an intercultural architecture of equality, dis-alienation, abundance, ecological sustainability, and freedom.

Through Marcuse, the Frankfurt School's critique of German fascism and antisemitism was augmented with a critique of genocide and ecocide in North Vietnam in a manner that prefigures the analysis needed today of U.S. complicity in Israeli militarism and Palestinian oppression. Marcuse's political-philosophical vision, cultural critique, and support for social activism continue to offer an intelligent strategic perspective on current concerns such as repressive democracy, political and racial inequality, education as a social control mechanism, and the radical potential of socialism—especially where issues of alienation, oppression, critical inquiry, critical media literacy, civic/revolutionary action, and war are involved. He maintained that the most important duty of the intellectual was to investigate destructive social circumstances—and be engaged in activities of transformation toward social justice. Critical knowledge is knowledge that enables the dialectical "negation of the negation" or the revolutionary negation of the social order's established systems of destruction that profoundly damage the core activities of human life. These core activities are neither being-toward-death as Heidegger once maintained, nor autonomous subjective thinking as Kant argued, but creative social labor, alienated as per the analyses of Marx and Marcuse. This is philosophy's contribution to critical pedagogy: education as alienation must become education

156 *Herbert Marcuse as Social Justice Educator*

against alienation, reclaiming life for our sense of satisfaction and social release, withing a commonwealth of social justice.

In 1972 Marcuse posed the question of whether the ascendency of a neofascist regime can be prevented in the U.S.A. He asked this because of his conviction that the U.S.A. had entered a period of reactionary, if technically precautionary and preventive *counterrevolution*. Marcuse proposed an antifascist vision of *intercultural solidarity against* the resurgent politics of white supremacy and oligarchic wealth idolization, as well as the toxic masculinism characteristic of authoritarian populism. In his radical socialist view, the *transformation of the labor process itself*—labor's liberation from commodification and alienation—*stands centermost*. As a species, we have endured because of our sensuous appreciation of our emergent *rational* and *ethical* powers: the power to subsist cooperatively; to create, to communicate, and to care communally within what we may rightly call an ecology of commonwealth.

Seeking Emancipatory Learning in Literary Art, Social History, Natural Science

What in the end does it take to be a social justice educator? We have reviewed Marcuse's confidence in the serious dialectical study of the *Geisteswissenschaften*, supported by familiarity with critical political economics and ecopedagogy. Marcuse emphasized first and foremost that there is an internal political factor within the liberal arts and sciences that may become emancipatory. This occurs when reason is permitted to pursue the real possibilities embedded within the established cultural practices that can enhance and protect universal human rights and socio-economic equality. What the future needs most is higher education in the liberal arts and sciences *with critical social purpose*.

Contemporary anti-fascist activist and critical educator Joan Braune (2024) has emphasized that even fascism

> may be bound up with questions of self, truth, and meaning suggest[ing] a need for philosophers to be engaged in the work of understanding and countering fascist recruitment and rethinking processes of disengagement from fascism. These are philosophical questions and the province of the Humanities.
>
> (Braune 2024, 15)

Braune sees fascism as a pathological way of coping with capitalist alienation and that countering fascism is, in part, a philosophical and educational task. Yet, she is clear that she is not advocating "kind outreach" to extremists. Because fascism "also emanates from the halls of power," the defeat of any fascist movement is a *political*, not merely pedagogical task (Braune 2024, 66, 73). Horkheimer and Adorno had of course famously pointed out in *Dialectic of the Enlightenment* ([1944] 1972) that the Nazis embraced both high German culture *and* concentration camps—Buchenwald was located only three miles outside of Weimar.

Marcuse's Critical Pedagogy as Social Justice Education 157

Marcuse supported Adorno and Horkheimer, yet his central educational tenet is that general education—especially through the Great Books tradition including literature, natural history, social history, and philosophy—can be generative of radically democratic political virtue and action. General education, thus grounded in the rational kernel of Hegel's historical dialectic and Marx's dialectical political economy, can emphasize *history as a way of learning* and social theory as a mode of critique facilitating an *emancipatory action* component.

Great art in Marcuse's estimation disclosed a realm of freedom and the *promesse du bonheur*, art's promise of happiness. Yet this promise *cannot* be realized by art alone: our *new aesthetic sensibility* must be accompanied by *critical political economy* and *social* and *ecological struggle* inspired by the most radical goals of socialism and reason.

The aesthetic rationality is thought to teach new sensibilities and radical action to recapture human freedom and dignity. The aesthetic dimension is a concrete reality which recovers a sense of the human material condition in its universal aspects. Marcuse theorizes that literary art provides a deeper kind of cognition—not through mimesis or by replicating worldly objects—but by retrieving *the species-essence of the human race* from its obliteration in the conventionally happy consciousness of one-dimensional philosophy and politics.

"The universal comprehends in one idea the possibilities which are realized, and at the same time arrested, in reality" (Marcuse 1964, 210). Art, understood most fully and concretely, is deeply dialectical. It unites the opposites of gratification and pain, death and love, freedom and repression. Only because of this can art honestly represent what Marcuse takes to be the conflicted, tragic, and paradoxical substance of human life. In Marcuse's view, the concrete and critical dimension of art discloses the inevitably conflicted condition of human culture. At the same time, the aesthetic ethos restores humanity's most rational enterprise: seeking the convergence of gratification and universal human need, social order and human dignity, art and politics: "... the development of the productive forces renders possible the material fulfillment of the *promesse du bonheur* expressed in art; political action—the revolution—is to translate this possibility into reality" (Marcuse [1958] 1961, 115).

Philosophy's first teachings on ethics are found in ancient African proverbs; the ethic of humanism (such as the *ubuntu/utu* principles) to make humanity *humane*. These subsequently served also as a critique of colonialism and neocolonialism. Like Plato in the *Republic*, Marcuse asks whether we are aware or unaware—enlightened or unenlightened (i.e. educated or not educated) regarding the fundamental human condition—such that we comprehend the conflicts rooted in our sensuous experience—its underlying dialectic of integrity and deception, kindness and cruelty. Have we cultivated the intellectual potential to understand both the given facts and the attainable, more humanely ideal conditions that the given facts have arrested?

158 *Herbert Marcuse as Social Justice Educator*

Without dialectical insights into these contextual dynamics, we have no critical philosophical understanding or account of our deeply historical and material human existence.

The Necessity of Critical Political Economy

Today, with the ever-looming crises of global finance capital, higher education must encourage students and faculty alike to examine the conditions that serve to perpetuate the increasingly stressed and volatile realities of political, economic, and cultural life in the U.S.A. and around the world, including the processes of U.S.-supported global war-making (in Ukraine and Gaza).

For both Marx and Marcuse, education had to become an education against alienation, mindful of our human core as sensuous living labor, i.e. an education to the fundamental conditions for societal self-consciousness and the necessity of social justice. Both Marx and Marcuse understood human alienation as estranged labor: sensuous living labor's separation from: 1) its product, 2) the process of production, 3) from our species need for the gratification of our sensuous, intellectual, political and ethical faculties (our species being or *Gattungswesen*), and 4) our separation from other producers, whom we now tend to see as competitive units of commodified labor (Marx [1844] 1982, 106–116).

The critical social theory of Marcuse and Marx sees the damage as being done by capitalism's core fetish with production for profit: profit before all else—gun manufacturers before victims in schools and churches—drug manufacturers before diabetics and opioid addicts. This obsession is a many-headed hydra: cut off one head and five more appear, e.g., control cigarettes, then vaping generates renewed profits for the tobacco industry. People define themselves in terms of consumption. McDonald's keeps expanding, and the rainforests are cut down for beef pastures. Private ownership of business is *not* necessary for the essentials of economic production, distribution, and exchange. Everything depends on labor.

The most militant, adversarial, and ultimately hopeful dimensions of Marcuse's philosophy emerge especially in *An Essay on Liberation*, where he proposes that the aesthetic ethos may become *gesellschaftliche Produktivkraft*, a social and productive force (1969, 126). Marcuse's philosophy developed a critical study of work and social alienation, looking at economic activity within the total complexity of other human activities and human existence in general. Marcuse's critical social theory has special relevance to U.S. culture today, centering on his analysis of the *commodified labor process* as a structural source of social inequality and cultural polarization. Labor has the power to liberate itself from commodification and exploitation and to make commonwealth the human condition.

If living labor creates all wealth, as John Locke and Adam Smith have maintained, then it creates the total "value added" that under capitalism is divided according to the capital/labor split, i.e. distributed as income to labor (wages and salaries), and the "surplus value" is funneled as income to capital (rent, interest, dividends, and profit). Marx and Marcuse stressed that labor is a *social* process, that the value created through labor is most genuinely measured by socially necessary labor time, and its product rightfully *belongs* to the working families *as a community*, not to private individuals as such, i.e. grounding a *socialist labor theory of ownership and justice*.

Marcuse likewise honors *Marx's philosophical humanism* as "the foundation of historical materialism" ([1932] 2005). Like Marx, he identifies a genuine concept of communism with a humanist worldview and looks to the supersession of alienation through the actualization of latent human powers. As I have repeatedly stressed, humanity's earliest ethical principles were those of partnership, cooperation, reciprocity, empathy. Our very humanity, our *logos* and *ethos*, is grounded in the legacy we have inherited from our earliest forms of collective labor and production in partnership societies with their ecologies of caregiving and commonwealth.

Humanity's *rights* to a commonwealth economy, politics, and culture reside in our works in common. Ecosocialism represents the (re)making of humanity in accordance with the commonwealth promise at the core of our material reality. This requires *new systems of shared ownership*, democratized ownership, common ownership. Commonwealth is humanity's (that is, sensuous living labor's) aesthetic form: workmanship and artistry, emancipated from repression, taking place not only "according to the laws of beauty" but also according to the communal ecology of labor underpinning philosophies of ethics and justice.

Marcuse argues philosophically that *labor is ontologically significant*—it is the *human mode of being in the world* (Marcuse [1933] 1973).

> Labor, as the specifically human "life activity," has its roots in this "species being" of man; it presupposes man's ability to relate to the "general" aspects of objects and to the *possibilities contained in them*.
>
> (Marcuse [1932] 2005, 96)

The social process of human labor is a lodestone with a fundamentally strategic role to play among the resources and satisfactions of the human community. It is not to be disparaged or displaced, especially while laboring humanity is nearly everywhere dehumanized and degraded. The liberation of labor from commodification is the ground of authentic dis-alienation and freedom, where satisfaction is restored to the processes of social labor and social wealth production—*not* solely or even primarily in terms of greater, more efficient production—but in terms of an ethics of partnership, racial and gender equality, gratification through work, and the political Eros of earth admiration.

160   *Herbert Marcuse as Social Justice Educator*

Marcuse's educational philosophy emphasizes that if democracy means the institutionalization of freedom and equality and the abolition of domination and exploitation then in this sense democracy remains "to be created" ([1968] 2009, 38). Traditional liberal arts curricula must be renewed and must be complemented with a serious engagement with social justice activism, critical political economy, ecopedagogy, and a vision of labor's true potential—not demeaned as some kind of utopia which can never be—but as a latent reality that may be *actualized*.

Few will today recognize the name of Elwood P. Cubberley—a man who in 1920 was one of the most prominent U.S. educational administrators. He was also an historian, who propounded an unapologetically business-friendly philosophy of education:

> Our schools are, in a sense, factories in which the raw materials are to be shaped and fashioned into products to meet the various demands of life. The specifications of manufacture come from the demands of twentieth century civilization, and it is the business of the schools to build its pupils according to the specifications laid down.
>
> (Cubberley, in Callahan 1970, 97; Reitz 1981, 112)

Cubberley was much less reflective than Dewey, an archetypal one-dimensional man. His approach (now updated according to the mode of neoliberal capitalism) has persisted as a rationalization for the reproduction of the unequal social division of labor and wealth in the U.S.A. Marcuse's critical Marxism helps radical educationists have an explanation as to just what is so unnecessarily damaging and wrong with this hoary and still prevailing approach to education—and *why*.

The Rationality of Ecosocialism/Ecopedagogy

In Herbert Marcuse one encounters two key features lacking in other members of the Frankfurt School: the critical analysis of the political economy of advanced industrial society and a profound concern for environmental issues. Marcuse advocated a fundamental opposition to global capitalism's underlying predatory and extractive economic order: "Authentic ecology flows into a militant struggle for a socialist politics which must attack the system at its roots … ." (Marcuse [1972] 2019, 5).

> Increasingly, the ecological struggle comes into conflict with the laws which govern the capitalist system: the law of increased accumulation of capital, of the creation of sufficient surplus value, of profit, of the necessity of perpetuating alienated labor and exploitation.
>
> (Marcuse [1972] 2019, 4)

His ecological materialism and critical naturalism operated with the methodologies of critical political economy, critical sociology, and radical ecology,

Marcuse's Critical Pedagogy as Social Justice Education   161

focusing on the complex and pivotal underlying structures of waste and exploitation inherent in a profit system's economic "growth."

> There is a feeling and a recognition that well-being no longer depends on a perpetual increase in production. The revolt of youth (students, workers, women), undertaken in the name of the values of freedom and happiness, is an attack on all the values which govern the capitalist system.
>
> (2019, 3; 2005, 174)

By its own logic, the tremendous productivity of modern capitalist technology *cannot* result in a rational reduction in or conservation of the use of natural resources. This technology becomes irrational and decadent. It destroys the ecological base and the humane dimension of our social lives.

Marcuse had a radical respect for our interconnected interdependence with the earth and our need for collective engagement in building an environmentally honorable future. He held that criticisms of pollution and unsustainable resource extraction implicitly or explicitly involved *system-negations* and that the restoration of *nature* hinged upon *humans* struggling for liberation from capitalism. He sharpened radical ecology in a classical Marxist fashion, emphasizing that wasted abundance and environmental degradation—when steadfastly investigated and opposed—give rise to a systems critique and a radical political engagement that Marcuse believed could become a revolutionary force. Marcuse characterized this form of struggle as *revolutionary ecological liberation*. Marcuse's work essentially aids radical philosophy in facing the necessity of building the ecologically conscious theory and practice for a new world order.

It is gravely difficult in U.S. higher education today to counteract an almost mandatory compliance with neoconservative corporate operationalism, including its almost categorical opposition to environmentalism. Catalyst groups of students and faculty within higher education institutions have quite remarkably struggled to move educational theory and practice forward in recent decades, especially through the anti-racist and anti-sexist multicultural education reform movement and through movements to protect and conserve the environment. New concepts in higher education arguing for the university's *ecological mission* are also emerging. Ronald Barnett's volume, *Realizing the Ecological University: Eight Ecosystems, Their Antagonisms, and a Manifesto* promises a "revolution in universities ... [seeking] to forge new relationships with the whole world, the whole Earth" (Barnett 2024, 2018). So too recent efforts at ecoversity.org challenge the reigning neoliberal, entrepreneurial conception of the university with an emphasis on critical pedagogy in the form of ecological learning within community.

There will be no restoration of nature and no re-humanization of our coarsened and divided culture without the radical regulation of globally financialized monopoly capitalism—or its *elimination*. Marcuse argued that the '60s spirit of

162 *Herbert Marcuse as Social Justice Educator*

rebelliousness expressed a Great Refusal regarding the totality of our efficiently functioning social world as such. The ecology movement could well become *the* driving force within it. Marcuse's work has helped critical pedagogy at every level, reappropriating and reworking the knowledge accumulated during prior stages of civilization. He seeks not their empty negation but sublimation at a higher level. Marcuse's writings help the social justice educator and social justice student appreciate the meaning of revolutionary ecological liberation and ecosocialism for the development of our humane character and the global commonweal— EarthCommonWealth.

In contrast to Freud's fatalist pessimism about dissatisfaction and unhappiness as permanent features of any culture—*Das Unbehagen in der Kultur*— Marcuse's emphasis on our political Eros finds attainable a radical and reasonable *Wohlbehagen*. Nature is an Ally. We *are* earth —conscious of ourselves as earth; social animals—conscious of our historically, ecologically, and ethically developed powers; *humans*—conscious of our *rational* and *sensuous* needs and capacities. Marcuse's critical pedagogy—as education for social justice—revitalizes our appreciation of social and educational philosophy as an emancipatory enterprise. It energizes our collective capacities for rebellion, self-recognition, social reconstruction, happiness, and peace.

References

Barnett, Ronald. 2024. *Realizing the Ecological University: Eight Ecosystems, Their Antagonisms, and a Manifesto*. New York: Bloomsbury.

Barnett, Ronald. 2018. *The Ecological University: A Feasible Utopia*. New York: Routledge.

Braune, Joan. 2024. *Understanding and Countering Fascist Movements*. London and New York: Routledge.

Callahan, Raymond. 1970. *Education and the Cult of Efficiency*. Chicago, IL: University of Chicago Press.

Dewey, John. [1916] 1966. *Democracy and Education: An Introduction to the Philosophy of Education*. New York: The Free Press.

Horkheimer, Max and Theodor W. Adorno. [1944] 1972. *Dialectic of Enlightenment*. New York: Herder & Herder.

Horowitz, David. 2010. *Reforming Our Universities: The Campaign for an Academic Bill of Rights*. Washington, DC: Regnery Publishing.

Kors, Alan Charles, and Harvey Silverglate. 1998. *The Shadow University: The Betrayal of Liberty on American Campuses*. New York: The Free Press.

Marcuse, Herbert. [1972] 2019. "Ecology and Revolution," in *Ecology and the Critique of Society Today: Five Selected Papers for the Current Context*. Philadelphia, PA: International Herbert Marcuse Society.

Marcuse, Herbert. [1974] 2015. *Paris Lectures at Vincennes University, 1974*. Peter-Erwin Jansen and Charles Reitz (Eds.). Philadelphia, PA: International Herbert Marcuse Society.

Marcuse, Herbert. [1968] 2009. "Lecture on Education, Brooklyn College. 1968," in Douglas Kellner, Tyson Lewis, Clayton Pierce, and K. Daniel Cho (Eds.), *Marcuse's Challenge to Education*. Lanham, MD: Rowman & Littlefield.

Marcuse's Critical Pedagogy as Social Justice Education   163

Marcuse, Herbert. [1932] 2005. "New Sources on the Foundation of Historical Materialism," in Richard Wolin and John Abromeit (Eds.), *Heideggerian Marxism*. Lincoln, NE: University of Nebraska Press.

Marcuse, Herbert. [1933] 1973. "On the Philosophical Foundation of the Concept of Labor in Economics," *Telos*, Number 16, Summer.

Marcuse, Herbert. 1972. *Counterrevolution and Revolt*. Boston, MA: Beacon Press.

Marcuse, Herbert. 1969. *An Essay on Liberation*. Boston, MA: Beacon Press.

Marcuse, Herbert. [1937] 1968. "The Affirmative Character of Culture," in *Negations: Essays in Critical Theory*. Boston, MA: Beacon Press.

Marcuse, Herbert. [1955] 1966. *Eros and Civilization*. Boston, MA: Beacon Press.

Marcuse, Herbert. 1965. "Repressive Tolerance," in Robert Paul Wolff, Barrington Moore, and Herbert Marcuse, *A Critique of Pure Tolerance*. Boston, MA: Beacon Press.

Marcuse, Herbert. 1964. *One-Dimensional Man: Studies in the Ideology of Advanced Industrial Society*. Boston, MA: Beacon Press.

Marcuse, Herbert. [1958] 1961. *Soviet Marxism: A Critical Analysis*. New York: Random House.

Marx, Karl. [1844] 1982. *The Economic & Philosophical Manuscripts of 1844*. Dirk Struik (Ed.). New York: International Publishers.

Mill, John Stuart. [1859] 1963. "On Liberty," in *The Six Great Humanistic Essays of John Stuart Mill*. New York: Washington Square Press.

Reitz, Charles. 1981. "Education and Communist Theory," *Humboldt Journal of Social Relations*, Volume 8, Number 2. Spring/Summer.

Index

Absher, Brandon 86, 91, 148
abundance 80, 102–03, 121–2, 129; *see* wasted abundance
aesthetic dimension 13, 27, 31, 34–5, 61, 136, 157
aesthetic education 31–2, 40, 62
aesthetic ethos 32, 65, 67, 118, 136–7, 157; as gesellschaftliche Produktivkraft 158
aesthetic form 67, 81, 159; as erotic life-affirmation 32, 50; and truth 41
aesthetic rationality 62, 157
affirmative culture 28–33, 36, 63–4; education 30; as political quietism and tranquilization 30
Africana philosophy 18, 122–4
Alexander, Thomas 125
alienation 2, 13–14, 17–18, 24, 73, 89–90; of artist 26–7, 32; art against 27, 62; education against 28, 31–2, 34, 51, 61–2, 81, 151, 153, 155, 158; life unburdened by 138; obsolescence of 134; socialism against 103–04
alienated labor 53, 118, 121–2, 155, 158–9
American Jewish Committee 58
anti-communism 12, 58–9
antiracism 65, 138, 145, 155, 161; no tolerance for hate speech 66; The 1619 Project 37
antifascism 57–60, 156
antisemitism 5–6, 9, 10–12, 66, 82n2, 118, 155; Charlottesville 11; false charges of 6, 11
anti-war 2, 14, 44, 49, 51–2, 59–60, 64, 77, 82, 90–1, 129, 151; *see* Vietnam
anti-Zionism 6–7
Apple, Michael W. 87, 141–2
Aristotle 14, 28–9, 81, 89, 108, 122, 134
Auschwitz 3, 12, 89, 127, 155

Barbie, Klaus 11–12
Barnett, Ronald 89, 161
basic repression 16–17
beauty 28, 48, 67, 90, 93–4, 98, 136, 159; as affirmative "beautiful souls" 26, 29, 30, 133; and ecosocialism 15–16; and Eros 14; and logic of gratification 32, 34; as political 81
beings-for-ourselves 52; *see* alienation; *see* critical pedagogy; *see* humanities
Bhaskar, Roy 40, 64, 86, 88–91, 93, 100–01, 114; critical naturalism 90, 125; ground state 124–5
Bildung 25–6, 151
Black Lives Matter 2, 8, 42, 120; as educative 51
Bloom, Allan 32, 37, 63, 76
bonheur commun 12, 15, 18, 19n25; and ecosocialism 134, 136, 138, 155; as EarthCommonWealth 155
Bowles and Gintis 87, 141–2, 144
Braun, Wernher von 11–12
Braune, Joan 156
Brecht, Bertolt 58, 77
buen vivir 128; *see* ecosocialism
Bushnell, Aaron 12
Butler, Judith 6

capital/labor split 112–14
capitalist system 4, 9, 13–16, 33–34, 37, 42–3, 45–7, 52, 66, 73, 78, 91, 101, 104, 108, 117; dysfunctional 43–4, 59, 68, 80; and fascism 59–60; global 14, 39, 95; and nature 52, 91, 95, 152; opposition to 68–9; as predatory 66; and prejudice 58
Cho, Daniel K. 36, 61
civil rights 9, 13–15, 24, 43, 63, 74, 120

Index 165

class 29, 36, 44–6, 53, 63, 65, 70, 73, 88, 112, 118, 142, 144, 152; *see* capital/labor split; *see* one percent
commodity 29–30, 75, 146; culture 1, 34, 41, 117, 148; dependency 129, 131, 134; fetish 101, 104, 126; production 73, 78; wage as 133; *see* decommodification; *see* one-dimensionality
commonwealth 18, 25, 35, 49, 52, 67, 70, 81, 97–8, 100, 122, 125, 156, 159; as comunalidad 52; economy 111–2; educated in 136; as ethic 135; form of free society 18, 117, 121–2, 135; form of labor, production and ownership 103, 121–2, 128–9, 131, 135, 155; humanist 104, 116; as social justice 156; *see* EarthCommonWealth
common wealth 48, 102, 125, 129, 148
commonwork 137
compensation 108, to owners and investors 114; to workforce 110, 112; *see* payroll; *see* profit
counteroffensive 17, 92, 135; *see* EarthCommonWealth
counterrevolution 37, 66, 81, 87
critical educators 38, 52, 76, 81, 87, 102, 145, 148, 151; critical education theory 110, 142; see Apple, *see* Bowles and Gintis; see Giroux, *see* Kellner; *see* McLaren
critical pedagogy 1, 78, 108, 142–48, 152, 155–6, 161–2; revolutionary 46, 116, 138
critical philosophy 35, 50, 77, 92–3, 141, 148
critical political economy 24, 32, 41–6, 157–8, 160
Critical Race Theory (CRT) 8, 37, 143; *see* racism; *see* antiracism
critical realism 64, 88–9, 93, 114; *see* Bhaskar; *see* Simmons
critical social theory 14, 24, 33, 41, 57, 61, 64, 80–1, 86, 88–9, 110, 125, 134, 142, 151, 158
critique of pure tolerance 82n2, 88; *see* repressive tolerance
critical teaching 70, 108–118; *see* critical pedagogy; *see* critical political economy
Cubberley, Elwood P. 160
culture war 5–9, 14, 81, 143

Daniel, Lloyd 76–77
Davis, Angela 2–3, 8, 69, 74, 141
Dayan, Moshe 4–5, 11
decommodification 48, 50–1, 66, 116–17, 120–2, 136–7, 144, 147, 156, 158–9; of wages 48; *see* commonwealth

DEI (diversity, equality, inclusion) 143; *see* multiculturalism
Deloria, Vine, Jr. 98–9
de-Nazification 58; *see* OSS
deprovincialization 76–7; *see* critical pedagogy; *see* multiculturalism
Dewey, John 36, 79, 88, 93, 152, 160
dialectics 24, 41, 43, 91–3, 94, 152, 157; *see* ecological materialism; *see* Engels; *see* Horkheimer and Adorno
Dilthey, Wilhelm 28, 40; and life philosophy 25

EarthCommonWealth Alternative 13, 48–50, 70, 97, 103, 130–2, 162; as aesthetic form of free society 116, 135, 159; as counteroffensive 92; as project 137–8; and labor 135, 155; as planetary comunalidad 52; as *telos* 131
ecocide 1, 3–4, 12–13, 24, 137, 154–5
ecofeminism 39, 125
ecological materialism 91–2, 95–6, 125, 160; Kosmos 96
ecological university 161; *see* ecopedagogy
ecology 3, 12, 48–52, 90, 92, 97, 104
ecopedagogy 24, 48, 52–3, 102, 160
ecosocialism 15, 17, 50, 104, 128; and earth's beauty 90; and ecopedagogy 102; and feminism 51, 68, 126; and humanism 132, 135, 159, 162; and reason 120–2, 160; as global alliance of transformational forces 51; as new world system 101, 116
Edu*Action* 40; *see* critical pedagogy; *see* Freire
Eisler, Riane 124
Engels, Frederick 59, 138; dialectics of nature 94–7; processes *not* things 92
equality 13, 46, 130, 137, 159; *see* aesthetic ethos
Eros 14, 35, 41, 66; effect 2; *see* political Eros
erotic energy 15, 133; *see* life-affirmation

Farahmandpur, Ramin 143
Farber, Marvin 88, 93
fascism, 9, 57, 59–60, 70, 74, 155–6; fascist rhetoric 66; *see* neofascism
Federici, Silvia 39, 125
Feenberg, Andrew 1, 78, 90, 125
feminism 68, 129–30, 143, 155
Foxx, Virginia 11
Frankfurt School 3, 12, 2428, 48, 57–8, 60–1, 68, 126, 155, 160
free speech 6–10, 153; fallacy 66

166 Index

Freire, Paulo 8, 40, 141, 148; directed dialogical method 143–4; see Meno
Freud, Sigmund 16–17, 40, 132, 136

Gattungswesen 17, 158; see species being
gay rights 155; see LGBTQ
Gaza 1, 4, 6, 10–14, 19n, 20n, 21n, 24, 42, 86, 129, 137
Geisteswissenschaften 25, 156; see Dilthey; see humanities; see literary art
Gemeinschaft 25, see Earth-CommonWealth Alternative
Gemeinwesen 138, see Earth-CommonWealth Alternative
gender oppression 24, 120; see feminism; see women's liberation
general education 14, 36–7, 40, 50, 53,123, 131, 157; see liberal arts and sciences
general interests of humanity 51, 65, 129–30, 155
genocide 1, 3–4, 6, 10–12, 42, 137, 154–5
German artist-novel 25–8, 61
Giroux, Henry A. 38, 46, 86–7, 141–3, 145–9
Gleichschaltung 28, 54n1, 73
Goethe 26–7, 94, 127, 136, 148
Great Books 32, 36, 136, 157; see general education
Great Refusal 47, 51, 60, 65–6, 74, 90, 127, 138, 143, 152, 155, 162; as global alliance of transformational forces 50–52, 68, 70, 90–1, 100, 103, 109, 120, 126; see system negation
Green New Deal 131
growth 34, 43, 52, 91, 104, 113, 134, 161; see Saito

Habermas, Jürgen 58, 60, 88–9
Hamas 6, 11
happy consciousness 77–8, 157; see one-dimensionality; see repressive desublimation
hate speech 6, 7, 9–10, 28, 58, 66, 82n7, 126, 153–4
Hegel, G.W.F. 40, 50, 54, 76, 79, 93, 120
Heidegger, Martin 41, 63, 76, 155
hermeneutic paradigm 41; see Dilthey; see Schiller
Horkheimer and Adorno 3, 28, 33, 35, 57–60, 71n6, 88–9, 125,157; on remembrance 127–8
Horowitz, David 8, 153
humanism 1–2, 13, 63, 70, 99. 121–4, 129, 145, 157, 159

humanities 34, 40, 61–3, 78, 80, 88, 148, 156; see Geisteswissenschaften
humanization 17, 25, 33, 35, 40, 80, 104, 144, 151, 161; see Bildung
Humboldt, Alexander 96–7, Kosmos 96
Humboldt, Wilhelm von 80; see Bildung

Ingraham, 110–11
immigration 14, 18n5, 46, 52, 57, 86; see multiculturalism
imperialism 2, 51, 59; see Vietnam
inequality 87, 114; origins 108; a structural relationship 110–11; wealth quintiles 111, 118n1; see Bowles and Gintis
income flows 45; structurally determined 112,114; distribution pattern 111; to labor 113; to capital 114–16
International Court of Justice 6
Intersectionality 32, 100; see multiculturalism
Israel 1, 3–6, 10–12, 14
Israelism 10–12

Jaspers, Karl 86
job creators 77, 116
jobs shell game 116, 131

Kahane and Cavender 76, 144
Kahn, Richard 32
Kangussu, Imaculada 14, 17
Katsiaficas, George 1–2
Kellner, Douglas 38, 58, 60–1, 79, 131, 141–3
Kerr, Clark 34–5
Kincheloe, Joe 141
Kors and Silverglate 8, 153–4

labor 18, 29–30, 32, 35, 43–5, 48, 129; alienated 16, 39, 43–4, 47; commonwealth 49; congealed 44; liberation 122, 130, 159; militancy 15; power of 28, 33, 103–4; precarity 24, 52; see sensuous living labor
labor objectification 128; exteriorization 104; see commonwealth; see commonwork
labor theory of culture 103; ethics 155; governance 128; justice 159; ownership 159; value 112–14
Lamas, Andrew 73
Langman and Lundskow 15
legitimation crisis 90, 104,
Leopold, Aldo 96–9, 130; earth as biotic system 96–7; land ethic 97
Lewis, Tyson E. 36, 61
liberal arts 8, 14, 24, 32, 34–7, 40, 53, 63, 81, 152, 156, 160

Index 167

liberation 1, 4, 8, 14–15, 49–50, 52, 67, 101; from affluent society 74; goal of education 24; of labor 18, 48, 121; of nature 50; goal of politics 67; *see* women's liberation
life-affirmation 13, 15, 50, 127, 134; see Dilthey; *see* erotic energy
life-chances 111
literary art 25–8, 30, 40, 61, 64, 110, 156–7
LGBTQ 18n5, 52, 135, 137–8
Locke, John 111–12, 114, 159
logos of humanism 121–2
logos of labor 159
logos of life 1, 90
Loughead, Tanya 86, 103, 148
Lukács, Georg 50, 78

Maley, Terry 73
Mann, Thomas 27–8
Marcuse, Herbert on ecology 3, 12, 17, 19, 48–49, 65, 101, 127, 129, 132–4, 160–2
Marcuse, Peter 5
Marcuse's Marxism 1, 13, 18, 29, 33, 45, 48, 95, 111–12, 117. 129, 159
Marx, Karl 24, 28, 45, 48, 50, 53, 88, 90, 95,103, 111–12, 117, 120, 124, 128–9, 148, 155, 159
materialism 31, 95–6, 102; dialectical 60, 93; ecological 41, 95, 125, 160–1; historical 96, 99, 159; *see* humanism
May Day 127
McLaren, Peter 38, 46, 52, 87, 116–17, 120, 141–5, 148
Meno 88, 123
Mies, Maria 39, 125
military 10, 42, 51, 102, 135, 139; in U.S. higher education 35; killing civilians 90; Marcuse in OSS 57; pollution 101; spending 12, 46, 108–09; suicides 12; waste 82, 109, 126
Mill, John Stuart 9–10, 53, 66, 153–4
Muir, John 96
multiculturalism 14, 38, 46, 50–1, 63. 76–7, 81, 131, 135, 143, 157, 161

national income accounts 112–13; standard economic data 110
nature 93, 95; as ally 94–5; as community 97; as educative 94; Bhaskar 40, 89–90; Dewey 93; Farber 93; Emerson 94; Engels 92; in Greek materialism 95; Horkheimer and Adorno 127–8; Leopold's land ethic 97; restoration 95, 101, 104, 128; under siege 127, 132–3, 161
Nazi Germans in U.S. 11–12, 14

neofascism 10–11, 16, 57, 59–60, 86, 126, 156; *see* antifascism
New Sensibility 3, 15, 32, 46–7, 60, 64–5, 68, 133–4
Nietzsche, Friedrich 28, 40, 63, 76
ninety-nine percent 125, 155; potential intercultural unity 87

objectification 128; *see* labor objectification
one-dimensionality 32–34, 43, 62, 64, 73–5, 78, 100, 109, 148, 160; as Gleichschaltung 54n1, 73
one percent 99–100, 110; as sovereign 87; as criminal 87
OSS (Office of Strategic Services) 58

Palestine 1, 3–4, 6–7, 11
payroll 112–16, 137
Peirce, Clayton 36, 61
performance principle 35, 62
Piketty, Thomas 111,
Plato 28–9, 80–1, 88, 122, 125, 157
pleasure principle 121, 136
political economy, *see* critical political economy
political Eros 1–3, 13–17, 32, 50, 65, 80, 90–1, 100, 125, 127, 132, 137, 152, 155,159, 162
profit 101, 104, 112, 114, 116–17; fetish 126; human need 117; maximization 125
promesse du bonheur 13–14, 27, 51, 64; of art 67, 157
proverbs, Africana 122–4, 157

racism 2, 8, 14, 51, 58, 60, 63, 102, 132, 135, 143, 145; reverse 8–9
recovery of philosophy 78–9
reality principle 69, 130
Renaissance 31, 95–6; and political Eros 32; *see* aesthetic ethos
repressive desublimation 16, 34, 63–4, 66–7, 77–8
repressive tolerance 7–10, 53, 153–4; *see* racism
reproduction *see* system reproduction
resistance *see* Great Refusal
revolt *see* Great Refusal
revolutionary ecological liberation 4, 49–51, 67, 93, 125, 127, 131–2, 138, 161–2
Robinsonians 111
Rufo, Christopher F. 8–9, 37, 87, 146

Saito, Kohei 47
Salleh, Ariel 39, 125

168 *Index*

Schiller, Friedrich 28, 36, 62, 67, 81, 93–4, 136; *see* aesthetic education
science 25, 38–40, 64–5, 75, 78–9, 81, 88, 92, 95; Bhaskar 64, 86, 90; and domination 33, 95, 100; to serve humanity 50,101, 128; method as ecological-evolutionary 92–3, 97
schools as factories 160
Sekyi-Out, Ato 123–24
self-actualization 91, 129
self-governance 11, 91
sensuous living labor 14, 18, 44, 67, 121–2, 129, 138, 155, 158–9
Sethness Castro 2, 5
Sherover, Charles 79
Sherover, Erica 5
Shiva, Vandana 39, 52
signature concepts 63–70
Simmons, Michael L. Jr. 87–9, 93, 101, 125
Singh, Savita 63–4
Slater, Judith J. 144
Smith, Adam 104, 111–12, 114, 159
Smith, John E. 79
social movements 118, 137; as civilizing 2, 51; ecology 132, 133
Social, Philosophical and Historical Foundations 87
social justice 2–3, 13, 30, 46, 112, 117, 138, 156; and critical political economy 41, 116; education 24, 156–8, 160; education against alienation 155–6, 158; and labor 112–14; *see* EarthCommonWealth; *see* ecosocialism; *see* labor theory
socialism 15, 51–2, 65, 82, 116, 133; democratic 131; needs feminism 69, 130; qualitatively different 69; radical goals of 28, 47–8, 68–70, 81, 116–18, 130, 132, 135, 157
Spartan, Stephen 108, 111
species being 14, 17, 50, 158–9
species-essence 35, 136, 158; *see* Gattungswesen
Stefanik, Elise 6–7, 11; *see* antisemitism false charges
Steiner, Stanley 144
struggle, educative power of 2,13, 51; *see* Giroux; *see* McLaren
student movement 2–3, 6, 8, 14–15, 45, 49, 51, 57, 59–60, 64–5, 91, 129, 137, 151–2
surplus repression 16–18; *see* basic repression
surplus value 16, 53, 104, 116, 126, 159–60
system change 45, 100–01; *see* multiculturalism; *see* system negation

system ecological 94–6, 99, 138; *see* Leopold; *see* Wildcat
system irrationality 65, 80, 82, 101, 134, 161
systemic negation 65, 69–70, 74, 87–8; as new general interest 51, 129–30, 155
system reproduction 29, 64–5, 87, 104; in education 65, 142–3, 161; *see* Bowles and Gintis

Tauber, Zvi 4–5
technology 25, 38, 39, 48, 50, 64, 61, 81, 88, 104, 129; and domination 64, 73, 78, 90, 101, 121; and liberation 65, 90, 95, 101, 117, 120
Thoreau, Henry David 96
torture 5, 10, 87, 109
transvaluation of values 15, 46, 65, 67, 131
Trump, Donald 10, 86, 141

ubuntu 123, 157
Unbehagen 17, 162
universals 80, 157
University of Buffalo 87–8
utu 123, 157

value added 112–15, 159; national income accounts 112, 115; surplus 159
value production 114; labor theory of 112
values revolution 14, 46–47, 65, 91, 131, 134
Vietnam 1–4, 14, 24, 35, 49, 51, 59, 86, 89, 120, 155; *see* ecocide; *see* genocide
Volpe, John Della 2, 137

wages-system 45, 113–14, 129, 131, 159; abolition of 117–18, 121, 137, 153
war crimes 2, 4, 6, 11–12, 86; *see* Gaza; *see* Vietnam
wasted abundance 114, 117, 126–7, 129, 133
wealth 44, 87, 102, 104, 110–11, 118n1, 141; distribution 40, 108, 111; income producing 104, 117, 128, 159; as common 48, 51, 112, 125, 129
Wildcat, Daniel R. 98–99
Winter, Rainer 10
Wohlbehagen 17, 162
Wolff, Edward N. 110, 118n1
women's liberation 15, 25, 45–6, 49, 51–2, 60, 64, 68, 70, 90–1, 99, 126–30, 137–8, 151; *see* feminism
Women's March 2
women's rights 13, 24, 68, 120

zoon politikon 89

Printed in the United States
by Baker & Taylor Publisher Services